Finding Myself
in Puglia

Author Note:

Laine B Brown was born in Middlesex and worked as a nurse and a counsellor. She spent four years living in Puglia with her basset hound Basil where she wrote her Italian memoir, *Finding Myself in Puglia*.

She currently lives in North Norfolk with her dog Basil and her cat Munchkin.

www.lainebbrown.com

Finding Myself
in Puglia

A Journey of Self-Discovery Under
the Warm Southern Italian Sun

By

Laine B Brown

Finding Myself in Puglia

First Published in 2018

© 2018 Laine B Brown

All rights reserved.

ISBN 978-1-9996548-1-8

For Christian, Elisa, Dean and Nelson

Contents

A Long Dark Pine Table

They sat at opposite ends of a long dark pine table
Polarised by the distance
A stranger sat at the end
She choked on the food that she put in her mouth
'I love you, but I am not in love with you,' he said
They sat at the ends of a long dark pine table
His words submerged her into the darkness of the table
Her head felt as though it was under water
Ten swords dug into her back and into her soul
They sat at the opposite ends of a long dark pine table
Long after his physical presence had gone
She smoked endless cigarettes
Her head bent
At a solitary end of the long dark pine table

Introduction

'We are the one animal that knows that we are going to die, and we carry on paying our mortgages, moving jobs about, behaving as though there is eternity in a sense and we forget, or tend to forget that life can only be defined in the present tense it is, is, and it is now only.

Nowness becomes so vivid to me now that it is an almost perverse sort of way, I am almost serene – I can celebrate life.'

Extract from a television interview conducted by, Melvyn Bragg with Dennis Potter in March 1994. Three months before Dennis Potter's death from pancreatic cancer.

I remember watching this interview in 1994 and being deeply moved by it. Dennis later goes on to say that he had been looking at a plum tree in his garden which he said had, *'The whitest, frothiest, blossomest blossom there ever could be.'* It seems as though the fact that he was dying was enabling him to be fully present with his surroundings and world.

So what if I wanted to be and needed to be more fully present in my world before I reached the last three months of my life. *Shit, I really need to take note of this; watch this; be mindful of this and be really present.*

I wrote down a few years ago in a journal when I thought that life was getting a little bit fraught.

'People are too busy living their lives to live their lives.'

I didn't heed my own thoughts until one day whilst walking up some steps of the hospital where I was working at the time, at some ungodly early hour to do a perpetually repetitious Sisyphean-like task. Sisyphus was forced by the Gods as a punishment for his proud and crowing behaviour, to push a boulder up a hill every day and it would roll back down the hill and he would have to commence his task all over again. That is what it was like for me pushing the boulder up the hill for it to just roll back down again. Every day seemed like this. I felt as though I couldn't breathe.

Suddenly, a thought developed in my head that said, 'I want to learn another language fluently before I die.' I had no idea where this came from, but I knew that it was something that I just had to do. That thought transformed into action and took me on a journey that I never thought I would take. I would start to learn a language that would take me to the country of its origin, Italy.

Having suffered the death of my marriage a few years before I had the sudden urge for a reinvention. It was hard to hear those words, 'I love you, but I am not in love with you.' And for your husband to leave the house and the home that you had built together with a guitar on his back leaving a wife, his teenage children, two cats, a golden retriever, years of memories and history.

That night I howled. A noise came from deep within

me. It was something primal and rose up and exited my body. I felt as though I was watching myself, my wounded self. What followed was an indescribable pain; emotional pain and then numbness. Everything I knew had suddenly fallen away like huge chunks of a glacier into the Arctic Ocean. Minutes seemed like hours and time slowed to a trickle. If I tried to futurise, I could envisage only darkness. I began to live my life nanosecond by nanosecond. The autopilot in me performing daily tasks and I paced like a polar bear in captivity. I paced, and I talked to friends on the phone to those who could bear to listen. No one can say anything to make it right because there is nothing to make 'right'. It was broken, ended, gone and I would have to learn to live through the pain.

Every morning I would wake up feeling sheer panic and out of control of my life and with a gnawing emptiness. The weight shed in pounds and then turned into stones. I lived my life in a fog. A divorce, a new house but the new pieces of my life didn't quite fit together. I had suffered a huge loss and felt lost. Autopilot madness. I couldn't read a book for two years never mind think about writing one. Even driving to the next town would send me into a panic. I started to have panic attacks on tube trains and in shops. The panic rising in me, made me want to run away and escape from everything.

I remember a colleague saying to me some years ago – when the emotional pain was still fresh – as we sat in a Buckinghamshire office of a local mental health charity, where I worked as a volunteer counsellor,

'I thought you would be your old self by now. You know, with you knowing so much about therapy.' She said this almost longingly – as though that 'old self' in me had gone and it had. My own internal therapist had left the building so to speak and I could only hear faint whispers of what I could or should be doing. I wondered what I was supposed to say in this situation, tears pricked my eyes, and I said something about not knowing what I was meant to be doing or how I was meant to be. My own reparation felt like performing an operation on myself trying to look at the parts that I thought belonged to me when they probably belonged to an 'other'. In reality, there was no 'old self' that existed, just a different self and trying to be 'me' that had many broken parts and was work-in-progress. As much as I tried to force the reparation it would be a long painful process.

It would be years before I had any idea who I was, outside of a relationship.

With my own internal therapist on vacation, so to speak, I had therapy. Difficult and tearful sessions where I tried to explore what had happened, why it happened and how I could get up out of the road from the car crash, away from the oncoming traffic. My therapist said – much later when the therapy was coming to an end – that she thought that I was so broken that she wanted to wrap me up in a blanket and give me a hug. The therapy was the hug.

Letting go of emotional pain can be difficult when it has been your only comfort and constant companion. Being and becoming a new forward thinking me and struggling to live in the present when my brain just looped back to the past in a vicious and seemingly never ending cycle; seemed impossible.

Exhausting nights and time slowed down into a torpid limp. My brain was bathed in so much cortisol that I didn't have any concentration and felt as though I had ADHD. I became impatient and impulsive. Irascible and mercurial and probably a right bitch to live with.

And then there was other people's impatience, yet another 'You should be over this by now.' From a relative, a close one. The words hanging like a heavy cloak and my feet wading through a bog of uncertainty. I was taking faltering toddler steps into a different way of being. Other people's impatience did not push me forward but made me feel achingly frustrated with them and myself. A passive-aggressive attitude of pull-yourself-together, just made me feel like a failure and was invalidating.

Divorce is like a death, but the other person is still around. A dead person doesn't throw barbed comments at you, change your marriage history or alienate your children intentionally, so that they lose a father, as in death. A dead person departs silently.

Eventually, the only thing left to do is to recover, move on and let go of the uncomfortable comfort zone. If time really is a great healer, then time did actually help me. I stopped recycling my thoughts and tried to process how I could be different and how I could embrace a different new me and ultimately, a different life.

I can't remember who said this – in the age of the internet, quotes that fly around like fruit flies around a rotten apple – but this resonated with me, *'Depressed people live in the past, anxious people in the future and happy people in the present.'*

The present is a lifeboat that has a spare place for you in it, as the vessel is going down; get in the lifeboat and don't carry on rearranging the deck chairs on the Titanic.

I yearned to regain my sense of humour instead of crying over a full ashtray of fag butts; a mascara-smeared-blubberer who needed to get out of her Bridget Jones' flannelette pyjamas (I did eventually dump these PJs as I really was a depressing sight in them). I have a friend called Julie (a friend of forty years and peppers every sentence with 'Darling') who would scoop me up and get me out of my pyjamas and announce, whilst waving her arms around, 'It smells like incest in here.' As I burned incense to get rid of the fag smells. I would call upon her on weekends and would find her in her own pyjamas and cry on her shoulder. If it was past 11am we would drink beer in her pergola that was covered in cobwebs and I would tell her the latest and greatest and she would listen attentively and finally announce, that she too, had to get out of her pyjamas. She would move on with her day and I tried to move on with my life.

I gained another dog (I already had an elderly golden retriever). A basset hound, that I named Basil and lost a boyfriend (maybe he didn't like basset hounds or maybe it was me that he wasn't too keen on). I found that a long-eared puppy can be very comforting when yet another relationship had failed in my life. I buried my head in those floppy ears and sobbed for a bit, well probably more than a bit and thankfully, the puppy was very obliging.

I needed something that would challenge and scare me more than the challenges of everyday life. I was living a life, but not truly living my life. I wanted something that was more transformational to move from the quivering anxiety of what I was, into what I had been, to a more solid centre of experience and older wisdom.

I decided to shed my old skin and give up everything that I knew. Ideas were forming and then some dying. Perhaps, France would be an option. But after the Battle of Waterloo maybe the French really don't like the English. I shared my musings with a colleague. 'You can live in France,' he said. 'But it gets bitterly cold in the winter and the temperature drops to -10c, and you won't be able to go out.' I had visions in my head of dying in France, alone under a pile of coats with a piece of French cheese in my hand. My only sustenance, because I hadn't been able to go out and probably sustained a long and agonising death, suffocated by mothballs and the dank smell of tweed.

Not that I was planning on dying anytime soon (although I had been known for me to have a nanosecond micro-sleep on the way home from a night shift as a nurse, on occasions), but I realised that I was heading towards the safety of what most of us think is necessary. To work until we are sixty-five, pay off our mortgages and develop a hobby of some kind. Not being a hobbyist, the thought of normalcy had begun to fill me with dread. What if I could do something completely different, unnerving and maybe a little scary.

One night duty shift, I drew a map for a friend who had decided to give up nursing and her PIN number (the registration number for a nurse) and had decided to travel with her husband. A life-changing decision. The map was a rudimentary, child-like drawing of Puglia in Italy.

I found myself saying, 'I have never been here,' pointing with a pen to the map, 'but I know that I want to live here.' The words just fell out of my mouth like an unconscious thought. The more practical side of me said, 'But what do I do with all my things?' The things being a lifetime of clothes I didn't wear and books I never read and an attic full of my children's drawings and letters to Santa and the Tooth Fairy. Oh, and an epilady. Have you ever used one? My advice is, don't unless you enjoy excruciating pain and a rash that you would never believe. I think I gave it to Self-Torturers- of-the-Undercarriage Anonymous.

She looked at me and said, 'But they are only things.' She was right, and the things found their way – if they weren't given to Age Concern – to a 70ft storage room. No 41 and that is where they would stay. Because if you are not using your 'things', then you probably don't need them.

A van eventually left the UK one bitterly cold January morning with a bemused basset hound in a dog cage; a bookcase; a John Lewis red cable knit blanket and a few bags of clothes. The van was headed to the heel of Italy, to Puglia.

'A journey of a thousand miles must begin with a single step.'

Lao Tzu

Dave Greenfield was the man with the van who kindly agreed to take most of my remaining 'things' down to the heel of Italy some 1,500 miles away.

The Italians say when you have a dream that you want to fulfil that you, *Realizzare un sogno*, realise a dream. And with a man with a van and my pared down life and a single one-way ticket to Brindisi with Ryanair, I was about to realise mine.

If it was a folly, then I was willing to take the risk. I was moving to a house that I had only spent a week in just over a year before. It was my second trip to Italy, and I was looking in different provinces and towns to see where I wanted to live. After a week's stay at the villa, I found myself feeling emotional and I asked the landlady, Lili, who rented the house to me whether she would consider a long term rent.

'How long for?' she said in fluent English.

'For about two years,' I said. I felt a huge wave of emotion and became tearful. I really wanted this to happen, and I really wanted to live in this little villa with its small enclosed manicured garden with luscious palms and even a bit of lawn. I had felt a strange kind of familiarity and a bonding with the place.

I had written in my notebook during my week's stay: *I want to write here, in this garden. This is where I want to live.*

I had looked at a flat in Otranto which was right down in the southern-most point of the heel of Puglia. The couple who showed me the flat were friendly but thought that if I lived in Brindisi, it would be a problem. A lot of crime they intimated and that I shouldn't live in a seaside village as there won't be anyone there in the winter, they advised. I listened but ended up just where they thought I shouldn't live, in a possibly crime-ridden dystopian place.

Fearing she would say no, she looked at me and said, 'You want a different life, don't you?' Somehow she had made that connection with me, she knew.

'Yes,' I said with my throat feeling as though it was tightening, as my emotions rose again.

That five-minute conversation was about to change my life.

Lili, who is under 5ft tall with big brown doe eyes and runs around like Bambi on speed, always doing something; cleaning mostly. Her mother says that she would clean the crack of an arse. Lili asked me recently, 'When you write about me, will you say that I am a crazy person?'

'Yes, but an adorable crazy person,' I said. And she is.

The country was unknown to me apart from three previous trips. I knew no one, and yet I had surety in my resolve. I wanted to feel fully present in feeling unsafe and comfortable with the not knowing.

I wanted to feel my way through a new language, although after three years listening to Linguaphone and Sarah and Lorenzo (the two main characters who took me on a journey through the Italian language), I was more interested in knowing whether they would end up together. Another friend once said to me (whom I will refer to in this book as the Writer), 'When you learn a new language, it changes your personality.'

It may have even changed my nationality as my daughter would breeze through the kitchen as I repeated the phrases on the Linguaphone – whilst putting some cobbled together dinner ensemble into the oven – and announce that I sounded more Polish than Italian.

I would become demonstrative and gesticulate in Italian rather than my stiff mumbling English. I would learn to lose my English vowels; roll my 'rrrrs' and keep my tongue behind my teeth.

I would learn to observe the Italian long table. A cacophony of noise and unintelligible dialect that would become music to my ears and I would learn to love a plethora of seafood, tossed in tempura batter and quickly fried. I would learn that red or white wine drunk with chunks of ice is perfectly acceptable to drink on a summer's day over lunch when it is 40c.

I would learn to value silence, be comfortable being alone, be more spontaneous and risk my life on the Italian roads. I would learn to laugh again, at myself and at others and to live in the moment where just being in the moment became the most important thing.

Ultimately, I would learn what it is like to feel part of an Italian family and an Italian community.

Dreams will remain only dreams if you don't take a risk and make them a reality.

To do great things, you have to fall off the edge of darkness; free fall and not worry about where you are going to land or if someone is going to catch you.

After the dark night of the soul, there is light – its luminescence from the self. The self that can look out across the sea and watch a majestic sunrise with smudges of pink, purple and blue merging into striking yellows and turmeric orange. Yes, the sun rises every day here on the lip of the sea. I can sit on a whitewashed wooden step and feel Basil nestling into my leg. His nose high in the air sensing and smelling a myriad of smells from all around us. The longing became an actuality. A fresh and vibrant reality and I can do the same thing tomorrow and the next day, and the next…

And if you have been kind enough to read this book. Remember you can be the creator and author or your own kind of magic. The gate is open, embark on the Fool's journey and don't look back.

'Live, as though the day were here.'
Friedrich Nietzsche

Chapter 1

ఎఓ

Dentist, Nursing, Men, and Italy

My dentist was looking intently as my dental x-ray.
'It's partially absorbed. It needs to come out,' she said,
referring to one of my back molars. And as I was
planning to leave for Italy in the following two weeks
– I declined her offer of an extraction – not wanting
to go to Italy with a yet another missing tooth. It's
an age thing, exiting teeth along with sprouting chin
hairs and a hormonal imbalance which gives another
connotation on, 'She's hot.' And not in a good way.

The thought of yet another tooth extraction
reminded me of a time of another tooth pulling. I
remember driving home on a cold winter's night with
a tampon-like swab sticking out of my mouth. The
tooth had had a fracture in it and had fallen clean in
half after coming out of my mouth. The dentist had
given me strict instructions, 'No alcohol'. Returning
home, I sat hugging my painful left cheek and sucking
white wine through a straw, along with the dental
tampon. My sister telephoned me the next day and
rather than saying, 'How are you feeling?' she said,
'What are you reading?' I was reading *The Dangerous
Passion*, by David M Buss (a book about evolutionary

psychology, a fascinating read).

A restless and sleepless night was followed by a sluggish day. The postman delivered *Wild Mary* by Mary Wesley and *Heartburn* by Nora Ephron – the latter who had died prematurely from leukaemia. I have always been a fan of the film *Heartburn*, and would say that it is one of my top three favourite films of all time, but I had never read the book. Nora was a funny, sharp and eloquent writer and I was looking forward to reading her book. My favourite quote from Nora is, *'Be your own heroine.'*

In other words, write your own story, whether literally or figuratively. I wondered what it would be like to be the author of my own story, to change my life and then write it down as a statement to it.

Mary, having written nine novels from the age of seventy, died at the age of ninety refusing food and only drinking warm water at the end. Mary Wesley was regarded as a late bloomer and didn't write her first novel, *Jumping the Queue*, until she was seventy years old. I looked up a quote from Mary that resonated with me, and it said, *'A lot of people stop short. They don't actually die but they say, 'Right I'm old, and I'm going to retire,' and then they dwindle into nothing. They go off to Florida and become jolly boring.'* Mary didn't retire but wrote ten novels and an autobiography. She led an interesting and full life when most people had retired. Although I wasn't at a retireable age, I was at an age, when I started thinking, *is this it? Is this all that there is?*

Don't offer me soup, or painkillers, just books. I love them. The feel and smell of an old book and the thrill of a new one.

My sister and I had spent hours as children reading books. Not just Enid Blyton, CS Lewis and Dickens but any books that we could lay our hands on. Of course, we played outside like normal children and learnt that a dock leaf was an antidote to stinging nettles, but equally, we were happy reading books. Usually, in my father's bed, whilst he was watching the Saturday horse racing. I remember his broad-shouldered silhouette in front of a flickering television; smoke curling around him from an ever present Rothman's cigarette in his mouth. My sister, Stella, and I would disappear downstairs to his bedroom in the old Victorian townhouse; the bedroom was on the ground floor. We would sit, lie and eat jam sandwiches and drink orange squash in the unmade double bed. Largely in silence wrapped in our own worlds and in books. I am not sure that he loved the crumbs and the sticky orange stains when he went to bed at night. Our remnants of the day in and on the bed. In his fifties and widowed, he must have been relieved that his two daughters were so 'quiet and preoccupied.'

My love of books has continued. Books will never reject you, but you may feel bereft when the book has been read, mourn and then look forward to the next one. Reading is one thing, but writing my own book might be an illusory folly of mine.

Nursing Back Story Ramble

As a student nurse in the 80s – the programme *Angels* had a lot to do with it – I was nearly defeated in the first two weeks of Introductory Block by hospital corners. And I never knew that I had to wash around the meatus (anus to the lay person) as demonstrated on Mrs Bedford a very unlifelike plastic dummy with a terrible brown synthetic wig. After the first six weeks, us newbies were eventually allowed to tackle real patients and a fellow student, and we put thirty thermometers in our unsuspecting patients' mouths all at the same time – we thought this would be more efficient – only to find that at least 50% of them had fallen to the floor by the time we had caught up with the first patient, and we chased pieces of quicksilver with paper towels for about two hours. I thought that I would never make it if I couldn't even take a temperature without giving the whole ward mercury poisoning.

As a student nurse, you wear your cape with pride, even though it smells like a dog's blanket and has probably never been washed. These capes were regularly stolen from the coat pegs, and another cape would be purloined in its place, smelling equally malodorous.

The first year student nurses were the amoebas and the lowest form of life in the nursing fraternity. We were all daft as a brush; as keen as mustard and as green as grass. The second years didn't speak to the first years unless to give orders. The third years would

look down on the first and second years with disdain
and pity and the staff nurses would look down on
us all with superiority, thinking that we would never
survive the training. All the newbies longed for the
white hat – that looked like a swan's backside and
would slide off at every opportunity – and the navy
blue belt with a silver buckle. If you were pretty
enough, you might even bag a doctor or the less
fortunate only being able to shag a porter.

Many years later, after being covered in a variety of
bodily fluids and demonstrating my worth, I became
a nursing Sister, which is a curious title. On queueing
up to buy a magazine one day – I can't remember
if it was *Hello* or the *New Scientist* – someone said,
'Hello Sister.' A fellow 'queuer' turned round and said,
'Blimey, I turned round and was expecting to see a
nun.' And there you have it, a completely useless and
nonsense title.

Nursing Sisters used to retire from the job or die
on the job. Not wanting to do either, I knew my life
had to change. Besides my uniform was made of
nylon and was itchy and very unflattering and seemed
to hang on to the hospital smells as well as my own
sweat.

The uniform wasn't the only problem; I was also
divorced, and my children had become young adults
and more independent and I seemed to be terminally
single. Although I did try to break the state of
being single. Even now I think that I have anti-men
Kryptonite in my pocket.

Dating Ramble
ৡৣৢ

Fifteen months after becoming single my sister and a best friend decided that I needed to try internet dating. Mysinglefriend.com seemed to be the dating site to try. But after a takeaway and several glasses of wine, there were both too drunk to write my profile, so I had to do it for myself. I think I wrote something like, 'Not so happy nurse, smells a bit; not a fan of nylon. Would like to meet a solvent man with a nice bathroom in order to wash in and who would be willing to buy future partner a new wardrobe. Must have a sense of humour, as you will need one...'

The first person I connected with became a four-month dating experience, before the inevitable, 'I am sorry, but I can't see this going anywhere.' Fair enough, he had big ears anyway.

Internet dating can become addictive. Even if you didn't want to date before, you would now. It's like crack – not that I have ever tried crack, but I am addicted to chocolate. Every Wednesday night I would go to my friend, Ally's, and sit on one of her dining room chairs in my MRSA-ridden uniform, drink wine and waggle a funny icon over the crotches of men on internet dating sites. Some of the weirder monikers being Conan-the-Librarian, Silver-tongue, and Desperately-Seeking-Susan. *Well, maybe Susan isn't on here, and you really shouldn't be that specific...*

I met an American actor who seemed perplexed that I didn't seem to know who Barack Obama was

– maybe it was the gin – I thought he was referring to a basketball team. After several sapphire gin and slimline tonics, I asked him about his line of work and asked him to repeat the word 'can't' several times in an English accent which sounded uncannily like the Old English word, 'c***'. Everyone will tell you that on a date a) you should never get drunk, especially on the first date and b) you should never repeatedly ask someone to repeat a word that you think – in your inebriated state – is a hysterically funny way of getting someone to say front bottom over and over again.

On the tube, he mimed a phone with his hands, which I think meant that he was going to call me. Thinking that I probably was behaving like a silly front bottom, he never did.

There was a man with whom I went out for a riverside drink, who was very unlike his profile picture. I was expecting a 6ft plus man who was standing at the bottom of a mountain looking vigorous and healthy. Instead, I was presented with a much shorter and skinnier man who spent the whole evening explaining the intricacies and workings of a pinball machine. He waddled out of the bar complaining of a sore back, and I wondered if he had difficulty in putting his socks on in the morning never mind climb a mountain.

I also made the mistake of driving fifty miles to the Cotswolds to meet a man with whom I had exchanged several emails with and seemed really articulate and funny. We arranged to meet outside a library in a town called, I Can't Remember. It was windy in the car park and in the days before satnavs had been invented. I had driven down with a map stuck to my face, whilst driving to avoid swerving in and out of cars that may have turned up in my path, whilst I was looking for the junction of the town with the name, I can't remember.

I found the car park and it had started to rain, and a gust of wind blew my route planner under the car. I was unsuitably attired for the windy and subsequently pissing-it-down-day, and I was wearing a short mini skirt and black boots. As I was crouching down under my car to retrieve my map that had blown asunder, I became suddenly aware of a presence. A man wearing an orange Kagool and Sou'wester and ominously steamed-up round glasses was hovering. He wasn't outside the library. He had seen me drive into the car park and decided to meet me at the car park to surprise me. Stalking behaviour, so early, unpleasant.

An awkward lunch and stilted conversation followed. He reminded me of 'Skipper', from *Sex in the City*. I decided that I wouldn't ever be buying him Captain Crunch for his morning breakfast and had to fend off an arm around the shoulder. At least he read my Tarot cards in the car as the wind and rain lashed around us. But seriously who has a deck of Tarot cards in their pocket on a date? To lighten the mood? Or perhaps he wanted to predict the second date, of which there was none forthcoming.

Maybe it was vanity or stupidity, but I would try and go on dates without the aid of glasses. I would misjudge drinks that were in the trajectory of the bar, but didn't quite make it. Be unable to find the slot for my train ticket and be unable to read a tube map and therefore could have ended up in Cockfosters on numerous occasions. I once walked into the men's toilets being totally unable to read the sign on the door. I slapped my date on the back and did an inspiratory snort finding the just-happened-men's-loo-mishap-story very funny, but only to myself. He looked at me as if to say, *Look, but don't touch, and you're really not funny. I'll walk you to the station immediately and put you on the train or push you under it…*

There was a man who licked his beer with a tongue that darted in and out like a lizard. And others, the non-drinkers; the boring and the humourless; the lotharios; the 'fishermen' – serial-dating-shaggers; the marrieds; the hopeless; hapless and the hopeful and the-I-am-still-in-love-with-my-ex-wife/girlfriend retaliators; revengers or rebounders. Oh, and there was one man who gave me a two-hour telephone interview to make sure that he wasn't wasting his time pre-date. The subsequent date was hard work, and I found that I was the one that had wasted my time.

There was one guy that I never even got to meet. He had the softest and most lilting southern Irish accent. He called me at work, and I darted in the cupboard where we kept all our sterile equipment and intravenous fluids. It was cold and drafty in there, but I melted when I heard that voice. Subsequently, he cancelled our date, 'Because he had to help a friend move furniture.' And so the voice would also be that, just a voice. I consoled myself by waxing my top lip and eating a bar of Cadbury's dairy milk chocolate.

There were also guys that I dated that, 'ghosted

me' which in more modern terms means that contact even by text dwindles to a trickle and then none. I would like to call these the withdrawers, the ones that withdrew like a cold cock in a brothel. There were also those men who behave badly in order to end the dating time (I hesitate here to say relationship because I feel that a relationship has more equality and perhaps a bit of commitment thrown in). The men who behaved badly. The guy that would get so drunk on a Saturday night that he had difficulty in remaining vertical – I also drank a little too much too, perhaps to keep up with the constant swaying. The guy who made me watch a two and a half hour documentary on American Foreign Defence Policy – which was mostly in black and white if I remember – and I realised that he was trying to tell me something. Or the guy who would text me just as I was about to leave on a date and cancel. He even tried to cancel once when I was already on the train and I refused to get off the train – as I had already paid for my ticket – and therefore forced a date night.

Transparency and openness would be so much easier. In conclusion of my very late in life dating experience; most men don't know what they want – or if they do they also want their cake and eat it – and women just need to know where they stand, so that ultimately we can move on. Don't leave a woman hanging 'just in case' we are not puppets and deserve a little more respect.

There are only so many times that I could tolerate standing on windy train platforms, freezing my tits off and waiting for a text or sending a text that said, 'That was lovely thank you.' Some things just have to end, and they had to before I contracted windy-platform-pneumonia and anticipatory-texting-anxiety-syndrome.

As you get older the dating pool consists of a much smaller pond with less interesting fish…

I once texted a lover/friend and said in my text that I wouldn't become *Tinatextalot* and then found that I did precisely that. There is an addictive process around cause and effect, the action and reaction from texting. There is a theory that it links into the dopamine receptors in the brain that give us the 'feel-good feeling' therefore if you get a reply from a text, you feel that you have been rewarded, and no reply leads to a feeling of loss or bereavement. Funnily enough, now, I hardly text and barely look at my phone and so the addictive need for texting has gone. I suppose it is like any form of behaviour really, anything that you do too much of is bad for you. I even put someone's name in my phone address book, *'Don't Text'*. Which I subsequently ignored. If I were an alcoholic I would probably still drink a bottle of wine that had printed on it, *'Don't drink'* – we all know what happened to Alice in Wonderland, when she drank from the *'Drink me'* bottle – the only real answer is delete the number or have no alcohol in the house. Remove the temptation.

It's far better to be alone, than with someone who doesn't appreciate you or makes you unhappy. You can also watch what you want on DVD – and preferably in colour. You can drink with moderation.

And most of all you never have to cancel a date with yourself. Especially if it is a special date night that involves a chilled glass of white wine, pyjamas and Michael Fassbender in all his glory.

Before I put in my phone, *Don't Text*, I had a fun relationship with Don't Text, and it was he, who introduced me to the idea of Puglia after first saying things like, 'Are you mad.' And, 'Have you done a spreadsheet.' I have always thought the last comment was a bit ironic. How do I do a spreadsheet on an unknown life? And if I did, I would probably embark on a new life-changing journey. It didn't seem spread-sheetable.

Shitey-Blighty weather and heavy snow fall before I left England prevented me from seeing many friends to say goodbye, but I did meet up with some ex-counselling colleagues in a restaurant in Bucks. I received special attention from the chef who provided a gluten free menu (he gave me the impression that he thought I might get an anaphylactic reaction from wheat products, rather than wind and bloatedness), I questioned myself, *why I was going to live in the land of pasta?* It's a bit like going to live above a sweet shop if you are a diabetic. Over a supper of salad and chicken, I explained to my friends that I felt as though I was going through an 'oxymoron' a *merry-meltdown* – as I had the mixture of feelings of excitement and trepidation with my impending move to Italy. I had previously asked the advice of the Writer as to whether he thought I was delusional, 'No, you are not delusional, illusional perhaps, but not delusional.'

I stepped out of the restaurant into the cold night, and I could see my breath hanging in the air. Frost and ice were clinging to the windscreen, and I comforted myself by the fact that illusory-dream or not it never falls below 0 degrees centigrade in southern Italy.

There is something that I would like to add here. The day I left work the Writer emailed me and said, *'Tell me how you felt when you left today.'* And I wrote back, *'A distillation of feeling – calm.'*

I had no regrets; I just felt relieved.

It was a big step out into the unknown. Fear and anxiety are often felt in the solar plexus area, where the solar plexus chakra is seated. This chakra represents our willpower and self-esteem, and the words associated with this chakra are: *I can.*

The calmness I felt embodied the feeling of *I can…* I can do this because if I didn't do it, then I would always regret it and probably block every chakra I have, and it would take a Buddhist monk chakra-plumber years to unblock it all.

Chapter 2

ॐ

Arrival

A white van left a Berkshire gravel driveway on a cold
and bleak January morning in 2013 with a confused
basset in a dog cage with Dave Greenfield, and I
took a flight two days later with my daughter and her
partner.

Some things in life just cannot be explained and
just feel intuitively 'right' and that is how I felt the day
I arrived in Italy. At home in every sense of the word.
On previous trips, I had felt 'at home' which is quite
indescribable really. I have struggled to convey this,
and the only thing I can compare it to is when you are
buying a house, and you walk in and get a sense of
Yes, I want to live here, this feels right...

I could bore the pants off you here by describing
every detail of unloading a van and putting my three
pieces of furniture, two small tables and a bookcase
in the house (which is describes as a 'villa' but is really
a ground floor apartment), but instead, I will share an
email which I sent to a friend and accurately describes
my arrival.

Whistlestop email:
Should have moved at the end of October. It didn't happen. Spent a month waiting, watching DVDs. Basil pissed up a box just before we left our Berkshire house, leaving a tattoo of the imprint on the box 'THIS SIDE UP', on the newly laid floor. Put a mat over it to cover.

I arrived at my sister's at the end of November. Brother-in-law complained about the boxes in the hallway – er weren't we moving them upstairs in the next 2 hours? I did a night shift after the move. Forgot to check with solicitors that everything had gone through. Woke up – checked – everything okay. Two months of purgatory followed. Brother-in-law grumpy; sister on a diet – Cambridge packets of sawdust – thought that Basil and I were going to be evicted after one week, due to basset barking – oops, sorry. Visited Mum, felt about 12, sobbed in her arms.

    Watched 22 episodes of 'In Treatment' – missed being a therapist in a previous life. Christmas came and went – thank the Lord – I hate Christmas, spent too much money.

January it snowed. Ate more dinners and lunches than Jo Brand on a good day. I said the longest goodbyes to some fabulous people – including my sister and brother-in-law. The difficulty was feeling as though I was in a departure lounge for two months and feeling neither here nor there. I wonder if I will ever get a discount at Brown's in Windsor – the bastards.

Basil left in a crate with Dave Greenfield together with his pet passport and a dog bed. He vomited and crapped somewhere in the Mont Blanc tunnel. Dave being a good guy cleaned him up and gave him a biscuit.

Arrived in Italy with Elisa and Dean. Late at night, tired and not in the mood for a big car at the airport (the bigger the car, the more dents you get). The man at the desk said, 'È strano' strange when I refused a bigger car. Hey, I have driven in Italy before, it is terrifying.

Elisa put some 'Let's get lost coordinates' in the satnav and we 'reached our destination' in the middle of an olive grove – didn't look like Santa Sabina to me. After arguing about the ways and wherefores of 'Where the fuck are we?' we eventually 'reached our destination'. Luckily, Lili and Mimo – my new Italian landlords – were waiting for us in their winter coats and hats and waved us in the right direction and I saved the destination as 'HOME' on the satnav. 'Come va?', How are you? Well, we are cold and hungry actually, I thought. L and M had installed a 2,000 euro wood pellet burner that was flickering away nicely and giving off warmth and a comforting glow. I had obviously created a good impression in 2011. A warm stove, hot showers, towels and bed linen provided, we were soon asleep.

The next day, the harbour village was like something out of 'I am Legend', the movie, not a soul… everyone must have been killed by a deadly virus. I imagined balls of tumbleweed bouncing down the street on eerie gusts of wind.

Elisa and Dean left on the Tuesday (three days later), and I must have sobbed for at least 30 seconds and then stopped. This is it, I told myself. Your choice, your life and there was the bed, and so I should lie in it!

L and M should be sainted. They have been so helpful to

me. They are always there at the end of the phone, which is good as they live in the town and are only 4 km away from me. L speaks very good English, even in the vulgar. 'Fuck!' she said one day after she dropped something. 'Did you say fuck?' I said. 'Yes, I know fuck. Fucking bastard. I know fucking everything.' Got to love her. L and M have driven me around looking for cars. I declined the 12-year-old Fiat with oil burning out of the exhaust for 2,500 euros. Hoping to get something nearly new. They have organised the internet for me. This involved drilling a hole through the foot thick walls. Basil farted during the proceedings, and everyone had to evacuate the house. I now have good internet. Access to YouTube and 8 out of 10 cats and QI…

Today I was meant to meet a Mr P, and Italian teacher that I had been in contact with on the internet (after searching for hours trying to find an Italian language school nearby) to discuss Italian lessons. I had arranged to meet him at the Villa Communale, a park in Ostuni – at 12:15, in the café. Ostuni is a very picturesque medieval town which is all called by the locals, 'La Citta Bianca', The White City. It sits proudly on a hilltop like a decorated wedding cake and is full of wiggly and winding streets. It is quite stunningly beautiful.

A cappuccino and nearly 45 minutes later he didn't show, so I left. The Sallysatnavslut took me up a blind alley in Ostuni old town, where I had to do a 5 million point turn and managed to scrape the side of the hire car, after reversing down another narrow alley to escape the blind alley. Fuck! She then told me to turn an impossible left. The car behind me was beeping with impatience. 'Scusi,' I said, 'Sono Ingelese.' I said it apologetically (although I don't know why I was apologising for being English). 'Dov'è uscita?' which means where is the exit. 'Dritto, dritto,' she said. Which means ahead, ahead. So why was the satnav slut telling me to turn left? I now frequently ignore Sallysatnavslut if she tries to take me into an alley-maze.

On getting home, I wiped the side of the car with a baby wipe (it was still dented and scraped), took Basil for a brisk and windy walk around 'I am Legendsville', installed a wireless printer by myself and reheated some ravioli – which is bad as I am wheat intolerant. Still, in Legendsville, no one can hear you fart.

I had my first Italian meal yesterday with Lili's Mum, Mary, 4ft 10 and adorably sweet. She cooked homemade ravioli stuffed with spinach (lordy) and ragu sauce. The meat was cooked on a log fire on a metal rack. The homemade red wine was an accompaniment (quite strong, robust and gave me an immediate headache) and I got lost in the chatter around the table. 'When the Queen comes to Italy,' she said –in Italian, of course, which was translated by Lili, 'She says she wants to eat ravioli.'

Salute to that.

Hope you liked your whistlestop tour,
Love Laine.

Chapter 3

❦

February Festival

The weather in February can be strange and changeable here in southern Italy. The sun is often shining in the morning and being English, and not being used to morning sunshine; I have taken to wearing shorts. However, by the time the sun goes down, the temperature drops dramatically, and I am often in double socks and at least two jumpers. Summer and winter all in one day.

February is carnival and festival time in Italy. Although I am coming to the realisation that the Italians don't seem to need an excuse to celebrate, as every day is a Saint Day, 365 days a year for a reason to celebrate something or other. I decided to enter into the festival spirit and find a festival to attend via the internet. I am not sure what everyone did before the internet or satnavs. Tours by the local taxi drivers perhaps? Although in this part of Italy taxi services are almost non-existent. Think of this part of southern Italy being thirty years behind the rest of Europe and you will be on the right track.

I have come to a *carnevale*, a festival in Francavilla

Fontana, and I am sat outside a café in the Piazza Umberto. This is a town with a pleasant centro storico, clock tower, and fountain, hence the Fontana bit.

Sweet stalls are scattered throughout the piazza, illuminated by energy saving bulbs. No parade has started as yet, but I have observed a twelve-year-old boy in skinny jeans; a mobile phone and slicked back hair – a pubescent Al Pacino. There is also a puppy basset hound that reminds me of Basil – who at this present time, would be howling in my house in Santa Sabina forty-five minutes away and probably dribbling on my cushions and shaking with anxiety. He has developed terrible separation anxiety since we have moved here.

There is an old man with a cloth cap and a winter coat opening and closing his mouth like a fish. If I were still a nurse, I would say that he had agonal breathing and perhaps in the throes of death, even though he was still vertical. He must have been waiting for the carnevale to start for a long time. The parade is meant to start at 4 pm, but in predictable Italian fashion, nothing will happen for at least another two hours.

I now have a prosecco in my hand to distract me from the fact that I am the only English woman here, with blonde wild and messy hair and speaking very poor Italian waiting for the carnevale.

Three men are now standing in the way and blocking my view of nothing going on. I am annoyed by this.

There are families with children – some even

with two children – out for an afternoon stroll, *la passeggiata*. This sight of two children is definitely in opposition to what I had read previously about one child families in modern Italy. There is a one child policy in China because of the bulging population and not being able to provide enough food for its people. Italy has the lowest birthrate in Europe. Therefore, two children will at least ensure future generations of Italians.

I have noticed that the women here in the south are tiny, minuscule, Polly-Pocket-sized with legs as thin as vermicelli. I had to buy a large jacket at the market back in Carovigno, and I am a size 8, on a good day when I haven't eaten too much chocolate. Most days I feel like a heifer walking next to big doe-eyed-beautiful-Bambi-like-creatures that toss thick manes of silky black hair, in a come hither-like way. They are gorgeous and really should have more babies!

All the old men in the piazza look alike, wearing dark caps and coats. No sign of the old man with the agonal breathing. He must have expired under a bush.

People have started to arrive in masks and clown wigs – probably my worst *incubo*, nightmare. Isn't everyone scared of clowns? I blame Stephen King for this. The toddlers and young children are waddling along in fancy dress – a princess, a witch and a little girl wearing what looks like a designer table cloth. The princess looks like she has an upside down cornetto on her head.

A man has just left his Vespa by the sweet stall –

which is right next to where I am sitting – shortly followed by a 50cc moped. The moped reminds me of when my mother used to ride a moped in the 1960s to get to work. She was the most nervous driver and probably lethal on a moped. Later on, when she had a car, she used to drive as though she had a box of kittens on her lap. My family has never been great drivers. My dad – whilst taking his driving test for about the fourth time – managed to empty a bag of cement over the lady examiner, during a poorly executed emergency stop. He failed the test. After eventually passing his driving test on the eighth attempt, I remember many a journey as a kid when he would put the car in neutral at 30 mph to save petrol, mostly down hills.

One hour later and still no sign of the carnevale. My fingers have frozen around the pen that I am holding. I may have to resort to counting the lollies on the sweet stall to pass the time.

I am also reflecting on how bad my Italian accent must be. When I asked the man in the café for a prosecco, he looked at me quizzically as though I had just asked him for a pork chop. Luckily someone came to my rescue and rolled the 'r' in prosecco – as in 'rrrr drum roll'. Mr P, my Italian tutor (we did eventually meet up after the first failed attempt), has also instructed to do this when saying bar. Say, 'ba-rrrrr'. I can flip peas with my 'rrrr' rolling now.

A little girl dressed as Mini Mouse has just walked by – how sweet. I would have smiled, but my face is frozen. Core temperature now thirty-three degrees centigrade and need a space blanket (the shiny blankets that they wrap exhausted and cold marathon runners in, a bit like Bacofoil). I am remembering my ALS course, Advanced Life Support course: 'You are not dead until you are warm and dead.' I can't be dead yet then and feel for my pulse. *It's alive; I tell you…* pulse confirmed. I am still alive.

An hour and ten minutes now into the vigil. I am now watching two dogs sniff each other's bottoms. Imagine if humans did that – stop it – I am obviously delirious due to hypothermia.

An hour and a half in and a man is staring at me now, quite blatantly (although I am getting used to being stared at in Italy, it seems to be a natural pastime). He must think that I am part of the carnevale with my blonde, curly and wild hair. Perhaps, I shouldn't have applied that last layer of lip gloss and look a bit clown-like.

Oh good, he has been accosted by three teenage girls in clown wigs. They talk. I imagine what they are saying.

The girls say, 'Is that woman part of the carnevale?'

The man says, 'No she has just frozen to death outside a café, waiting for something to happen, when clearly nothing is happening.'

He then moves on.

Core temperature now thirty-one degrees centigrade (about the same temperature as a defrosting chicken). I put my hands in my jacket pockets. The stream of fancy dressed children continues. Juliet walks by and Leonardo, one of the Teenage Mutant Ninja Turtles. I am wondering how much more of this anticipatory excitement I can take.

Eventually, there is some movement, and it is getting dark. I push through the crowds to the front and nearly knock over a man who is seated on a plastic chair and drinking a liqueur, and I want to grab it out of his hands to warm up my internal organs. I hope all this suffering is worth it.

The actual parade was a bit of a let-down. There were small children in what looked like a cage – reminiscent of the Child Catcher's cage in *Chitty Chitty Bang Bang* – being pulled along by a tractor, very, very, slowly. There were men dressed as women with beards or women dressed as men, as women with beards, I am not so sure. All this weird beardiness must have some Pagan significance. I took some shaky photos and had confetti thrown at me – small punch-holes of magazines and newspapers in reality.

After all this painfully slow processional spectacle and after my organs had thawed out, I realised that I needed a wee and had frostbite on at least three fingers. It was going to be a long forty-five-minute drive home.

Sallysatnavslut took me the rural route home. No street lighting, the darkness behind me and in front of me, through the Puglian countryside. The car speckled with confetti, the remnants of my first Puglian festival experience.

Chapter 4

୨୦୯

Italian Lessons. Hello and Farewell to Mr P – Ciao

I finally tracked down Mr P at the café in Ostuni once again, and we walked through the park and zigzagging this way and that through Ostuni's historical winding streets until we reached a blue door. A door to my learning Italian, a door through which I would walk through and feel illuminated and fluent in the Italian lingo in a few weeks. This, I found out, would not be the case.

Mr P was a pleasant middle-aged man with a bit of a pot belly (lots of excellent Italian cuisine no doubt), and he would make me coffee every Thursday afternoon and waft his hands about as though to circulate the air of the wonderful '*Ah profumo di caffè*, the perfume of coffee,' he said. He also said that he 'would not' be speaking English to me. Fair enough, maybe I would be able to manage with my few practised sentences and scant knowledge of the Italian verbs. How many verbs are in my verb book? 500. How many have I learnt? Five… in truth, I had learnt about two and a half verbs. It really is a long dark tunnel of verb conjugations. I realised that I knew almost nothing, zero, zilch, fuck all.

However, his lack of willingness to speak English to me at all became like a huge barrier. I was feeling a bit isolated, only having been in Italy a month or so. If anyone spoke English in the harbour, I would walk towards them in order to hear some familiar tones. I wasn't integrated or immersed into my new life. I wanted Mr P to talk to me occasionally and ask how I was doing in English, at least once. I was beginning to feel at bit desperate. I imagined conversations:

'How are you,' said Mr P.

'Not too bad. Actually fucking awful. I haven't spoken to anyone all week. Basil was nearly attacked by three dogs. I miss my family, baths, and the cinema. I wonder if I am going mad or if I have made the right decision. I feel emotionally unravelled and close to tears… I can't do my homework. Can you give me a hug?

'Don't worry. Tell me all about it. Let's see if we can sort you out. Don't worry about the homework. That's the least of your worries…'

Followed by an imaginary bear hug (he was a bit of a big-bear-huggy type) and me blowing my nose…

Every Thursday afternoon, I would turn up in front of the blue door and rap on it to announce my arrival. Mr P would shout down at me *'Buongiorno, Elaine'* and dangle a front door key on a piece of string from the upstairs window so that I could open the door and walk up the limestone steps to my Italian lesson. Week by week it all became more of a struggle for me. Each footstep seemed harder and harder as though I was being weighed down emotionally and physically.

By the sixth week, I felt as though I had come
to a frustrating halt. I did my homework religiously
and pored and sweated over verb conjugations and
pronunciations. Mr P was becoming equally frustrated
and said that I should be more fluent by now – the
Italians can be quite direct and even blunt. I also
thought he said, 'What are you doing in Italy?' Or he
could have said, 'What have you been doing?' And
in my insecure and emotional-tipping-point state, I
'heard' the former, which felt a bit accusatory. Exactly,
what was I doing? Where was I going and was this
all just a folly, a nonsense, an illusion? That was it, I
broke down and cried in front of a relative stranger,
feeling child-like, alone and all-at-sea, up-the-creek-
without-a-paddle and eventually driven into shaking
sobs, a-right-bloody-lemon.

Observing this sodden-English-mess, Mr P's
resolve softened and miracle of miracles, the English
came out, and I immediately felt more connected
to him as my teacher. Between the sobs, he offered
me more coffee and glasses of water. He asked what
could he do to help? Would I prefer group classes?
I explained how alone I felt and that it was difficult
for me to carry on at that time. I simply couldn't
come to the lessons anymore. In truth, I was finding
it difficult to cope in the early days, not just with the
lessons but with adjusting to living alone, in a strange
country. I was performing toddler steps into my new
life and felt as though I was continually falling over.
No roots had yet formed, and I was feeling adrift. It's
a bit like landing on a completely different planet, all

that was familiar was absent, and all that was left is the not knowing. I was getting used to being stared at (not just because I am English, this is a national Italian preoccupation) and getting used to struggling to communicate, but I realised that I was faltering and needed to regroup, to take time for myself to work out what I really needed and what was really important to me.

Learning Italian was occupying my every living moment, and I was trying too hard to be a 'good student'. I hadn't allowed myself time to settle to my new environment and learning a new language, although important, should not have been my main focus. I had also developed 'Italian paralysis' – which I understand is quite common – when I could understand what was being said and yet, could not construct a sentence with which to reply.

I left behind my lessons that day and felt relieved that I had taken some pressure off of myself. As I walked back to my car, I had a little giggle to myself about some of the funny things that Mr P had said. *Hymen*, instead of hymn and the way that he demonstrated the verb, *imbucare*, to put something in, or to insert something, by putting his finger into a hole on the opposite hand, which in English, as a gesture means a totally different thing!

Ciao, means hello and goodbye in Italian. Mr P looked defeated as we went our separate ways. *Don't worry Mr P; you can't polish a turd…* He tried and I failed, at least for the time being.

Anna
༦~ঙ

Anna is my new English teacher. I got back on the horse of learning Italian. Thankfully, she is bilingual and speaks fluent English having lived in England for many years and having two children that were born and brought up in England. I needed this; I needed to be able to express myself in my own language and let my teacher know how I was feeling or even just to connect with someone in my own language. It takes years to be able to express yourself well in a language emotionally (this is my belief anyway) as so much can be simply lost in translation or culturally 'misunderstood'. I needed Anna as much as I needed air to breathe and it turned out that she was just that, a breath of fresh air.

Anna says that in order to grow olives, you only need silence, sun, and stone. Her villa, set in a hectare of land and including two little trullis, not only has the silence and the Puglian sun but somehow she managed to haul huge pieces of limestone to line the driveway (even though when she first renovated the house she was already in her sixties). Olive trees with deep green leaves and silver-grey undersides are dotted everywhere. A mimosa tree dips it head full of yellow mimosa flowers, nodding towards her front door. Herbs circle beneath it as if in tribute to the tree, sage, rosemary, and thyme. Trees that bear persimmon, pomegranates, oranges, lemons, figs, and almonds add to the scene and Italian bucolic picture, a gorgeous fruit basket of smells and colour. *Il suo paradiso*, her paradise.

Anna is busy making coffee, *caffè lungo*, a long coffee which involves coffee made in the mocha pot, hot water added and then after heating milk in the microwave, 'ping'. This whole process takes quite a long time and seems quite ritualistic, but it is worth the wait. I am not keen on the small oil-slick-like espressos that are consumed within thirty seconds; a strong and bitter taste. The big buckets of cappuccino that have become so popular in the UK seem like a distant memory. I couldn't imagine drinking that amount of coffee now.

We sit opposite each other to drink our coffee. Biscotti have been freshly turned out on a plate, and I look at Anna, who is diminutive and dark haired and reminds me of my aunts (I am sure that there is some Italian or Spanish blood in my family somewhere).

We have a conversation about our lives, and Anna informs me that she used to be a nurse, and it turns out that she did her midwifery training at the same hospital where I did my student nurse training in north-west London. A small world, we say.

'I can't believe,' she says without using the word 'it' and Lili does the same. I wonder why the 'it' never gets included.

Anna insists that we go back to the beginning with my Italian. *Is my Italian really that bad?*

Soon she has me reciting the Italian alphabet (really back to basics here), and I realise that my pronunciation is appalling. Anna tells me that I need to pronounce every word correctly otherwise I won't be understood. *Anno*, meaning a year, if mispronounced can sound like *Ano*, anus and it would be easy to say that I have fifty anuses, Ho cinquante ani, instead of *Ho cinquante anni*, I am fifty years old. I became aware that I could be one 'n' away from making a complete arse of myself.

On leaving, she gives me quite a bit of homework and say, 'Buon lavoro.' This literally means 'good work', in Italy they say this quite often, although it is considered to be bad luck to say, *Buon pescare*, good fishing, as the fishermen believe that they will return without any fish.

The bag I am holding when I leave is heavy; it contains an Italian verb book and other textbooks on Italian grammar. Once again it seems like an uphill struggle. I feel more than a little overwhelmed.

Anna and I kiss, the Italian kiss on both cheeks and I have to bend down to hug her.

As I leave, the chalk flies up behind me from the driveway and I know that I still have a long way to go, in more ways than one.

By the second week, the alphabet has been left behind, and we look at some simple Italian phrases. As I sip, my *caffè lungo*, Anna corrects my pronunciation at every turn. Still stumbling and grappling with Italian pronunciation I worry that I may, *'Posso avere il tuo pene?'* 'Can I have your penis?' Rather than, *'Posso avere la tua penna?'* 'Can I have your pen?' Although, on second thought the former may come in handy. Anna was right; pronunciation is everything.

Anna tells me a story about an experience she

had whilst in England teaching English children to speak Italian. The children would be accompanied to the lessons by their *nonni*, grandparents, who were from all over Italy. In Italy, each town and province has its own dialect. Children learn the town's dialect that is spoken as the main language at home and Italian. Consequently, as standard Italian wasn't widely spoken, the older generation of Italians tend to be more proficient in dialect than in standard Italian. Even today, dialect is widely spoken and preserves the local heritage and is communally bonding. It's a sad fact that the Cornish language has died out through lack of use, whereas in Italy they preserve the traditional dialects. I recall Mr P telling me about an old Italian woman in Ostuni who could only speak dialect, and he said that he could not understand what she was saying. Small microcosms of heritage.

Even if dialect is spoken at home by the young, they speak standard Italian outside of the home, with articulacy and precision (I am not saying that Italian slang does not exist – it does – sexual slang words abound). Unlike English youths, who speak a mumbly-bumbly-slang-youth-talk that is changing all the time and new words are entering the English Oxford Dictionary at a great rate of knots.

Anyway, back to Anna's story. At this school, a new teacher had been appointed having a degree in Italian. All the children had completed their homework, and she was correcting a little boy's homework and didn't seem too pleased with its content. 'Who helped you with your homework?' the teacher enquired.

'*Nonno*, grandfather,' the little boy replied.

'Your grandfather is an ass,' she said.

The little boy's grandfather was watching through the window with tears in his eyes. The homework had been completed in dialect and not in Italian. The grandfather was humiliated by the new teacher.

I have noticed that there is a hierarchy in Italy and even snobbishness among Italians between the educated and the uneducated. Any teacher is thought of a 'professor'. Everyone wants to know what you do for a living, and an image and a judgement is then formed. The educated are venerated, and the uneducated are scorned. *All men are equal, but some are more equal than others...*

At the end of the lesson, I leave with an arm full of herbs from Anna's garden and more homework to do. My relationship with Anna just feels 'right', it feels more nurturing. I can share how I am feeling in English. Having Anna in my life feels like a friendly dock in a harbour that I can tether my 'adriftness' to. Keeping me steadier and a bit more grounded. My new life and a new path are opening up in front of me, and I am not going to lie and say that I am not a tad scared at times. I have shed all that I used to know. Like any transformation, it feels like leaving behind my old self and yet my new self and new life has yet to form fully. I don't have a map for this, just my instincts. I need to adapt to a new way of living and being. I want to learn the *bella lingua* and immerse myself into this new life that I have chosen for myself.

I can't remember who said this – but it encapsulates how I feel:

'It's paradise if you can stand it,' said Gertrude Stein to Robert Graves (thanks, Google).

Chapter 5

❦

April and Torre Guaceto

Winter has long since passed, and the newness of spring is here, and I am no longer alone. An Italian woman who lives in the next street sought me out and invited me to come for coffee. *Tu sei sola?'* 'You are alone?' she said. This question comes so frequently that I am beginning to wonder whether I should have it tattooed on my head. *'Sì, sono sola.'* 'Yes, I am alone.' Being alone and living alone by choice seems to be confusing to the Italians and they can't fathom why I would want to come and live in a foreign land entirely alone.

Lina is in her sixties and has a mop of white hair, and she always seems harried, as though she has forgotten something or needs to be on to the next thing. She has a house here near the sea and one in the country. She is always busy whether it is frying *peperoncini*, hot chili peppers, in her outside courtyard garden (in southern Italy the 'frying' seems to be done outside), or cooking masses of lasagne to take to her family in Rome. Lina's house is spotless, and the dining room is dominated by a large dining room table, which always seems to have some sort of food preparation on it. The kitchen is tiny (as is mine) and it seems that in Italy, where you eat has more importance than where you prepare the food. These small kitchens are utilitarian by design and not particularly aesthetically pleasing and suggest perhaps, that only one person is meant to be in the kitchen.

I am getting used to the dark and pungent coffee which I am encouraged to add sugar because it is good for the stomach according to Lina. We have short, fragmented conversations during our morning coffees as Lina speaks no English, and my Italian is still in a place that is not easily accessible. But this doesn't seem to matter; we manage to communicate the sense of a meaning and a gist of a conversation develops. Lina speaks slowly and is very patient with me. I gave her a small dictionary from which she learnt, 'Do you want coffee?' And that was sufficient for her. The dictionary now sits on a shelf gathering dust.

I inhaled deeply today. Early April and I am sitting on the small patio – which I have discovered captures the afternoon sun – the smell of magnolia, sweet and pungent is dancing and stimulating my olfactory nerve. The smell is reminiscent of evenings spent in Spain with my father in the 1960s when he had a bar and my sister, and I would spend a couple of weeks with him in Benidorm before it was 'Benidormised' and before package holidays and air travel were commonplace. The smell is so evocative and stirs me. I feel blessed today, blessed to live in such a beautiful place. I lie on my back on a sunbed that sags in the middle and watch the pushing clouds and reflect on the last time I actually watched the clouds in this position, being in the moment with not much else on my mind. Being fully present, just me and the clouds.

This morning, Basil and I had been for a daily walk, and the sea was stunning like a jewel. Turquoise and azures mingled into the sparkling water's edge. The tethered fishing boats were bobbing gently up and down on the ripples of the sea. The seagulls were cawing and swooping overhead looking for fish near the surface. Apart from Basil and myself and two builders we had this little piece of Italy almost to ourselves. I felt as though I was walking on a wave of beauty, which was fractured by the sound of the stray dogs, gang-like creatures, snarling and baring their teeth the hackles rising on their backs. Basil has yet to recognise aggression in other dogs and always wants to play. I am beginning to think that he has a form of dog Asperger's syndrome. Luckily the builders were there to fend them off. The beauty and the inferno, it would seem.

Torre Guaceto Nature Reserve

I decided to take a drive out to the local Torre Guaceto Nature Reserve, which is about four miles from where I live in Santa Sabina. I have parked about half a mile away – which might be a bit of a trek for those day-trippers visiting with picnic baskets, blankets, parasols, and children. Because it is a reserve, there are no permanent cafés or hotels or seaside villas. In the summer, I believe you can buy drinks and an ice cream from a hut.

On the walk up to the beach, there are farms on either side of the small tarmacked road, and wildflowers nestle in the roadside edges. There are a couple of small whitewashed flat-roofed houses with white plastic furniture outside. Aged farmers are tending their fields – rich, reddish brown soil and sprouting green crops of something edible in the future. Tractors trundle along in the distance. I can see an old farmer wrestling with a hose and using his stick to steady himself. Further along, reed beds appear with reeds reaching up to the cloudless sky, their fronds swaying happily in the midday breeze.

The sand is white, and the sea is beautifully calm with licks and curls of waves gently washing in the shoreline. Sandcastles on the water's edge wait to be decimated and drowned by the incoming sea. Presumably, there are no toilets here, and I imagine hundreds of people peeing in the blue waters during the summer.

I wonder if this is one of the best times of the year. It must be 19-20c with a slight breeze and very comfortable to walk around in or sit by the shoreline and muse. Walking yesterday in Santa Sabina, I realised that my quiet afternoon sea walks would soon be disturbed by hundreds of Italians on their summer holidays, covered in Ambre Solaire, playing music and soaking up the sun. Easter Sunday demonstrated this to me. The harbour was packed with Italians enjoying *la passeggiata*, a walk (la passeggiata is a national, late afternoon pastime), eating ice creams and necking coffees; drinking wine and having a late lunch. It was like an English summer afternoon for me, and I was in shorts and a T-shirt and the Italians were all wrapped up in scarves and heavy overcoats to protect them from the possible threat of pneumonia.

A couple wearing cargo pants and matching hats and shirts are walking along the shore. I imagine them saying, 'Take a picture of me in the foreground.' And they predictably took pictures of each other in the foreground. I have several pairs of cargo pants and wonder if – like this couple – I don't look too great in them. Maybe cargo pants should only be worn on safari or during an exploration of the Amazon.

I am perched on a piece of driftwood or more precisely it is half a tree trunk. It looks as though it has been placed here for a magazine travel shoot. Just as I am daydreaming about my log/tree an English woman scoops up a pair of children's shorts next to where I am sitting. 'There they are! I have got them,' she exclaims, paying no attention to me. The difference between the English and the Italians is that the Italians will always greet you. A polite nod of the head or a smile with *buongiorno* or *buonasera* – whichever is the most applicable depending on the time of day – the English on the other hand, do not do this in general unless you have a dog in tow, and then they become a little less frosty. I am not sure where the English attitude comes from, probably the cold, damp weather and the fact that there are millions of us crammed onto a small island. The only time the English seem to be bonded is when they have something to moan about or if they are in a queue, and if the queue is moving slowly mutually sighing and eye-rolling and perhaps a bit of tutting, maybe the only exchange. The Italians, on the other hand, will miss no opportunity to greet strangers and within thirty seconds of meeting you they will have extracted a potted history of your life, and you wonder how that happened.

I walk up to the end of the beach and take my shoes off as my feet sink into six inches of white sand. Thankfully, it's not the hot-burn-the-soles-off-of-your-feet kind – too early in the year. Alas, they have yet to pick up the rubbish from the headland. As in Santa Sabina, no one seems to clear up the plastic bottle detritus from the humans out of season. It is heart sinking.

I observe my fellow beach dwellers. A woman is massaging a man's shoulders. He appears to be asleep or unconscious. I always wonder why people engage in foreplay in a 'beach situation'. Maybe it is the warmth of the sun redirecting the blood supply to the genitals. Another woman is sunbathing in her bra. How does that ever happen? 'Oh it's a nice day, I think this calls for a sunbathe in the bra situation.'

I walk back to my driftwood/tree. The man is now on top. I am beginning to feel like David Attenborough watching some sort of animal courtship. Perhaps, I shouldn't be watching anyway – I am clearly spending too much time on my own.

The beauty of actually living in a country like Italy – which has long hot summers – is that I don't feel the urge to lie on the sand, splayed out like some washed up starfish. Sunbathe in a bra and knickers; get sunburnt, heatstroke and spend the next two days in bed with dehydration and a temperature. I can sit here, tap the sand out of my shoes; take some unprofessionally shot photos and observe life. I look down at my legs. Oh God, English shaved daily on the front and Germanic hirsuteness on the back. My split personality legs due to the fact that I can't wear my glasses in the shower. I decide to walk back and perhaps get out the razor when I get home to tackle the back of my legs and deforest the 'Forest of Dean' that seems to have sprouted surreptitiously.

The waves are now lapping the sandcastles which may be saved for another day as the tide is going out. I take a left turn and find a magnificent view of another white sanded beach, occupied by a few dots of bathers. The Byzantine tower, *torre* sits prominently on the headland, the sister tower to the one at Torre Santa Sabina. Both built in the 16th century a perfect place to look across the Adriatic for incoming marauders. The reserve is a marine protected area where turtles and stingray and other marine life swim around in crystal clear waters, perfect for snorkelling and scuba diving – not for me though I can barely do the breast stroke. At the moment, it remains totally unspoilt. There are miles of beaches around this area that as no construction has been permitted, the area has been allowed to prosper in its wild and natural state.

Just below me is a freshwater reed bed with a myriad of fish and I am greeted with a frog or toad chorus who remain hidden beneath the reeds. Only the song of their people can be heard. I am relishing this out of season meander around the reserve; a walk in nature. On the way back to the car the old farmer is still struggling with his hose. A daily battle I feel.

Chapter 6

❦

Italian Neighbours and Food

The Italians say, *'Se non cucina, non mangia.'* 'If you don't cook, you don't eat.'

A man came to my gate one day selling pots and pans. He opened the box of shiny cooking implements, and they glinted and winked at me in the late afternoon sun. Only hundred euros he told me – for that price I would want him to cook for me. I don't cook I tell him.

'If you don't cook, you don't eat,' he said.

I shrugged my shoulders, as though it were my only form of defence.

'Are you the Dalai Lama?' he enquired, which I thought was an odd thing to say.

'Yes,' I said, 'I only eat air.'

Of course, only eating air is a falsehood. I eat salads and lots of fruit and put all different types of seasonal vegetables in a pot and make soup – or warm goo, which may be orange or green depending on what's in it. Why I don't cook is not a mystery, I don't have to, and therefore, I elect not to. I like to eat, but not necessarily to prepare food, cook it and then eat it, wash up and then wonder why I have gone through the whole process. Perhaps I don't have a positive relationship with food. I have met a lot of men who get a kick out of cooking and experimenting with food, and I enjoy someone cooking for me. I think this is preferable rather than me turning sweaty and panicky wheels in the kitchen and serving up something that is inedible and unidentifiable to my victims.

In my minuscule kitchen in Italy – which will only fit me and perhaps Tyrion Lannister – I have an impressive Puglian Cookbook called, *Puglia in Cucina*, the English title being, *The Flavours of Apulia*. It sits half open and propped up on the kitchen counter – the openness suggests that perhaps it should be opened more fully, or perhaps its semi-openness will tempt Jamie Oliver to cook something from it if he were to pop by. The book is beautifully illustrated with pictures of little old *nonne*, grandmothers hugging each other or making the local *orecchiette*, little pasta ears. My favourite recipe is probably *melanzane sott'olio*, aubergines in olive oil as it doesn't require any cooking.

I haven't always been *non cucina*. For my daughter's first birthday I made my own jelly out of gelatin and pineapple juice, a cucumber crocodile (I should say here that one-year-olds really shouldn't be given raw cucumber; possible choking hazard, especially if swallowing a whole one). I slavishly made all the fairy cakes, decorated with jelly tots and biscuits that were so hard you could bounce them off the carpet. A rather sad looking sunken birthday cake was another one of my creations. The huge divot disguised in the centre with a huge layer of icing. All my appalling efforts were played around with by the babies – they became feral after a bit of sugar – who then proceeded to mush everything into the carpet as though they were making a Jackson Pollok painting.

Dinner parties were a nightmare. It took me four hours once to cook French onion soup when I should have gone for the easy option of prawn cocktail. I also once made the mistake of buying kidneys instead of liver for homemade pate – has anyone ever heard of kidney pate? I have even made my own after dinner chocolates – now that is a really sad fact. I obviously tried too hard and felt guilty if I hadn't made the butter; bought my own cow, milked it and waved a muslin around the kitchen for half an hour. My ex-husband did all the cooking for the last three years of our marriage – although I had done it for the twenty years – he then joined Martyrs Anonymous for undertaking such a task. My children now deny any memory of their mum ever cooking anything…

My mum was and is a very good cook. I refer to her as Mum here as she brought me up selflessly as her own child from a very young age along with my sister. She already had two children of her own and her family doubled in size overnight after the untimely death of my mother after childbirth. My sister and I were the cuckoos in the nest.

In her working life, she was a school cook. Occasionally, when I was off from school (I used to get this awful eczema on my hands), I would watch her bake huge oblong trays of chocolate cake with

chocolate icing, assorted biscuits in their hundreds
and my favourite jam roly poly – this is also known
as dead man's arm, which sounds like the sort of
pudding that might be served on *Game of Thrones*. I
am tempted here to crack a joke about another regular
dish, Spotted Dick, well I will anyway, but a man
should really go to the GP for that, for a prescription
of topical cream and penicillin shot.

Even though she had been in a hot and steamy
kitchen all day, she would come home to four fussy
children who would ask for different things to eat in
the evening, and she would then cook four separate
things – complete madness on her part. To give her
a break and as I was the last one to leave home, I ate
orange and banana salads for a couple of years. She
must have been relieved.

My mum expresses love through her cooking, and
so do the Italian mothers. Despite now being in her
late eighties she still cooks regularly and loves baking.
She continues to make over a hundred mince pies
at Christmas with her aged and arthritic hands and
will make at least three Christmas cakes for anyone
who wants them. I admire my mum for her prolific
baking wizardry, however, as a child I would witness
her being in the kitchen all day cooking on a Sunday
and it all seemed like such a chore. Fortunately,
having a big lunch on a Sunday in the middle of
the day has gradually died out in England. When I
did bung something in the oven for my own family
on a Sunday; it would be in the evening. The older
generation of Italian women who still have masterful
culinary skills are also slaves to the kitchen and

although I have great admiration for their culinary prowess and the love of cooking, the feminist in me thinks that women need to get out of the kitchen. Hence, railing against the idea spending too much time in the kitchen – actually more than ten minutes is too long.

Luckily for me, the Italians love cooking, and so I get to eat Pugliese cuisine. Italian neighbours and food seem to come together. The Italians think that it is rude not to offer a guest something to eat or drink. All the guest has to do is answer the many questions that may be fired at them and accept that this 'nosiness' is just part of Italian culture. My daughter said recently, and I think that this is a truism, 'English people mind their own business, and the Italians mind everyone else's business.'

My neighbours, Ferdinando and Rosetta, have invited me to lunch at *all'una*, one o'clock and I am prompt. I rub my arms nursing a few angry bites, after a couple of wasp stings from that morning. The wasps had decided to build a nest in my gate and then attacked me as I walked through carrying a bowl of cherries. Previously, I have been allergic to wasp stings and had even carried an epi-pen. At a barbeque in England a few years ago I was stung by a wasp on the leg – which I think was attracted to the smell of alcohol and a friend called an ambulance. The ambulance crew arrived and after examining me thoroughly; diagnosed slight intoxication, hypochondriacal hysteria, and hyperventilation. After being stung, this time, I waited half an hour in case I died from anaphylaxis. I didn't die, and so I made it to the lunch date.

Ferdinando and Rosetta are both retired. He was a quarryman at the local quarry and Rosetta used to be a nurse. As with many other local people, they spend the winter at their house in Carovigno and the summer months in Santa Sabina. Ferdinando is a big talker and waves his arms around a lot as though he is conducting an orchestra. They both often talk in unison, and I often listen to them from my house and wonder if they are arguing all the time, or just having a discussion. It's a bit difficult to tell most of the time as it always sounds dramatic, but they could just be discussing what they are going to have for supper or threatening to kill each other, who knows.

Ferdinando offers me an *aperitivo* (I once asked for an *apertive*, which means an aperient and no wonder I received a strange look from the waiter), a ready-made Aperol spritz which looks like Iron Bru and he buzzes around me attentively. Rosetta is in the kitchen (another small kitchen), and Ferdinando tells me that he produced fifty-nine quintales of olive oil from his land last year. We eat green olives from his land with the aperitivo, and he says that the food is the best in Puglia, Calabria, Sicily, and Tuscany, not in the big cities like Rome or Naples. Rosetta joins us, and then they develop a two-pronged attack and tell me that I am thin because I don't eat pasta (I have learnt that the Italians are not shy about commenting on how someone looks). However, despite this, I am served pasta, *orecchiette*, little ears (not *occhi*, eyes as I mispronounced it. Otherwise I would have

been eating a bowl full of eyes), with ragu sauce.
Homemade red wine is served with the pasta. Now,
this I have had before, you can really feel it when it
hits your stomach and flushes through your body –
and this effect is immediate. The wine, Ferdinando
says, helps the food go down, and he jumps up and
down to demonstrate that the food is going down
somewhere. He tells me that he and Rosetta have
been married for over forty years, and he says that
by now his liver should have exploded, and I am left
wondering whether he means that an explosive liver
is a consequence of the marriage or because of the
wine.

More wine follows and more food, the meat which
made the ragu sauce with Italian cucumber cut into
lengths (not watery like English cucumber), chicory
leaves and stalks followed by a *tartini*, a flat omelette
with *zucchini* flowers which are popular in Puglia.
Fresh fruit finished off the whole thing and some
mandarincello liqueur, just in case I hadn't had enough
alcohol with my lunch. I now understand why the
Italians are so fond of a siesta in the afternoon, or as
they called it a *pisolino* (which sounds like having a wee
on a hard floor).

Absolutely nothing happens in Italy in the
afternoons after lunch. Offices and shops close, and
you can hear a pin drop in the afternoon slumber
time.

They love their life they say. La dolce vita, I say.
I feel like I have been initiated into a small part of
Italian life that involves love and food. If only we
Brits could love life and live more completely and

more in the moment, instead of rushing through life and eating hurried meals. Ferdinando says that if I live in Italy for two years, I will be fat! Together, they both demonstrate my impending fatness by puffing out their cheeks and curving their arms around their bodies to accentuate how large I am going to become. I am beginning to believe this, as I have a muffin top alert.

In the evening, Ferdinando takes me to his olive grove in the country in Serra Nova where he has over four hundred olive trees which nestle in thick, cloying reddish brown soil. He proudly shows me all that he surveys. He has tomato plants, capers, and parsley and various fruit trees. The evening is warm and still. In retirement, he still has lots of work to do he says, *molto lavoro*. He goes to the olive grove every day and tends to his plants and trees. In November he will harvest the olives for olive oil and sell off the excess. There is something to be said for producing your own food for consumption, and I wonder if the future generations of Italians will do the same and I doubt it.

A few days later I have been invited to another lunch – dear God I don't think I have quite fully digested the last one. Rosetta says that lunch is like a ceremony and is very important to the Italians. Lunch is the main meal of the day, and the whole of Italy will stop for lunch and the evening meal is less important. More pasta – my poor intestines – with tuna, olives, capers and garlic. They serve me the best digestivo, *Amaro Lucano*, which is a liqueur made from herbs in Lucano in Basilicata. Most Italians in this region make homemade liqueurs from almost anything that they can get their hands on. In supermarkets bottles of 95% alcohol can be bought – imagine that in Blighty, there would be supermarket car parks full of drunks lying in shopping trolleys – and small amounts are used to make the liqueurs, from myrtle, fennel, liquorice, lemons, mandarins, strawberries and the alcohol content can vary from 28% to 40%. These liqueurs are not for the faint-hearted and are meant to aid digestion after a heavy meal, but in effect they act like an anaesthetic and knock you out for a few hours.

All this food at lunch time is making me feel as though I am slowing down and addle-brained, I definitely could not do this every day. The Amaro Lucano is going down, but perhaps not that well. It slides down my throat like antiseptic and seems to be sleep-inducing, and I am struggling to stay awake.

Through the haze of alcohol we start to talk about the Italian language and how Italian grammar is difficult. Rosetta says that even for Italians, Italian grammar can be difficult to learn. *'Oh good, I'm not such a thicky,'* I think to myself.

I am proud to say, or not so proud to say, that I have taught my Italian neighbours how to say fuck off.

'Come si dice vaffanculo in Inglese?' 'How do you say fuck off in English.'

'*Si dice*, fuck off,' I say.

And for the next ten minutes, you fuck off; they fuck off; we fuck off is the topic of the conversation. No sentence now being spoken without saying, 'Fuck off.' I am now laughing so hard that tears are streaming down my face.

And then there is 'Dick'.

Dick has been adopted into Carovignese dialect after there was a military base in Brindisi after the war and a lot of Americans were stationed in the local area. Dick was then used and integrated into the local *parolacce*, swear words. The Carovignese are very fond of saying, '*Non rompere mi dick*,' – don't crash my dick, or don't break my dick, which is a bit like saying don't break my balls. Soon, dicks and fucks are flying around the table and by this time I am laughing hysterically.

The next day while I was washing my car and Ferdinando walked over, grinned and told me to 'Fuck off.' Showing off his new ability to say two words in English, and thought it was funny. Lili, who was passing by, overhead this profanity and was visibly shocked and said, 'What have you been teaching them?'

My head bowed in shame and a bit of foot shuffling… well, it all started when…

Maybe I should stick to saying very little during lunch, drink less and stay away from the 'F' word references and keep dusting my Puglian cookbook, which is still sitting idly on the kitchen counter.

Chapter 7

৩৯৫৫

Summer: Zanzare and the Beach

Before summer gets into full swing and everyone has
to retreat into their houses to escape the fierce heat
of the daytime sun, the *zanzare*, mosquitoes arrive
and usually en masse. They wait patiently in showers,
under towels, and on bedroom walls, for a human to
pass in order to satisfy their appetites for blood and
are a bloody nuisance.

Every night I go into battle with the *zanzare*. It is
the beginning of May, and already I have had a fever
(I know this because I took my temperature with a
recently purchased thermometer) from two bites on
my arm. Fearing cellulitis, I deduce from an internet
search that it is probably 'Skeeters Syndrome' and
abnormal immune response to the mossie kiss. I use
a huge torch to search every corner of the house in
search of the unwelcome interlopers. Having found
them, I swot them or spray them. The former leaving
ugly blood splatters over my whitewashed walls.

Every year the Italians spray their gardens and
houses with some sort of insecticidal spray – which is
probably not good for the humans and certainly death
to the mosquitoes – I am holding out on this course

of action for the moment in case it is something else that I am allergic to.

The *zanzare* obviously like English sweet meat as I have three bites on my foot, which has now grown into elephant-like proportions. I have dutifully applied the insecticidal lotion on my exposed parts, and still, they nibble and nip at my flesh. Another internet search informs me that *'people are genetically susceptible to mosquito bites.'* Also, they are attracted to carbon dioxide emitted by every human breath. I can't hold my breath, surely? It is suffocatingly hot at night, and I can't bear the thought of going to bed fully clothed, and so a net will have to be the answer. Lili suggests that I might have to go back to England, bugger that, I will not let the *zanzare* beat me.

Internet suggestions for mosquito bites:

Spit on it, get someone to lick it – I rather like this suggestion. Put alcohol on them, ice, a cold compress, a crushed aspirin, baking soda, cold tea, mouthwash and toothpaste, salt water, vinegar, baking soda, wet soap, lavender oil, basil leaves, aloe vera and lastly – and most bizarrely – making friends with the mosquitoes. Will I have to throw a party for them or shall I just lie on the lawn and invite them to dinner, English sweet meat on the menu. The best thing is to avoid the Z monsters in the first place. Have ordered a hat with a net from England and plan on sleeping in it – attractive.

I have ditched the hat, as it is more uncomfortable to wear than having mosquito bites. A white mosquito net hangs over my bed to keep out the bloodsuckers. Unfortunately, I wake up every morning wrapped up in it as though I am a fly that is ready to be eaten by a giant spider. It seems as though I can't win.

What Do You Do All Day?
༄

'What do you do all day?' This was a good question posed by Lili as she deadheaded my purple petunias, petulantly tutting. She was probably thinking that I am a lazy cow for not doing my own deadheading. In truth, I hadn't even noticed that there was a need for it. I wonder where my head is half the time. Drooping indolently in need of love and attention probably.

What do I do all day, a summary:

• Awoke to the sun shining relentlessly in the sky. The sky is blue, naturally. Pulled on my favourite cropped trousers – the knee is going, and the seams have been sewn up several times.

• Put on for the second day running a white scooped necked T-shirt from Zara – a recent purchase.

• Took Basil for his morning walk. He shit in the woods – I know that a bear usually shits in the woods – and I feel slightly guilty about this having not scooped up the poo with a little black bag.

• Avoid the man who has been trying to chat me up with the line, 'Do you need somebody to love?' Obviously, he has been using Google translate. And

although no man has visited my pantry for a while,
I do have standards.

- I clean out a cupboard in the bathroom and wash
  all my towels for the fifth time. Why do they always
  smell musty? Put them on a 60c wash.

- Eat a coffee ice cream out of the freezer and put
  bicarbonate of soda in the leftover cup to soak up
  the damp.

- Kill a mosquito on my mosquito net. Obviously
  waiting there for its supper.

- Skype my sister who shows me around her house in
  Worthing.

- Think about going to the beach, but realise that
  I am not on holiday, I am supposed to be working.
  Think about setting up a Facebook group called,
  'Beach Dwellers Anonymous.'

- Read an email from a creative writing group. Among
  the top ten tips for writing a successful novel is
  'Turn up for work every day.' Well, I turned up
  and now I'm just distracting myself. My 11th tip
  for being a successful writer would be, 'Don't
  get distracted by the Italian lifestyle.' Or 'Don't
  deceive yourself, when you know that you are just
  procrastinating.'

- Forgot to eat lunch so have an apple and some

cheese.

- Read an email from a friend who has read my writing and has declared that he has 'Tightened up some of the sentences.' Very kind, but I quite like my rambling writing style. I don't want to sound like Jane Eyre on an Italian respite, whilst recovering from consumption.

- Wash Basil's ears in soapy water. He tends to pick up the sand like a little sweeper with his basset ears. Cover them with Sudocrem. The dog looks puzzled and smells like a chemist. Reward him with my discarded apple core, and he leaves it on the mat with a look of disgust.

- Think about having a shower and look down at my recently infected toe, which is now peeling several layers of skin. Get distracted by the swing seat.

- Try to read Julian Barnes on the swing seat and have a guilty and rather weak white wine spritzer.

- Retire back to the house as the kids next door are screaming. Fall asleep for half an hour and decide that it's not officially long enough for a proper 'Nana Nap.'

- Think of an idea for a screenplay and a novel and scribble a couple of sentences on a yellow Post-it note.

- Try to read Julian again and can't decide whether it is, in fact – good. Maybe a great novel or novella is subjective. Although I reflected, that I had recently read and thought that The White Hotel, on completing it on another hot/swing seat day – that it was a masterpiece.

- Reflect that books are like art. Does art have to be aesthetically pleasing or beautiful in order to be art? If I left a red ball in the middle of a gallery and entitled it pretentiously 'The Red Orb' and declared that it was a symbol of the red, sensual pulsation of life – in reality, that is complete bollocks and it is just as it is – a red ball.

Clearly, I have too much time on my hands and in my head. But I will never have the opportunity to do this again and savour every moment of doing very little, and not really achieving anything. The beauty of doing fuck all. La dolce fuck all.

The Beach
ৡড়

I have walked to the beach for the first time in six months without Basil, just to sit, to be, and to write. Usually, I have a 6 am walk – or even earlier and a second, 6 pm walk with Basil. My mattress is hard; you can bounce tennis balls off of it, so sometimes I only get four hours sleep, six if I am lucky. I am not working in the normal sense of the word, and I am not physically tired when I go to bed, and therefore sleep is as elusive as the Scarlet Pimpernel. I do, however, love my early morning walks, the solitude and witnessing the birth of the day. I like to watch the sun emerging at the edge of the sea, which seems like the edge of the world – a glowing orb of solar maximus. Sometimes, the sea takes on Jaffa cake-like tones, the sun burnishing and burning off the exiting night.

In the earliness of the day, I can observe my early birders. An octogenarian jogging in a shuffly-way, carrying his loose brown skin, his trainers incongruously white. An avid sunbather setting up at the water's edge at 6 am and erecting the pole of his umbrella – a prime spot before anyone as everyone else isn't even awake. The beaches are cleaned early, the debris of the previous day drawn up in the mouth of a digger. Men sweep the roads and snatch an early morning coffee as the café opens. Dogs are walked, including mine. Although Basil is often hoovering up leftover rolls or an abandoned chocolate crepe; a dried dog turd is also appealing which I always make him drop from his mouth, fearing sickness and disease. But actually, it is also disgusting and gross.

The old, don't seem old here. They remain very active well into old age. Their joints well oiled by olive oil and antioxidants consumed with the Mediterranean diet, with lots of fish, vegetables, and fruit on a daily basis. All the Italians seem to cycle, young and old. The elderly are up ladders doing repairs on their houses or going for brisk walks. I have yet to see a zimmer frame.

On a previous visit to Puglia, I observed a man having dinner on one warm October evening. He had been walking up and down, alongside the harbour restaurants and eventually settled at a much-visited table, eating a free pizza and beer or so it appeared. He chain-smoked constantly, even when he was eating. His speech slightly slurred – not through alcohol – but as an after-effect of a previous stroke. He limped. He approached my sister and I as we sat at our table for dinner. At the time my Italian being even worse than it is now, I said, '*Non parlo italiano.*' 'I don't speak Italian.'

'No,' he said and then paused. 'Hello, good morning, good afternoon and good evening.'

A bit David Frostesque, although David probably said something more on the lines of, 'Hello, good evening and welcome.' I was touched. We reciprocated and thanked him. I saw him the other day, a crutch supporting his weakened side. Still smoking, still alive and walking. I am sure that it is the sedentary lifestyle that kills the English.

Early morning walks also mean stray dogs. They have to eat and nose their way through the bins for discarded pizza and *panini*, sandwiches. I now have a whistle, yes a whistle to blow in the ear of any dog that might want to attack Basil or me. A tartan umbrella waved in their general direction also seems to scare them off. Yes, I am the mad English woman with a whistle and a tartan umbrella. Basil had been previously jumped on by three dogs (owned by a local restaurateur) who had been let out to roam freely and were looking for trouble. It was my body surging with adrenaline that kept Basil away from their gnashing jaws. I somehow held him – with one arm – 2 ft off of the ground. The restaurateur smiled but in an almost mocking way and asked if I was okay. I said yes, but felt badly shaken. Basil didn't seem to mind (he probably thought that it was bit of rough play). The dogs here are not socialised with other dogs or trained as a rule. The English (and I am generalising here) tend to treat their dogs as a member of the family. They are walked regularly, let off the lead to run freely in large green parks and may even have their own coats with their names on them. Italian dogs are pampered only in the minority and are often let out for walks on their own and are rarely allowed to romp and play with other dogs. I have to remind Basil that he is not in a park in rural Berkshire.

It is now mid-July. I have been in my Italian bubble for six months, and I have come to realise that this time next year* I will have to think about returning to England. Maybe Cornwall, live in a log cabin and sniff a fisherman's jumper; get fat on pasties. But for now, I am here. Today is a sharp contrast to the January that greeted me. Santa Sabina/Legendsville. Although there is something quite comforting about a closed down resort. Silence in a self-soothing hammock. The shutters closed on every house, the beachfront hotel hibernating for the winter, an emptiness which I find comforting.

---

* I actually didn't go back after two years, but ended up staying for four years.

Santa Sabina began its awakening in April. Italian weekenders cleared their paths and roadsides. Pruned their trees, painted their walls and cleaned their houses. The cafés slowly opened, and the harbour became more alive and vibrant.

I am sitting on the terrace of the beachfront hotel, sipping a chilled prosecco. I can now order one with aplomb now that I have perfected the rrrr rolling. It is at least thirty-two degrees and a slight breeze from the sea is my only relief.

I don't even notice my hot flushes in this heat. The two temperatures – mine and the environment – merging into a cacophony of blended diaphoresis. It's lovely. I glisten, perspire and sweat like a horse. I order an espressino freddo. Something cold. It's a small cup of whipped ice cream, laced and tumbled with an espresso shot. Much needed coolness and caffeine to perk me up a bit.

I am looking at the Torre. A Byzantine tower which dominates the headland. To its immediate left is my favourite fish restaurant the Miramare. This restaurant is thankfully open all year round. Its neon light glimmers welcomingly, when everywhere else is dark and abandoned in winter. The fish dishes are amazing at the Miramare: swordfish, cuttlefish, octopus all laid out on the plate with fresh deliverance. The fish in Santa Sabina is so fresh that it can be bought straight from the boats, with the immediacy of a fresh catch. Equally, fish is caught using harpoons in the sea by my wetsuited neighbours. You know when you are in a different country when you can see your neighbour walking down the road with a pair of flippers sticking out of his backpack, a harpoon in his hand and with a bucketful of octopus intended for the lunch table.

I am touching my hair. Blonde as a child and highlighting it since. It's now caramel – the colour of a toffee penny from a Quality Street tin. Before I came to Italy there were three things that I was apprehensive about and indeed thought that they were essential:

1) Clean and dry clothes – it can get cold and damp here. Where's the tumble dryer? There isn't one and tumble dryers eat electricity which is really expensive here. Cheaper option – a Lakeland heated clothes airer; godsend, so I don't smell like a damp tramp. I could also mention here my washing machine that looks like a cheese grater and lives in the bathroom, but does the job.
2) A car. Aygo purchase. A bit tinny, but a great little run around.
3) A decent haircut and colour. Cue, the Italian hairdressing experience.

I long for the day when I can summon up the courage to go my natural colour. Which at the moment I think is a mousy brown, although I still kid myself that I am blonde still and every three months I have my *mesce*, highlights done. I hold up a picture of a delectable twenty-five-year-old with the look that I want to achieve. 'This, I want this.' And I point to it, but I would probably need a plastic surgeon and not a hairdresser to achieve the 'I want this.'

'The colour is *troppo freddo*, too cold you need more hot – *caldo*,' said Mimo, the grey haired and spritely Italian hairdresser whilst brandishing his scissors and touching my hair as though it was beyond saving. It was March, and, two months in, my Italian was limited to that of an amoeba. The walls in the salon were orange. I hoped that I didn't end up with burnt umber hair like the walls. Two girls, worked on my hair and putting in the foils, as though they were trying to save a seagull from an oil slick.

'Ah, cocktail,' Mimo announced shaking a plastic bottle in his right hand. The contents of which looked suspiciously like orange hair dye. I acquiesced. I sold my house, gave up my job, I could shave my head if it all went wrong. The colour was thankfully, pleasing; a warm blond and not a carrot top. I asked for a *riccia*, curly blow dry. And after much moussing, diffusing and head tipping. Shirley Temple left the salon.

After another recent visit to the hairdressers here in Italy, I noticed after having the foils put in and washed out, that there appeared to be something indescribable that looked like green gunk in the sink. I had asked for golden. In reality, the 'golden' had become a mixture of the green gunk and a bit of orange from a bottle. The young girl who was rubbing it in – a bit too vigorously I might add – seemed to be at it for rather a long time and it felt more like an Indian head massage. The green gunk and orange became ginger, or should I say a Renaissanced-Titian. I hoped that it would wash out.

The next day I was considering wearing a hat for a few months and met Lili at my gate.

Lili said 'I like it. You look like a little dolly' as she observed my new mop of copper.

Not quite the look that I was looking for...
Thinking 'Whatever happened to Baby Jane.' Bette Davies – I shuddered.

And so whether my hair looks like toffee penny or Titian, I always hope that it will wash out, and it does eventually.

Back to the beach...

A small toddler of about eighteen months is rifling through my little leather Italian bag – a recent purchase, and I can't get anything in it. She babbles like Boo from *Monster's Inc*. We have an equal parity in our parlance of the *bella lingua*. She cups her hand in and out as if to say, give me your money, or if not your sweets. I have neither. Papa scoops her up to prevent her from a life of crime.

There are a myriad of technicolour parasols. Cuban music blares out from the hotel terrace. Why is this? We are in Italy. Puglian traditional music is divine. Tangostic/Greek influences with The Pizzica and Tarantela which has an orgasmic crescendo. Why Cuban? Even in my local Berkshire Italian deli, they would play Cuban music. Maybe it is generic. Evocative of hotter climes, sweaty bodies and blue skies and oh dear speedos. What is it with speedos? I much prefer surfers' knee gliders. Should Stephen and the Twins, really be trussed up so close to the body and in a tangled mess. No wonder the Italian birth rate is on the decline.

The toddler is back. We have a babble-talk in incomprehensible Italian, and we both agree that the Italian verb conjugations are a mystery. Her hand is in the bag again. Little podgy fingers – got to love her – but seriously get out of my bag.

The Italian language still being a mysterious tongue twister, any slight inflection in voice or mispronunciation of a vowel and I met with 'What the fuck?' kind of stares. This, I am becoming used to. The toddler shrugs her little shoulders; even she can't understand me. Masculine, feminine, plural, tu, lei, voi. I continue to constantly mix my personal pronouns. Anna says that the use of *voi* – you plural, today was used as a way of discerning the educated from the uneducated. Even in families Papa/voi was used instead of tu and was a used as a form of respect. Voi being used both as a form of reverence, but also as a form of submission. *Schiavo vostra* – I am your slave would be used as a form of supplication. I guess it is a bit like the word Boss being used instead of Sir in the English vernacular. Both of which I am not a fan of. I mix my personal pronouns like the hokey cokey and never know if they are in or out. Usually, I put my whole self in and suffer the consequences.

The beach dwellers are 'bronzed'. The high consumption of tomatoes giving some protection to the rays of the sun and hopefully some sunblock. The children are bronzed too. Not a T-shirt sun protecting fabric in sight. The children run around freely in the midday sun, cooling off their little brown bodies in the sea or in the beach showers dotted along the beach. Their skins may be overexposed but they won't starve. It is 3 pm and food is offered as a bridge between lunch and dinner. The children are being constantly fed from foil wrappers containing panini with cheese and prosciutto inside. Everyone seems to be constantly eating, chatting and popping in and out of the sea. A man is approaching the beach dwellers with a basket in one hand and a large bucket in the other. His back is scorched from the sun – lobster like – obviously he doesn't eat enough tomatoes, and his wife has hidden the sunblock. *'Mandorle e Coco,'* ' Almonds and coconut,' he shouts. I stroll over – vacating my little roadside step that smells vaguely of dog wee – he offers delicate slices of coconut and a small net of almonds doused in iced cold water. This really does top a British Mr Whippy and a 99 flake. A delicious little work of art.

The speedos are in competition with the Brazilian bikini bottoms, which barely cover the cheeks, although marginally better than a thong. How do these young Italian women avoid the cellulitic orange peel dimples? Wrinkle free, superbly shaped brown bums abound. Not a pear in sight – only peaches; perfect peaches.

My observation of Italian health. More risk of skin cancer due to speedos and Brazilian bikini bottoms. Offset by a rich Mediterranean diet, lots of exercise; swimming, cycling, and walks. Increased morbidity due to limp cigarettes which seem to hang out of every male mouth on the beach. Although they don't seem to be inhaling; they just seem to hang there like a symbol of masculinity.

I walk home and watch the bright pink and yellow kayaks that are traversing the bays. A schooner with an aubergine sail glides across the horizon, and I avert my eyes from any approaching trussed up Stephen and the Twins in speedos.

It Gets Hotter and I Think
I Am Going to Die
༄

It is nearing the end of July, and it is hot, and I mean really hot, road tar meltingly hot. 'Only mad dogs and Englishmen go out in the midday sun,' as Noel Coward once penned in a tuneful ditty. It is 40c during the day dropping to only 26c at night. I can't get the air conditioning to give out more than a few farty warm breaths, so I leave the doors open and let the air circulate. An overworked fan attempts to keep me from going insane in my bedroom overnight.

At lunchtime I can hear the 'click, click' of Rosetta's hob as she prepares yet another sumptuous lunch and wonder who wants to cook or eat in this heat. I am as torpid as a sloth. I feel as boneless as an omelette and spend all afternoon trying not to slide off of the plastic patio chair, whilst attempting to read a book.

It is so hot that beach life has continued past

sunset and heads can be seen bobbing in the sea at nine-thirty at night. People are cooling off and their bodies submerged in lukewarm water. Dark shadows in a pewter sea.

I have recently bought a bike, an *Itala* – which I assume is an Italian make. It is powder blue, classic looking with a basket on the front 'a la Jean Brodie'. I can't get on it at the moment, because I don't have the strength and I imagine my bum melting into the seat. Maybe later at dusk, someday, anyday when it is cooler. My daughter said that I need a helmet the only time she can remember me riding a bike was in the woods when we used to live in Berkshire. I turned the corner, and she met me with my body on the ground – like road kill – having no cycling skills. I ride a bike like a fish and swim like a cyclist. I hope the bike doesn't turn out to be a white elephant. It looks nice in the shed though, all shiny and new. Everyone rides here, the old, the young, mums and dads with small children perched on a little seat in front of them. This part of Puglia is quite flat and dozens of cyclists ride along the country roads in colourful biking gear. Whizzing past dry stone walls and olive groves at break neck speed usually.

Recently, I made the mistake of riding through a throng of people during *la passeggiata* and had the back of my bike hit by an angry walker. Obviously, I should have got off and walked. In retrospect, perhaps the safest place for my bike is in the shed.

Here's my own little ditty:

Putting yourself out there in Italy

Putting your handbag on the floor will make you poor

Putting your feet on a cold floor when you have cystitis will make it worse

Putting your hand out to be taken by a man (as a formal greeting) will end up with several crushed fingers

Putting sugar in your coffee is good for the stomach

Putting a liqueur in your coffee is even better for the stomach

Putting yourself in a car on Italian roads is hazardous

Putting yourself on a bike on Italian roads is even more hazardous especially during la passeggiata when you shouldn't be riding your bike anyway

Putting a limb outside of the mosquito net will lead to a midnight feast by the beasts

Still putting myself out there

Chapter 8

෨ஓ

Men, Boys, and Dogs

September has arrived with cooling breezes and the occasional spot of rain. In another month or so, I will be thinking about putting on my stove, and I look forward to quiet walks with just me and Basil. The Italian kids will be going back to school, and the beach dwellers will return to the town. The summer cafés will close, and all will be calm, as Santa Sabina settles into a winter sleep.

I learnt yesterday of the death of my neighbour's dog; a yellow labrador called Ricco. I surprised myself at how upset I was at hearing this news, but he was part of my Italian experience in my little Italian bubble. I had recently been asked to help look after him during the coming winter if his owner's moved back to Carovigno and I was looking forward to bonding with this brown eyed, tail wagging mutt. Ricco's barks and howls would punch through the air anytime day or night and rather than being irritated by this I was becoming accustomed. A familiar sound. He would howl in unison with passing ambulances or a car alarm, and if he barked in the night, I felt safer knowing that he could alert me to any intruder.

He would be sitting at his gate diligently and patiently at the beginning and also at the end of my walks. I would tickle his ears through the gate, and he would bound around his patio and find an old shoe or a piece of garden hose to present to me, like a handsome gift. I would have taken him for a walk with Basil if it weren't for the fact that they were both intact males and probably gone in for a bit of 'my balls are bigger than your balls' banter, and may have had a little tiff and gotten into a bit of ball biting. Probably after they couldn't decide which ones were bigger. Although I have to say Basil would have won the ball size competition by a long chalk.

As Santa Sabina is going to sleep, I had been looking forward to the winter and seeing his face pressed against the gate anxious for an ear rub and looking at me quizzically whilst I spoke to him in English saying, 'Who's a good boy then?' He was a good boy, a strong and athletic dog that died suddenly in his sleep. Bless him. Basil now gets extra ear rubs and a lot more declarations of, 'Who's a good boy then?'

Tonight Basil and I will play hide-and-seek in the garden – his new game of choice – because we can.

A Beach Reflection
୬୶

I look for seclusion and anonymity and find it on the headland of my favourite beach – the Mezzaluna. Unable to find a support group for Beach Dweller's

Anonymous on Facebook, I find myself on the beach at 12.30. I have a sense of the summer time running out. It is already more chilly in the evenings, and my thoughts are turning to socks – although I wonder where my order has gone, for six pairs of black thermals as they haven't arrived yet – in anticipation for the winter. Only mad dogs and Englishwomen are out in the midday sun, but after two days of rain, I find myself in need of the sun's embrace and the comfort of Graham Greene. I am still in love with real books. Paperbacks and hardbacks and I'm sure that I am keeping Amazon's profits up, by the amount of books that I order. Although I did recently baulk at ordering a 'used' copy of Anais Nin's, *Delta of Venus*, for fear of contagions and DNA evidence from the previous owners, who may have enjoyed the erotica a little too much.

It is much quieter now in this idyll-beach-dwelling-place. A man is walking gingerly over the rocks, so not to cut his feet – surely flip-flop wearing would prevent him from this peril. An elderly man is slowly easing himself onto a sunbed, as though he is in fear of someone snatching it away from him, as in musical chairs. I used to hate musical chairs at children's parties. All that rushing around, adrenaline rushing, anticipation, and inevitable cake vomiting. The man lifts his legs up towards the sun, as if to prove to himself that he still can. His everyday in the sun, Italian tanned skin hanging off his skeletal frame, no longer supported by collagen. Is this my fate too? A wobbly gait, an anticipatory sit and husk like skin? I feel another ditty coming on:

Bask in the sun,
Bob in the sea,
Take time out,
They are all doing it – as well as me,
Lip, lap sings the Sea,
Just stay here and be…
My mind is obviously wandering.

Today, I am looking forward to some quiet beach time, time to reflect and to be. I should be at my place of work, my Italian table, which is covered in books, diaries, Italian textbooks and a few crystals to stave off any negative energy. Having thoughts of writing a book, painting a picture and climbing a mountain.

This is a small place and not the sort of place where it is possible to have a liaison and then not bump into 'that person'. 'That person' being my first fling in a foreign land, probably a mistake in retrospect – a bit like having a fling on a desert island when there are only two palm trees to hide behind. In Graham Green's *The End of the Affair* – the current paperback read – the protagonist Maurice Bendrix lives a mere 500 yards from his ex-lover. It's not quite that bad; 1km is close enough, too close. Close enough to make me wince and my skin prick at the thought of an awkward, bump into, 'that person'. Not that 'that person', is a bad man in any sense of the word. But it would be nice to be in a larger a more anonymous place where these things could be avoided, like Australia for instance or Siberia. As a teenager a rule should be made, 'never kiss a boy in your class'. The 'bumps into' can be a daily occurrence with rushes of awkwardness, feelings of stupidity, and ensuing embarrassment. I kissed a classmate at a summer party when I was about thirteen. At this age, you can guarantee that all the girls will be at least four inches taller than the boys as the boys wait for the hormonal surge to kick in, and then literally grow some balls. In the meantime, we exploratory girls are stuck with the shorties with unbroken voices and awkward mannerisms and behaviours. I was once struck on the cheek by a flying stone across the playing fields, by a good looking boy with a David Cassidy style haircut. He was trying to attract my attention, but very nearly removed an eye. I must have forgiven him as I married him six years later. Once the haircut had gone, and the manners had improved.

Back to the vertically challenged kiss. 'Summer Breeze' was playing on the record player, and I remember a slow dance and the boy's head was resting on my shoulder. I didn't so much as lean into, but lean down for a kiss. The liaison was brief, and once the summer was over, and school began, awkward glances turned into comments such as 'Elaine's a geek and a snob'. It was the end of the affair.

So here I am hiding behind a sand dune on the headland. I realise that I will have to leave soon as a man who looks like Hugh Jackman has placed his beach towel within spitting distance. I hide my head under my Andy Capp-like cap and peer underneath. The Italians have a superb gene pool. Strong shoulders, slim waists, and very small bottoms. Englishmen, by comparison, look like misshapen potatoes. A combination of a poor diet and mixed genes from a multiple of insurgencies over centuries and probably too much pub time. I am beginning to believe that the British man doesn't abide by the rules of evolution and natural selection. If they are not bald-beer-bellied men, they are often golf-jumper-wearers – I am obviously talking about men of a certain age here. The Italians, on the other hand, are nice to look at – in general – from Rudolph Valentino to Franco Nero, although I would prefer the latter. Even older Italian men have a certain allure about them…

I perform a quick nipple check as my *bikini top is far too small, and my breasts are unfettering and behaving like two school boys fighting under a duvet. I lie on my front but have a morbid fear of snoring. Although I sleep on my own most of the time, I have been told that I snore. An ex-boyfriend once said that when I slept, I sounded like a little pig shitting. Not very appealing, which is probably why he is an ex-boyfriend.

A beach seller is now hovering above me trying to sell me anything from dresses, bracelets, umbrellas and hats. Several of the hats – at least six of them – appear to be balancing on his head. I say 'No grazie' and do another nipple check.

I glance over, and the Huge Jackman look-alike has gone. I imagine myself looking like a sexy Helen Mirren gazing out to the Salento coastline in a sultry ruby red bikini – this is a famous newspaper pic, and she did, indeed, look very lovely. When in reality, I am an unfettered-bosomy-type woman, who shouldn't

be let out in a bikini and in all likelihood, absolutely
no one is looking at me, not even the Hugh Jackman
look-alike. Maybe it is time for me to draw a line
under the *bikini wearing anyway.

I console myself with the fact that most Italian
men are either far too young for me, married or
live with their mothers. I cover myself with a white
kaftan – didn't Princess Margaret wear one of these?
And look forward to thermal socks, leggings, a
thick blanket and good book and being absolutely
anonymous and invisible.

---

*I was actually wearing a 'Tankini', which is not really
for tanks, but for women who want to keep most things
undercover for fear of scaring small children on the beach.
How Elle McPherson still wears a bikini God only knows,
perhaps she keeps her intestines in a little beach bag.

Chapter 9

҈

Footprints in October and in Search of Chestnuts

I am alone. Only my footprints are left in a diagonal story across the sand. The sand is being rippled by a gusty north wind from Albania. The sea's turquoise and aquamarine hues pulled up by a white frothing, whipping wind and incoming tide.

The beach café is closed. The shutters are down until at least the end of May or the cusp of June next year, No more white rum mojitos or *espressinos*. The *espressino* (by espressino I mean the hot coffee version, and not the *freddo* version, which is essentially ice cream), being a peculiar to southern Italy with more coffee and less froth than a cappuccino.

A boat lies in front of the decking as though abandoned by a local fisherman who had forgotten that the tide had gone out. It's not a seaworthy vessel and has a crack in its hull, a break in its azure blue body.

The noise and singing of sea combines with my own tinnitus. An ever present reminder of my declining hearing. I now, often have peculiar conversations with my sister – whose hearing is also declining, probably at a more rapidly descending rate. Whilst staying at my daughter's in England I had spilt coffee from the stairwell which then proceeded to trickle down her newly painted wall. My sister had come to pick me up for lunch, and she found me swearing and trying to clean up the mess and oddly, she started to film me on her smartphone.

'Why are you filming me?' I enquired as I bent over the stairway with a cloth in my hand.

'I thought you said – can you film me,' she replied whilst still filming whatever she thought she was trying to capture.

'No you daft, cow. I said – Elisa, is going to kill me.'

I now think that it will be difficult for us to have any kind of normal conversation unless we are both directly facing each other and cupping our ears. Oh, the joys of getting older.

I would like to go off on my tangent here about smartphones – as I was filmed committing and subsequently, trying to cover up my coffee spilling crime – it is my belief that smartphones and the older generation have a bit of a struggle. Smartphones are gentle, touch sensitive pieces of equipment and I have often witnessed the elderly stabbing the screens with their index fingers as though there are demons inside that they need to exorcise. Or performing exaggerated swiping motions across the screen, as though every page has porn on it or maybe some elderly men are using Granny-Tinder and are looking for someone who still has a pulse and doesn't have a face like a ploughed field.

I too have a smartphone, and I find it impossible to perform swift texting with my thumbs like my daughter does, and I too stab at my phone with my index or middle finger. I think that they should develop mobile phones as big as mobile phones in the early 90s with huge buttons, so that some of us of a certain age can use our thumbs again. My son says, 'If your mum doesn't have a black leather cover on her smartphone and doesn't use her index finger to text, then it is not your mum.' I defy anyone over the age of forty to be able to use their thumbs to text.

The orange and yellow striped sun loungers are abandoned and stacked in an untidy manner. The ever present blue sky has a heavy skirt of watercolour painted clouds, the white mixed with swirling shadows of grey and a hint of runny pallid purple.

I count the bottle green recycle bins every morning, a statement to who might still be here. I feel a slight hollow emptiness as autumn has begun and summer has left for the underside of the world. I guess it is about endings, seasons changing and although I yearn for solitude, with every change comes a need for adjustment and adaptation. Everything changes and nothing stays the same.

In England, Shire churches will be full of fruit and vegetables in celebration of Harvest Festival – or as my children would say, 'Harvest Vegetable.' The stacks of the five-a-day on a decorator's table at the altar. The vegetable array broken up by the odd tin of soup, some busy mums really have been too busy to go to the supermarket. I always gave my kids a tin of soup. But it was always Big Soup, so in theory, the vegetables were given as an offering but in a can.

I went back to school myself this week, in a picturesque Masseria near Ostuni for a Creative Writing Workshop, run by an experienced writer and also a book editor. The thoughts of school transporting me back to the childhood new school term. Brown tuffs, itching white collars, pristine socks and a baggy jumper that was always two sizes too big so that it would last longer. Now I can go to school with tanned legs and bright orange sandals and drink chilled white wine with my lunch.

I brought pens, paper, and an ageing laptop with a very short battery life and wore my favourite pink shimmery lip gloss. Would be scriveners and scribblers worked on their prose under the watchful eye of the tutors. Concretising our sentences and making us aware of our chimes. Chimes – not a shopping centre in northwest London – are repeatable words and phrases that will bore the potential reader into discarding your paperback or Kindle into the nearest bin or immediate deletion from the digital page. Their review being, 'repetitive and didn't hold my attention.' You need to edit, rewrite, sweat, submit and wait; this is the message from the more experienced. Writers, on the whole, do not make money we are told. I have come to the conclusion that writing is like masturbation, *you have to do it for yourself and enjoy the process.*

At the 'end of school' after dinner reading, I chimed as though I had several carriage clocks in my pockets. The after dinner prize of a notebook going to a very deft and fellow newbie writer, who wrote a hilariously comical story even though at the beginning of the week, she said 'I don't do comedy.' In a gravelly voice much changed by tobacco as she flicked ash over me on the Masseria steps during a coffee break. A totally different style in comparison to her emerging novel on Forensic Psychiatry/Serial Killers – which I imagine might be entitled, 'She was only a farmer's daughter, and he chopped her up and put her in the freezer.'

We all trilled and clapped rapturously. Never was a better story told about 'The Tenalady Detective Agency.' So funny and bladder-stimulating was the storytelling that we all could have done with an extra protection of three-ply wadding in our knickers.

My bum is now numb, and the wind has rearranged my hair. I have enjoyed my little storytelling and musing by the sea.

I walk back across the sand, not retracing my steps, but creating new ones. I will fill my emptiness with Italian chocolate. It's just a feeling, and it will pass.

Every time I feel anxious, and I wonder what the hell I am doing, I say to myself, 'You won't remember this, this moment of anxiety and doubt.' And I don't.

In Search of Chestnuts
ৡৡ

It's an early start 05:30. I am on a *Pullman* – a coach
with my Italian neighbours. I have no idea why we are
leaving so early, but we are all headed to Monticchio
in Basilicata, a neighbouring province in Italy to
celebrate the arrival of the chestnuts in the autumn.
As I have said before the Italians will find an excuse
to celebrate anything and everything. The chestnuts,
in my opinion, should be celebrated as years ago
when the south was much poorer, chestnuts were
used to make bread and puddings when there was
very little else to eat. Chestnut festivals are held every
October all over Italy.

Basil has been safely deposited at Anna's the
night before for his first Italian sleep over. He has
three acres to explore and lots of olive trees to pee
up. Anna said that she would be delighted to have
him, and I have given him strict instructions not to
pee in the house or lie on the sofa. Last night, we
walked around Anna's property under the light of a
full moon. She is reluctantly selling the property due
to her age and her ill health. She has a great love for
the place. It seems as though this is a common theme
here in Puglia. People retire here in their sixties, grow
their own vegetables, pick their own fruit and harvest
their own olives and then ten years on it all becomes
too much to handle. A dream is shattered, because
we all have to grow old. Anna's trullis cast domed
shadows in the moonlight, and I know that Anna has
been very happy and contented here. She completed

a lot of the renovations herself, and it will be a sad day when she has to leave it all behind. The place that feeds her soul, her home country.

Trullis are unique to Puglia and the Itria Valley. They are limestone buildings with conical rooves. Originally built by farmers with large slabs of the local limestone. No cement was used back in the 17th century so that they could be quickly demolished to avoid housing tax; if no building was standing, then there would be no tax to pay. There are over a thousand Trullis in Alberobello, which is a UNESCO heritage site. Lately, these trullis have been bought by foreigners and converted into homes or holiday lets. I love them, and they are unique to Puglia. Anna has a small trullo to the back of her property that she escapes to when she has guests. Anna and I have had a discussion about how it would make an ideal writer's retreat. Peace and tranquillity amongst olive and fruit trees and only the whirring of the crickets to disturb you. The downside is that the internet signal is poor, and Anna has to sit on the roof in order to write an email. Internet access tends to be a bit patchy, and when my internet goes down at home, the story usually is that three men are up a pole trying to fix it, and I wonder where this pole is and why it takes three men to fix it. My conclusion is that it is a typical 'Italian arrangement' and may involve a metal coat hanger and some duct tape.

Anyway, before I go off on another tangent about 'Italian arrangements' and how if any piece of equipment goes wrong, some Italian with a screwdriver in his hand, will come to look at it and then shake his head and declare that it is a mystery and then walk away. Let's get back to today.

As I step up onto the coach at such an ungodly hour, I reflect on the fact that it was only last week that I took another coach to a different destination, to Bari, with the same gaggle of Italians. Not in search of chestnuts, but in search of Swedish soft furnishings and furniture in Ikea – pronounced *Eekayah* by the Italians. I went to Ikea in pursuit of blankets, candles, and a mattress. The mattress being essential as I have had disturbed sleep for the past nine months in a bed with a mattress that feels as though it is made of concrete. I have suffered in this princess-and-the-pea-bed, and I fear that there will be no prince to marry at the end of my torture and no queen to declare that I am actually, a real princess. If this mattress fairy story is to have a happy ending I just need to get a new one.

I am also glad that mossie season is over, and I took the dreaded mossie net down. I would find myself wrapped up in it every morning, like Miss Havisham's wedding dress and would fear a visit from her offering me rat infested wedding cake. I realise now that I haven't had a good night's sleep in months.

A visit to Ikea in Italy is an orderly affair. Everyone goes in the same direction like shoals of fish. Unlike me – after having lost everyone – went against the flow like a salmon upstream and was given some disconcerting looks. I had also apparently stuffed some display cushions into my yellow Ikea bag – which had been marked 'For Display Purposes Only.'

I really don't understand the Ikea shop etiquette.
Dogs were in abundance in trolleys and on leads. Why
take a dog shopping to Ikea? Probably, to choose
their own rugs, blankets, and sofas. At the end of the
blanket and rug hunt, the dogs exited the building,
like they were attending an event at Crufts.

I ask myself whether I am actually fond of
chestnuts, but I am gradually becoming an Italophile
and am happy to celebrate almost anything, even the
opening of an envelope. In the past, I have only eaten
chestnuts or *castagne*, as the Italians call them, from a
seller with a burning brazier in London. Black fingers
and a burnt tongue are always the after effects, and
I wonder why people buy them, as everyone looks
as though they have been in a fire afterwards. I also
had a chestnut binge as a child when fallen chestnuts
were inadvertently cooked and burnt in a fire in the
garden at my dad's. I ate so many that I vomited in
the rhododendron bush. I haven't been that fond of
them since.

I wonder what the collective noun for chestnut
hunters is – conkerers? Anyway, here we are in pursuit
of the shiny brown things. Conkers, are in fact, from
the horse chestnut tree and are inedible and have been
banned from schools in England – not in case they
are eaten – but because the yearly game of conkers
can lead to injury. I hear now that a child cannot
enter a sack race unless they are wrapped in bubble
wrap, and egg and spoon races have been banned in
case a kid develops 'low self-esteem.' I personally,
enjoyed the slow cycle race, which meant that the
slowest competitor won, and that event rather turned

everything on its head.

Now we are all seated and accounted for on the coach, the chatter in the charabanc quietens as the Sunday morning benediction is listened to over the radio, Radio Maria, very aptly entitled. The opening morning prayers are in Latin, *Benedicat vos onminpotense Dei* – Omnipotent God may bless you. It's 6 am, and I have the feeling that it's not the pope as he doesn't get up that early. I am not a Catholic, although everyone else in the coach is and I feel soothed by the benedictory offering over the radio waves.

I am not religious, but I do believe in a higher power. I make the sign of the cross when I enter a church; even though I count myself as an 'areligious'. I visit churches and cathedrals in Puglia as much as I can. One of the cathedrals that I like to visit is the Basilica concattedrale di Santa Maria di Assunta, which sits on the highest point of the old town. Ostuni was built in medieval times and has warren-like wiggly streets where you can find artisan ceramic shops, cafés and restaurants and dominating and imposing piazza. The cathedral itself was built in the 15th and 16th centuries and renovated in the 1960s. I am not sure if they ran out of money or whether it was a 1960s shortcut, but I was slightly disappointed when touching the walls and the columns in the cathedral, that I discovered them to feel warm and not cold like marble. The walls and the columns had been decorated and cleverly disguised to emulate marble. I also hadn't realised that there is clothing etiquette (probably because I couldn't read the sign which was obviously written in Italian),

until a girlfriend entered the cathedral – after paying
1 euro – she was deemed to be too uncomely and
exposed in her low-cut dress. The woman in the kiosk
handed her a large piece of kitchen roll in order to
cover up the offending items. The sign, which I had
been unable to read, probably said 'Please cover your
boobies, in order not to offend God and Mary.' It was
all a bit undignified, therefore, after that embarrassing
episode, I now, always carry a scarf to cover up any
offending décolletage.

I am so soothed and soporific by the benediction
over the radio that I fall asleep on my companion's
shoulder. The coach rides over a bump in the road,
and I suddenly wake up with a start and realise
that my mouth is open, and I am dribbling slightly.
Narucia – another Italian neighbour, generally a
jolly and funny person, and my current head resting
companion – gently pushes me off with a bit of
disdain and my head bangs rhythmically against the
coach window. My eyes are opening now and then
when the banging gets too incessant. My mother
always used to say that I could fall asleep on a
washing line because as a child I was always falling
asleep and she thought I had a case of narcolepsy. She
would have taken me to the doctors, but I probably
was never alert enough to get there.

Once fully awake I notice that the olive groves
being replaced by fruit trees and vineyards.
The landscape is becoming less flat and more
mountainous. Broccoli florets of trees dotting the
mountain tops and lolly-stick-like wind turbines
are scattered on the hills creating energy for the

surrounding houses. The reddish brown soil of
Puglia replaced by the dark chocolate truffle soil of
Basilicata.

We stop on the autostrada for a coffee. *'Scendi, scendi,'*
Someone pipes, urging us all to descend out of the
coach. 'Shandy, shandy,' I repeat, intentionally as I
like to keep them all amused. Everyone laughs. The
Italians are now openly sniggering at my bastardising
of their beautiful language.

We alight and arrive at a comically named pitstop
called 'Sarni'. I stretch my legs and wipe away the
dribble from my mouth, drink a coffee and eat a
Twix. My fellow travellers are eating *Corneto* which
is not an ice cream, but a croissant like pastry and
afterwards join an orderly queue for the toilet – it's
not true that the Italians don't queue. In banks there
seems to be a protocol of horizontal queueing, which
results in utter confusion and polite questions of
'Were you before me?' or exasperated tutting and
enquiry, 'Am I last?' English vertical style queueing
would relieve the confusion surely? Get in a bloody
straight line; then you would know who is next.

Post bladder relief, I make a quick phone call to
Anna to see how the dog sitting duties are going. 'If
only a man would look at me with those eyes,' she
coos. Clearly, she is in love with the short-legged,
long-eared Basil. What's not to fall in love with apart
from the farting, the drool, and the baggy balls. Just
like most men really.

Finally, we arrive at Monticchio which is picturesque.

A lake has formed in the mouth of an inactive volcano. A large white convent nestles in the trees on the top half of the mountain, and I use my camera zoom lens to see people hanging out of the windows. Are they tourists or escaping nuns?

We all stop and have a picnic which mostly consists of bread, which I refuse. Why? *Grano intolerante* – wheat intolerant, I tell my fellow picnickers. I am not dying, and therefore they all look at me as though I am being fickle. I eat cheese and ham and drink a glass of homemade wine. I have an instant hot flush and have to disrobe. I have given up on trying to explain that I can eat a small amount of pasta, but not every day and that I never eat bread.

'But you ate pasta at our house,' Ferdinando says as he pours yet another glass of hot flush-inducing liquid.

I am also tempted to tell them that apricots don't agree with me and that following an ingestion of apricots I can perform the Apricot Bum song, but unfortunately I don't have the language skills to tell this comedic story and I just shrug at Ferdinando. Which really means that I have given up trying to explain my bowel symptoms and whether my bowels are just irritable, fed up or angry.

The next stop is Melfi – still in Basilicata – where we go in search of food. They are plenty of food stalls and plenty of bread. I satisfy myself with another glass of red wine and realise that I am becoming a little bit tipsy. I am tempted though by chestnut ice cream which is being sold in the gelateria. I order a cone and one scoop of chestnut ice cream which is speckled with small pieces of chocolate and decide that my indulgence will help to soak up the red wine. My dessert after the cheese and ham. I refuse a bun with a mashed up sausage and *pettole*, which is a local delicacy, which looks like a doughnut that has been squeezed through a ringer (the pettole that I am used to, are small dough balls). I wonder why all the food here seems to look as though it has been hit by a hammer.

After what seems to be like a very long day the sun is setting on Melfi. My feet ache and I take my shoes off when we take a rest stop and look over to see a dog slumped on the grass. We are all chest-nutted out, although I am pleased with my chestnut associated purchases, a chestnut fridge magnet; chestnut chocolates and chestnut liqueur which I intend to consume over Christmas.

When we leave Melfi, and I muse about the chestnut sellers that we have encountered on our chestnut hunt. A man with a large nose and a green felt hat, who had very shiny chestnuts. An old man with mould on his chestnuts who spat chestnuts remnants as he spoke (he ate whilst he sold them) and a fit young man with bulging arm muscles and a large fiery brazier, stirring his chestnuts with a large wooden stick, whilst wearing a yellow apron. I think I prefer the latter as his chestnuts were hot!

The next day I pick Basil up from Anna's. He ignores me as I drive up and continues to cock his leg up Anna's herb garden. Anna greets me with a double

Italian cheek kiss and an English hug. 'He's been a good boy,' she says. And Basil wags his tail in agreement and disappears into the garden.

She invites me inside, and Lesson 11 begins. 'You must sing the verb changes and phrases.'

Here is the song about chestnuts that she invites me to sing:

Sonno riccio spinaso
Ma frutto gustoso
Mi trovo in Campagna
Mia chiamo…. Castagne

Which roughly translates into:

They are spikey
The fruit is delicious
They are found in the country
I am called chestnuts

(not to be confused with a pole dancer advert from Norfolk)

This little rhyme, I hope, will help with the unfurling of my English tongue so that I don't mix my tenses like a man on amphetamines tossing a salad. All this talk of singing reminds me of singing 'Show me the way to go home', at the picnic in Monticchio yesterday, which I performed at Lili's request and after a couple of glasses of red wine. She must love my singing. I realise that I am not ready to go home. Not yet.

I sleep more soundly now with my mattress topper from Ikea and pull a blanket up to my chin every night, the cooler nights allowing me to have a good night's slumber.

Chapter 10

≪≫

November, Olives, Chicken and Pup

I have always had a romantic and idealistic idea
about picking olives. A warm, maybe hot afternoon,
a knotted hanky on my head, sunburnt shoulders;
perched on a ladder, surveying the strong arms and
broad shoulders of young Italian men picking olives
for extra pocket money. Instead, it is a weak watery
sunny afternoon and I am at the family olive grove,
with Lili, her mother Mary and a nice, handsome
young Ghanaian, called Manuel who came to Italy via
Lampedusa and sends all the money he earns home
to his family. I also imagined huge nets and shaking
olive trees to get them to give up their sumptuous
prize. But instead, rakes are used to gather the already
fallen olives. Years ago, the olives were picked off
the ground by hand. Hard- back-breaking work, with
women on their knees for hours on end. Had the rake
not been invented?

It's the end of November. I am doubled up on
socks and jumpers and wearing a rather unflattering
long green Parker. My nose is red and cold. The sun is
peeking through the sliding doors of late autumn and
early winter and the ground is damp and covered with

a carpet of green, brown and black olives. The olives are already on the ground ready to be scooped up, along with leaves and earth and dispensed into plastic stacking boxes. As an observer, I am not getting my hands dirty – although on reflection it would have added to the experience. I imagine an Amazon review, 'lazy cow, didn't even help with the olive picking.'

All the olives in Italy are harvested between November and March – not the summer pursuit that I had imagined – the coldest time of year. Although, I later found out that the olive season was cut short due to the wet and stormy weather and all the olives fell to the ground. Also, the olive yield would be poor this year due to the lack of rain during the summer.

In the region of Puglia are over 60 million olive trees that produce 40% of Italy's olive oil. We are on the land today belonging to Lili's friend who is unable to pick her own olives due to illness. There are 40,000 square metres of olive trees here, some of them are over 2,000 years old. Lili will be paid about 23 euros per *quintale* – a *quintale* being 100kg. The olives, once collected, will be taken to the local *Stabilimento* – I don't know what the correct term is, but let's call is an olive squishing plant in Carovigno where they will be pressed and turned into olive oil.

I wander around the grove. The olive trees seem to have personalities. Twisted, gnarled and bent over by the wind and weathering. They are dry to touch; some have huge caverns and caves carved deeply into their trunks, and yet they still produce olives. Wild marigolds punch out through the red soil to give way to thick black jewelled carpets of olives. I squeeze an olive and am surprised at the reddish purple stain on my fingers and note the faint smell of the oil.

A dog is watching us in a dry and sunny spot – I seem to attract dogs. His face tilting towards the warmth of the sun. I scratch his nose and tickle his ears and think about the little black pup that gave me a visit a couple of weeks ago. The little black pup had followed me to my gate, wagging his tail and looking to be loved. I do love dogs, but you kind of get used to all the strays after a while. Occasionally some of them get rounded up and taken to the pound in Brindisi, and I always wonder what their eventual fate will be.

Seven dogs were sunning themselves one morning on the beach; I usually give them a wide berth once they form a pack of more than three dogs. There is always a risk that Basil might get set upon, and I have been charged a few times by dogs with their hackles rising and white teeth flashing. On this particular day, I decided to get some control of the pack and said in Italian, 'Enough, go away.' (Which is actually *basta* in Italian which sounds a bit like bastard and is very satisfying to shout.) And eventually added the command, 'Sit!' (all in Italian, but I did have the English dog trainer's voice of Barbara Woodhouse in my head at the time – for those of you who don't know her she was a posh dog trainer). Surprisingly they all sat down one by one and stayed sitting until I passed.

I assumed that this particular errant pup had broken away from the pack, and as I shut the gate and I went to go into the garden, the little interloper slipped through the bars of the gate, wagged his tail again and waited patiently for some attention. If my heart had strings, then it would be definitely playing like a harp, and the little black pup nuzzled through the undergrowth in my garden, familiarising himself with what could become home. Basil made the final decision not to welcome the pup into our home, by being a bit unfriendly and showing some dominatory behaviour. I began to realise that the puppy was – in all likelihood – going to be bummed by a randy basset. In order to save the pup from a bum-rape fate, I carried him to the end of the path (where he came from) and sat him down on the pavement and gave him a little pat on the head. I rang my daughter afterwards full of remorse for my guilty-non-British-like-you-must-like-a-puppy deed.

Three weeks later he came back to my street, and I saw him being fed by an Italian neighbour, and he greeted me with enthusiastic tail wagging. His coat was like black velvet, and his legs were longer, and I had to force myself not to steal him away and keep him a secret from Basil by hiding in my bedroom under a warm red cable knit blanket. Another guilt-ridden phone call to my daughter, who assured me that he would survive without me adopting him.

Another two weeks went by, and I saw little black pup being chased at great speed, passed my gate by Brando, an Italian Segugio hound. Segugio hounds are like a cross between a greyhound and a basset – luckily a greyhound body with a basset-like face and not the other way around, which would just be weird.

Brando can run like a greyhound and chased the little black pup back into the field. More guilt ensued and I looked for the little black pup in the fields, but to no avail.

A few weeks later, I saw the little black pup again – or his identical twin brother – in the back of a Jeep under the watchful eye of a large Italian Mastiff who was now his new companion. The little black pup had been happily adopted by a good Samaritan and was no longer languishing in a field, getting wet in the storms and waiting to be fed by any kind stranger with a bowl full of kibble or rummaging through bins looking for leftovers. Guilt assuaged.

There must be something about my gate that makes the local animal population think that I am Dr Dolittle as later that week I found a chicken in my garden, whom I named Cynthia. Now Cynthia wasn't a good house guest and pooped on the patio, did a lot of head nodding and scratching and wasn't going to be caught easily. Although I wondered what I would do with her once I caught her. Would she fit in a pot in the oven? Luckily for Cynthia, I am not much of a cook and tend to prefer my chicken prepared and packaged and on display in a supermarket cold counter. I thought that Basil might be able to chase her out of an open gate, but instead, he's pinned her against the garden wall and she appeared as terrified as Chicken-Licken waiting for the sky to fall in.

Then I heard a young voice shouting 'Lina, Lina.' Obviously, my neighbour's son had been alerted by the terrified clucking of Cynthia – Cynthia was, in fact, a Lina, the errant chicken – I assume that Lina is a derivative of *gallina*, which is the Italian word for a hen. She had been missing for three days, the little boy said. With much relief, he scooped her up and took her home for a worm supper and a nice bed of straw, or a lie-down on the sofa to watch Rai TV and a bowl full of chicken feed.

Back in the olive grove, a lot of olives have now been collected. 170 kg of olives in total and put into stacking boxes and thrown into the back of Lili's much abused Fiat Punto, and I follow her to the *Stabilimento* and on to the next stage of their journey.

I enter the olive pressing plant totally unquestioned, without a hard hat or Wellington boots, although it may be a good idea to wear them as there seems to be a lot of oil spurting out of the mouth of a giant mechanised press. Lili's olives are emptied into a huge grate, weighed, and a conveyor belt takes them to a machine that separates the fruit of the olive and the oil. Leaves shoot out one end, olive fruit from another and the oil is centrifuged and pumped out like liquid gold from another much larger metal shoot. The noise is deafening.

Traditionally and probably a more artisanal method, olives are crushed using large millstones and after grinding the olive paste is then pressed in large fibrous discs to extract the oil. The best way to extract the oil is through cold pressing, however, generally the olives are pressed through a process of hot pressing which affects the quality of the oil.

The pulp that is left from the pressings is called *Sansa* and has a bit of a funky and foetid smell. Until recently this pulp was re-pressed and mixed with better quality oil and sent to other countries disguised as extra virgin olive oil. This doctoring has now been clamped down on, but it has tainted the reputation of Italian olive oil.

The Greeks were the first to extract olive oil from olives over 5,000 years ago. Extra virgin olive oil is produced by simply pressing the olives, and nothing else is added. Extra virgin olive oil should have a clean olive taste and not be contaminated by other variations in taste. If it doesn't taste like olives, then it is not extra virgin olive oil.

I can't imagine Puglia without its olives groves or the Puglian cooking without olive oil and wonder if I am ever going to learn to cook a Puglian dish, or whether I am just going to toss another salad in olive oil.

The olive trees in Puglia, however, are under threat from a bacterium called *Xylella Fastidiosa*. This bacterium is particularly affecting trees in the Salento region of Puglia. The bacteria affects the root system, and so the olive tree cannot adequately soak up water. The tree then becomes desiccated and dies. Although some Italian officials are now arguing that the desiccation is caused by pesticides and not by the bacteria. Either way, olive trees are dying, and if the Italian government literally does not get to the root of the problem and work out a solution, then millions of olive trees in the Puglian region may have to be destroyed to prevent the spread of *Xylella Fastidiosa*.

According to the *Olive Oil Times*, the world production of olive oil is now exceeding 3.2m tonnes, which is a shit tonne of olive oil. Maybe we are all just becoming a bit more health conscious and aware of the benefits of olive oil in reducing low-density cholesterol in our bodies and preventing heart disease. Or maybe everyone is just embracing the peppery taste of olive oil and beautiful variation in colour from yellow straw to deep greens. Although it has been documented that some extra virgin oil is 'doctored' with low-grade oil, soya and even vegetable oils, I can assure you that any Italian could tell you whether the olive oil they are using is of good quality without a chemical acidity testing kit, but just by smelling it and then tasting it.

Olives that fall to the ground affect the taste as the oil in the olives starts to oxidise, and it tastes acidic. A good virgin olive oil should have an acidity of less than 0.8% and in ideal conditions, all olives should be picked from the tree and not collected from the ground.

I look around again at the machinery in the *Stabilimento*; my shoes are now sticky at the bottom from the olive oil which seems to be shooting out of machines, and I wonder how anyone can decide which olive oil is theirs once bottled, or maybe it all just becomes Carovignese olive oil and nobody cares.

Anna produces her own olive oil from her olive trees in her garden and she once had 9 litres of olive oil in her suitcase to take back to England. I relieved her of 3 litres of the oil, in order for her not to incur a huge excess baggage charge and also to stop the plane from sagging in the middle from the extra weight.

It's time to go, and Lili has sped off to collect more olives, and I drive home to a solitary basset, minus a chicken and pup and toss a salad in olive oil for supper.

Chapter 11

༄༅

A New Year's Eve Reflection

I had settled down to a quiet New Year's Eve – this
is my first one here in Italy – with lots of candles, a
bottle of chilled prosecco in the fridge and a flaming
pellet stove emitting enough heat for the whole house.
I reflected on previous New Year's Eves when I was
either working or coming back from work, or going
to work depending on the shift system. One particular
New Year I had completed a thirteen-hour shift and
didn't even have the comfort of a hot bath as my
boiler had broken down. The house was freezing. I
dressed and washed the essential triangle and walked
across the road to my neighbour's house. My feet
ached, and everyone was drunk and singing Karaoke
songs. My worst nightmare. I grabbed a warm glass of
white wine and clutched it to my aching body, wishing
for the midnight hour to come and go, so that I could
escape.

I became cornered by my neighbour's friend who
talked 'at me' for an hour about the virtues of being
a perfect wife. Having been divorced and having
had an empty bed for several years, I felt as though
I would have rather woken up with my head sewn to

the carpet than listen to this diatribe. How can you
be a perfect wife? Unless you have been replaced by
a multiple orgasming Stepford Robot? Gobsmacked
and thoroughly bored by the absurd right-brained
perfect wife tale, I retreated to my cold and fridge-
like house and dove under several blankets and put
on a woolly hat. Quite honestly, my worst New Year.
I could sense the MRSA bacteria seeping into the
bedclothes, escaping from my unwashed body.

So here I am at a party in my Italian adopted seaside
village looking at a red plastic plate. It is empty
because I have already eaten, having received a late
invite. Despite saying, *'Ho già mangiato'*– I have eaten
already, several times, and yet food is still pushed
towards me. Seafood salad, with octopus and every
kind of fish you can think of; cold meats; cheeses
and a huge seafood casserole. Anyone would think
that I lived by the sea. The mussels are eaten raw with
just a squeeze of lemon juice. Everyone is eating in a
belly-god-like fashion. Lili has a huge plate of them
and tells me how she was hospitalised after eating
fourteen oysters at a wedding and spent four days on
a drip. There's obviously a price to pay for eating raw
seafood, and I am so relieved to have already eaten.

Hot green peppers and tomatoes are also served.
The green peppers are very hot I am told.

'Is it true that hot peppers make you hot in the
bedroom, like Viagra?' a man at the end of the long
Italian table enquires (I can't actually see who is asking
this question as there is a cloud of cigarette smoke
at the end of the table, due to an Italian bad habit of

smoking whilst eating).

'No, it's not true,' I reply.

This conversation prompts Lili to tell the story of how on Christmas Eve she introduced me to yet another 'single' man – he may have been single, but I didn't think that he had long to live. And I had exclaimed how come she only drags up unattractive men, to which she replied that there aren't any attractive men in Carovigno and that this is all there is.

There is one thing I have learnt whilst being in Italy, and that is any personal information and, or gossip will be repeated over and over again, usually whilst in the presence of the victim (you really shouldn't reveal your deepest secrets to an Italian). The said victim will smile sweetly and accept that this is just the way it is and that the Italians just love to talk and gossip about everything so openly (even if it causes acute embarrassment). As your secrets are endlessly regurgitated; the seafood may also come up and out at a later date in a regurgitative manner, especially if eaten raw.

I feel a bit incongruous with my empty plate and agree to two inches of wine as I am driving – although in theory, I could have walked. A large bottle of Casa Di Whoever is on the table. I am writing on a serviette, as I don't have my notebook, and the babble of the Italian language is all around me, and I still feel at times as though I am drowning in a sea of words and which leads to my inevitable miscomprehension. I refuse any more wine initially. The police won't stop you tonight, they tell me, and I feign having my hands in handcuffs, to demonstrate that I won't risk it. Although after gentle persuasion and several two fingers of wine later, I am certain that I am at an arrestable limit.

Christmas in another country is different. I hung Christmas decorations on a fir tree next to my door, which then blew off in a tremendous gale. I had fish for Christmas dinner and minus the Christmas crackers. Lemon sorbet to cleanse the palate between courses, a delicious *dolce torta*, sweet cake – without any Christmas pudding or mince pie in sight. Followed by an Amaro Montenegro liqueur or I could have had the house liqueur which was ice cold liqueur made from *finocchio*, fennel which settles the stomach after a heavy meal. I enjoyed a short coastal walk home with my grown up kids and didn't have to suffer any Christmas repeats on the telly.

A British Christmas is a much more strenuous affair. Friends and family have bought and wrapped presents by November. Someone is planning how to puree the food for Granny and get her to the toilet on time before the Queen's speech. Credit cards are bludgeoned to death like a Ripper victim in Whitechapel and queues are formed from Argos to Debenhams for the latest must-have-whatever-that-maybe. In the internet world, Amazon works 24/7 flogging seasonal workers with no toilet breaks and cardboard covered gems fly through the letter box. Mothers cry in frustration; children scream through boredom and husbands doze off outside changing rooms, whilst their spouses shop for the perfect Christmas Day jumper or dress.

Over the years, I gradually developed a deep dislike of Christmas and usually worked. You would always find me in Sainsbury's on Christmas morning buying the food for the staff at 6 am, wondering how many satsumas could be consumed over Christmas and would buy three bags. I would then carry the said shopping up to the Cardiac Unit where I worked and passers-by would always say, 'Having a party?'

'No, I always come to work carrying several bags of food, that no one will have time to eat because we are always so busy.' A true statement. Festering piles of food over the Christmas period was the norm. My kids were sick of me saying, 'And I didn't even have time to change a tampon.' Quite often I wondered whether they secretly wished that I had died of toxic shock. In the year that I left nursing, I told my staff that I was going to have Christmas Day off, and a member of staff looked at me as though I had just declared that I had shot Bambi's mother. Someone else will have to do it; I told her and gave her the instructions of how to get to Sainsbury's in Taplow.

My NHS Christmas days would consist of snatched mouthfuls of satsumas and nuts, orange juice, fighting with the hostess to give a woman a Christmas dinner whose husband was dying and they had been married for fifty-five years: dropping an oxygen cylinder on my toe. Having said toe examined by a Consultant, who was a patient. No break. Organising a transfer to Harefield Hospital for a patient who needed a heart transplant. Dancing the Bangra for an Asian lady to cheer her up – several times – she was very down. Punching the teddy on the raffle prize display out of frustration. Smiling sweetly at management, whilst receiving a box of Quality Street. Smiling more sweetly whilst receiving a free car pass after I had to work Christmas Eve, Christmas Day and Boxing Day due to staff sickness and realising that it all had to end.

I have never told my kids that I don't believe in Santa. Even though one year I received a dressing gown from Brentford Nylons, my faith was unwavering. In Italy, Santa came and deposited presents wrapped in red tissue paper into much loved and used Christmas woollen stockings.

San Nicola is the patron saint of Bari. Otherwise known as Babo Natale, Father Christmas, or as he is more popularly known, 'I am the guy in the red suit.' The red suit being an invention of Coco Cola in 1921. Up until then, you could always find him in blue-striped pyjamas.

It is said that San Nicola – who was very rich – tossed sacks of gold coins down the chimney which then fell into socks which were hanging to dry by the fire, therefore commencing a tradition of gifts in socks/stockings.

In my family and when I was little, we had a coal fire. My dad, who was a Geordie, would shout, 'Are you up there, Jimmy Pie?' And a hot twopenny piece would fall out of the chimney. Much to our amazement and I still don't know how he did it. The twopenny pieces were always hot from the fire. But then all four kids would look around for our real presents. Magic tricks weren't enough and then we would scrabble to find our pillow cases stuffed with presents under the tree – which was usually made of white tinsel, and my mum would decorate the tree with something called 'angel hair', highly flammable and a fire hazard. But a lot of things were hazardous in those days; explosives in chemistry sets and oil burning trains that would give any kid third-degree burns by Boxing Day.

On Christmas Eve in Italy my son and I went to a party that was being hosted by Lili's sister, Concertina. Usually, on a British Christmas Eve, you would expect the hostess to be Nigella Lawson like – slurring her words – not actually looking perfectly groomed and wearing the latest dress from Monsoon. Poor Concertina had her head in the fire cooking *pettole* – small little balls of dough mix, which once cooked are covered in honey and are delicious.

Her head was in the fire because the oil is in a huge pot on the fire and her face is as red as San Nicola after a hard night tossing around gold coins. This is Lili's family's Italian Christmas tradition. Every year, Concertina does this and risks third-degree burns to her face and arms making dozens of little dough balls.

My daughter was missing from the *pettole* cooking bake-off. There had been a flood at Gatwick, and the power was out in the whole of the airport. Her luggage could not be booked in, and she missed the flight, due to 'the head down let's ignore this horrible situation' British incompetence. Apparently, there was only one toilet functioning, and I could imagine the Brits queueing for a pee and exclaiming in disgust, 'What do you mean, there is only one toilet?'

The internet came to the rescue, and we managed to get her another flight, and she arrived late Christmas Eve via Rome, and San Nicola corroborated with Santa Claus and Father Christmas to deliver gifts.

It's now creeping towards midnight on New Year's Eve, and I say farewell and wish everyone, *Auguri Tutti per Capodanno* – Best wishes for the top of the year to everyone and raise my glass.

As I leave the New Year's Eve party, I tread in dog poo. 'That's lucky,' Lili says, 'You will have much luck and money in the New Year.' And I hope so. Otherwise, I just have dog shit on my shoe.

At home, I toast myself with the prosecco from out of the fridge at midnight and go outside in the hope to view the large and impressive fireworks being let off at the sea shore. I can't see anything because of the dense cloud cover and just experience the tremendous cannon fire booms and flashes of strobing light. I raise my cold glass of prosecco skyward in a salute to the turning of a new year and hope for a very good one.

Chapter 12

❧

Year 2 and Beyond

I kept putting off when I was leaving and four years
soon rolled around.

Resolutions and Writing
❧

Every year I have had the same New Year Resolution
– to write a book, paint a picture and climb a
mountain. The latter two aspects of my resolution,
perhaps I would never reach, but the former has
become a preoccupation. 'All writers are miserable.'
The Writer friend once told me, as we sat in his damp
cottage in Wales, sipping wine, of his intention of
writing a book on commuting and wondering what
happened to that sweaty man on the platform and his
quotidian trek to the office with his briefcase in his
hand.

'What are you going to write about?' he asked.

'I'm going to write about living in Italy.' Realising
at the time that many others had dreamed of living in
Italy, and some perhaps making that dream come to
fruition and then also dreamed about writing about it.

Was it all just a dream? Too many dreams – too many dreams in a sentence.

Here I am on the swing seat on a January morning at the start of my second year in Italy, and I am always thinking about writing if not actually tapping at the keys. I am wearing a Mickey Mouse onesie – horrible things really onesies; you have to disrobe in order to have a pee – with factor 50 sunscreen on my face and my leg pushing the swing seat to and fro and being lulled into a meditative state. The sun is out, and it is unseasonably warm. The cushions of the swing seat are giving off a musty smell, post many a rain storm and wisps of clouds eclipse the sun occasionally.

As a 'would-be-writer', I have had some miserable times, especially when I spilt coffee on my laptop and swiftly took it in the garden and turned it upside down. I panicked and turned circles in the garden and kept staring at it. The keys were stuck, and the laptop was dying a slow death, and a game was playing, which seemed to be in Korean or Japanese. I rang everyone that I knew, thinking that some sort of mechanical-CPR would save the doomed laptop. Maybe if I hung it from a tree and wafted it with a napkin, it would survive. The next day it sputtered, crackled and popped and eventually gasped its last. Ten days off-grid followed, writing notes on bits of paper, reading books and immersing myself in Ian Hamilton's poetry:

Resolve

ഏ

You used to know. You used to know.
My other room, my books,
My altered times of day.
You used to know my friends.

You used to know how hard I tried
And how foolhardily I'd swear
That this time I'd not falter. You could tell
What lay in store for me , and what I'd spent
And what might be retrieved.

The poem reminded me of what I used to know and now, 'I know nothing' just like Jon Snow. Nothing is structured about my days now. I choose when I want to get up and what to do. The elasticity of time can feel daunting. Nothing is known, and everything is new. For the first time in my life I have an open path ahead of me and no idea where it will take me or for how long.

I recently read on someone's profile on Instagram, 'Life begins at the end of your comfort zone.' This is true for me, my life is beginning again in strange and exciting ways and I am way out of my comfort zone.

I spent years looking for my own Ian Hamilton.*

---

* I would like to add here that The Writer whom I refer to in this book is a tall drink of water; doesn't smoke, but likes a drink. He is as erudite and writerly as any one that I know, but is also mercurial and cynical. Traits that come with the writing territory, 'all writers are miserable'…

A tall erudite man perhaps, but without the love of drink and chain smoking. Someone who could sweep me off my feet with words and wanting. And then I realised that my own resolve would have to be to let go of any poeticised-tall-man chasing vagary and to chase my writing folly.

Men are strange I would tell myself. They don't know what they want and women – like myself – just need to know where they stand. I do, however, resolve not to refer to men, as men in a collective noun – or resort to all-men-are-bastards – as they are all as different as they can be indifferent.

I continue to walk for two hours a day, no matter what the weather. An hour in the morning and an hour in the evening and 'contemplate my navel' as my dad would say. Sometimes the sea is angry, fast and furious and sometimes still and smooth as mirrored glass. The colours on the surface of the sea change with the time of day, silvery-flickers, aquamarine hues, grey and clagging dense waves and transforming into oranges and purples as the sun sets.

The fishermen zip out on their little powerboats at sunrise to catch the fish that have yet to wake up fully. My fellow seaside villagers stand on the volcanic rock on the sea's edge with fishing rods dangling in the sea, hoping to catch a lunchtime treat.

Often I would meet up with an old Italian woman called Melina. She always wore a head scarf and a coat no matter what the temperature was. Her legs browned and bowed like the legs on a Victorian table. She would speak to me in English usually and whistled and rasped as she spoke. I wondered if she had a respiratory condition, but she always said that her chest would be sorted out with a morning espresso, as if a cup of the morning black stuff had healing powers.

I once took Melina to the police station as she said that she had something very important to tell them. I realised that maybe her memory was fading and that she had begun to greet me, as though she was meeting me for the first time. She seemed happy after she had a chat with the *Carabinieri* and swore me to secrecy, although I had no idea what 'the secret' was as she didn't tell me.

I dropped her off at her house in Santa Sabina, and she whistled and wheezed as she undid a huge chain at her gate. A cat greeted her. 'What's the cat's name?' I asked.

'Cat,' she said, as though she was stating the obvious and didn't turn round to say goodbye, or give a courteous *grazie*. And that was that.

After the visit to the *Carabinieri*, I never saw her again. No one in the village seemed to know who she was when I asked about her. I have always wondered what happened to her.

Because of the sad demise of my laptop, my sister was in the process of sending me a replacement laptop from the UK. Not an easy task as it was refused passage by the Royal Mail because of the lithium battery. Lithium batteries being refused as air freight by the Philippines, Thailand, and Italy. Also excluded are nuclear warheads; large bags of tainted money-laundered fivers; terrorist bombs and huge hauls of drugs stuffed inside cuddly pandas. The aforementioned list was quoted by a post office worker in a sleepy West Sussex post office. DHL eventually came up trumps took the risk to dispatch the laptop at the same cost of having its own airline seat and own cabin crew service.

The Writer said, 'Use the time off-line to walk, scribble and enjoy the process…' So, I read *Going Solo* by Eric Klinenberg. Which rather than leaving me feeling emancipated and uplifted, dragged me down to a feeling and resonance that people alone, die alone. People who live alone end up with no one at their funeral and if their ashes are not claimed, then their ashes will be interred into a mass grave. Therefore, not only are writers miserable, solo living ones are exceptionally miserable. I comforted myself after reading this, by eating a jam tart that has been lying idly in the freezer. The tart was my prize for euthanizing a neighbour's basil plant after she had left it in my care. When she came to collect it after the summer, I handed it to her solemnly, *'È vecchio'* 'It's old,' I said. I had forgotten about the plant on my patio that had been trusted into my care to be watered and nurtured – oops! She looked at it as though she had just picked up a near-drowned kitten. I shrugged with English inadequacy and apology.

The computer was tracked from Gatwick to Bergamo, to Bari and then on to Brindisi. The track then stopped. It had been signed for and not arrived. I cursed the courier service thinking that someone had signed for it and pocketed my laptop. It eventually arrived two days late and with *Windows 8. A modern software installation that I have yet to become familiar with, or friends with.

I set up the computer myself (having saved all the important things on a separate hard drive before the previous laptop died) and reflected on how I would usually defer such a task to someone else – whether male or female, let's not be sexist here – should I have pat myself on the back for this? Probably not. Within an hour, I was Facebooking and emailing. No longer off-grid and connected back to the social media world. Reflecting on my ten days off-line was enough to make me feel isolated and disconnected, as I have become used to the action/reaction which is almost instantaneous in the steroidal social media world. Although I have to say that I didn't miss the photos of people's dinners or of pot plants or Facebook updates that say, 'I have just hung the washing out. Now for a cup of tea lol.' *Oooh what a treat…*

The Italian's wouldn't be able to live without their cell phones, and the English wouldn't be able to live without the internet. The Italian's being great talkers and face-to-face socialisers, whilst the English are beginning to live a much more disconnected and

---

* I would like to add a caveat here on writing up this piece, much, much later that there is now a joke going around regarding Windows 10 that I wish to share with you:

Fifty shades of nerds (or something like that)

'You have been a very naughty girl,' he said.

'And I am going to have to punish you.'

And then installed Windows 10 on her computer

avatarial life. You can have 1,000 Facebook 'friends' and yet still be alone. There is a sign that pubs in England sometimes put outside their entrances, 'Pretend it is the 1990s, talk to each other.' In modern times you could spend a whole evening with someone without actually talking to them and just looking at the flickering blue light being emitted from the smartphone of your choice; a sad reflection of how connecting with people in the real world seems less important, or even of no importance.

The more time I spend alone and getting to know 'me', the less alone I feel. Perhaps I just felt disconnected from the world that I knew, because I still connect to everything that is 'familiar' via the internet. I can still talk to friends and family via Skype or watch *Mock the Week* on YouTube. I wonder how 'comfortable' I would have been if I had moved to Italy ten years ago, before I could do any of this. Maybe I would have sat in cafés more and spoke to the locals more, and experienced a deeper immersion into a new and different culture. Whereas now I can shut my front door and sit on my sofa in my cosey lamp-lit corner and still feel connected to my old life and my English culture (I am referring more to popular culture here). Am I copping out by doing this? Or am I just keep myself sane with the familiar?

I am always amazed at what people will take on their desert island on *Desert Island Discs*. Julie Burchill said that she would take a still so that she could make alcohol out of the coconuts and I suppose if you are in a drunken stupor then loneliness won't have such an impact – you could just bounce off of the palm trees and say 'Ooh excuse me. I didn't know you were there. I thought I was on a desert island.' My luxury item on the 'desert island' would be glasses as there is no point in having the complete works of Shakespeare and the Bible if I couldn't read them. And a huge tub of Vaseline to keep my lips moist.

I would like to say here that I don't have 1,000 Facebook friends. I have ten, and nine of those I met at a bus stop.

The sun has now gone in and it's time to get out of my onesie – at last – and go for a daily walk and think about writing a book, painting a picture and climbing a mountain. Or I might take a picture of my lunchtime salad and post it on Facebook...

Chapter 13

෨෪

Yoga and Expats

I have read about all the benefits of yoga for improvements in posture, muscle strength, flexibility and stress relief and heard about yoga classes in the nearby town of San Vito Dei Normanni and decided to give yoga a go. My only form of exercise currently being walking having given up running when I reached the milestone of fifty realising that I would only be safe running after that age without an ambulance following me and a charged defibrillator at the ready.

I enter the yoga class with my yoga mat under my arm and look forward to all the possible health benefits of the class even though I have the flexibility of a petrified tree.

'I have never been to yoga before,' I falteringly admit, hoping that the instructor may go a little easier on me.

'That's okay. Come near the front, so that you can see what I am doing,' the instructor, Liz, replies with kindness and a little look of 'this-lamb-is-definitely-going-to-the slaughter'. She is probably looking at me very sympathetically, but this point my imagination is running wild.

Being at the front is my first mistake. I nervously position my yoga mat not really paying attention to whom I was next to, but I should have done. An American lady who had also positioned her yoga mat at the front looks down at me with disdain, and I think I even notice a little bit of lip curling. Anyone would think that I had just pooped next to her yoga mat. She then says rather loudly – not for my benefit as I had suddenly become a non-person – but for the benefit of the others,

'I swing my arms around a lot you know, and I would hate to hit you with my arms.' A threat of violence already and I have only been here for five minutes. She then demonstrates any possible arm fall-out injury by swinging her arms around in a winding grandiose fashion, and I am glad that I am not standing close enough to sustain a black eye during the arm swinging demonstration.

'She,' she says, (which feels like verbal pointing) and moving her yoga mat as if from the imaginary poo, 'obviously needs to be at the front and I don't.' She huffs off, or should I say in an amazing flounce-bounce and I am left looking down at my socks.

A humiliating first day at school feeling ensues, similar to the five years that I spent at a north-west London Comprehensive, where survival of the fittest meant that I didn't fit in for five years (*Hunger Games* had nothing on this school). Considered to be too posh – even though I lived in a council house at the time – and would say 'haven't' instead of 'ain't' and would actually do my homework and take a pen to each lesson. My sister looked up the prospectus for

this miserable school some years later to find one
of the prerequisites for being fully equipped in the
classroom was stated in the school prospectus as;
'Please bring a pencil to every lesson'. She also noted that
at the end of the indoor school swimming pool there
was a large notice that said, *'No smoking.'* I imagined
several non-pencil carrying, 'ain't' saying miscreants
smoking Benson and Hedges in the shallow end,
whilst trying to drown the fellow pupils who were still
saying 'haven't'.

With no smartphones to amuse the boys at
playtime in the 1970s, the boys would cut their skin
with glass and drizzle in Indian ink to spell words like
'hate' and 'acab' (all-coppers-are-bastards), although
none of them were brave enough to tattoo in the 'F'
word.

I found that going to violin lessons also made me
unpopular, especially at home when I played 'Pop
Goes the Weasel' – the only piece of music I ever
learnt – for several hours, which was so bad that even
the local cats were throwing themselves in front of
cars in a plea to stopped the incessant wailing of a
resined bow on the strings of a cheap violin. The
jet black case in the shape of a machine gun case
ostracised me even more amongst the self-tattooists.

I left five years later with a bunch of CSEs
and O'Levels being grateful that I was never flour
bombed in the corridor or had my head pushed down
the toilet. My saving grace was perhaps the fact that
I learnt to say 'ain't' and would occasionally wear
platform boots and a stick-on tattoo to school.

So, here I am at the front of the yoga class. My

glasses are in my handbag, and the instructor is a blur, and suddenly I have forgotten my right from my left. I seem to be pointing in the wrong direction at every turn and after twelve downward dogs in quick succession, I wonder if I try hard enough, whether I will become flexible enough to kiss my own bum. I also seem to be doing a windmill action when everyone is gliding like swans from one position to the next. I am moving off of my mat with every yoga position and hurtling towards the back wall.

The relaxation bit is a nightmare for me, and I mentally do a shopping list and count the compartments on the stellar ceiling. Everyone's breathing has settled in a quiet ebb and flow, and I seem to be panting like a dog on a hot day. In an attempt to quieten my mind, I think about the expats. Who are they?

Expatriate (as defined by Wikipedia) – *An expatriate (sometimes shortened to expat) is a person temporarily or permanently residing in a country other than that of the person's upbringing. The word comes from the terms,* **ex 'out of'** *and* **patria 'country, fatherland'.** As of January 1st, 2013, it was recorded (by istat.it) that there were 4,387,721 residing in Italy out of a total population of 60,626,442.

In the Province of Brindisi in Puglia where I am currently living in the Municipality of Carovigno, there are 496 foreign nationals 3.06% of the total population of 15,929. In the Municipality of Ostuni 1,064 foreign nationals 3.36% of the total population of 31,709 and in San Vito Dei Normanni 315 total foreigners 1.62% out of a total population of 19,494.

Out of the whole of Puglia, which has a population of 4,050,803 only 2.4% are foreign nationals – the Brits and the Americans being a small part of the population with much larger numbers of Albanians, Romanians, Moroccans and Polish. And despite tales to the contrary as the locals calling San Vito Dei Normanni, San Vito Dei Inglese, only 1.62% of the population are foreigners and a much smaller amount are from Blighty. Maybe it is the Brits causing a 'sticking out like a sore thumb' impression being a nation of colonialists and complainers.

I recently asked an expat friend, Angela – who has had a property in Puglia for about ten years – her thoughts and she said, 'You end up in a small place with people that you wouldn't necessarily choose as friends in the UK.' Having said this she also said that they had been wonderfully supportive to each other in times of crisis and especially for women that had come to Italy for a different life with their husbands, or were now divorced. And as the Brit expat population ages, they can find support amongst each other in times of bereavement, illness or infirmity. When Angela arrived in 2002 – she went on to say – there were virtually no Brits in Puglia, but thanks to Ryanair flying to Bari and Brindisi and expat population gradually grew. Lured by the warm weather, the friendly southern Italians and a simpler and less hurried lifestyle. The Brits came in small numbers and set up holiday villas or earned money looking after other people's villas. They used their skills as plumbers, builders, and electricians. Some have taught English to Italians, and some have never learnt *la bella lingua* either due to apathy or ignorance. Those that only socialise with fellow Brits find themselves in small expat communities that further isolates from the Italians, and their sense of belonging to Italy is probably tenuous. The expats that fully immerse themselves in Italian culture, not only become fluent in the Italian language, but also become more readily accepted by the local Italian population. The expats that choose only to socialise with their English and American counterparts tend to moan about Italy and the Italian system and are not well integrated. As a Brit, I feel that we are expert moaners and groaners. You can take the man out of Blighty, but you can't take Blighty out of the man.

This is how some expats feel about living in Italy and being an expat:

Christine, who is retired and teaches English to Italians, her husband John who will come and tinker with your electricals. Dee, who spends part of the year in Italy (a writer, journalist and photographer) who has a beautiful villa on the Tuscan/Umbrian border. Maureen who spends six months of the year in Puglia and the winter months in Lanzarote with her husband; they are both retired.

Christine:
The trouble with being an expat is the assumptions that others make about you. You don't even need to originate from the same country; it's the language that tags you. And English speaking people are often drawn to each other, simply because of the ease of communication. The downside of this is that one ends up associating with some people with whom you would never have

become friends in England. I remember on one occasion, caught in the airport, waiting for a very late departure, I stupidly started talking to the couple next to us. In my defence, this often happens in airports when timetables are disrupted. I thought that these two people were mother and son. Picking through the clues in their conversation, I actually discovered that they were husband and wife!! He was also ex-Puglian and had nothing good at all to say about this beautiful part of Italy, but that he was going to return here. She told me that she had a skin complaint that meant she couldn't expose herself to the sun and would only come here in the winter. It was at this point that I considered extricating myself before undying friendship was offered, which unfortunately was before I could find a suitable excuse.

'Oh, I can see we're going to be great friends,' she enthusiastically spouted. Over my dead body, I thought.

Inspiration arrived, and I slightly modified my telephone number and thankfully I've never heard from them again. However, I do know some English people living in Puglia who carefully keep their scope of acquaintances to a healthy mix of Italians and Brits. This works well for language practice, and it also means that they are in the driving seat when it comes to choosing with whom they wish to associate.'

All I can say is shame on you Christine, who is as fit as a butcher's dog in her seventies and is bendier than Gerri Halliwell doing yoga and has a wonderful ebullient personality. Christine speaks fluent Italian with a wonderful cut glass English accent. Both hysterically funny and endearing. Jam and Jerusalem!

Dee:

Why do expats move to Italy?
Italy, Thailand, Portugal or Spain, expats that find the courage
and determination to relocate by choice, invariably all want the
same thing: a better life.

There are many obvious attractions to Italy. 'Tuscany' is a
word heavy with the fragrant appeal of the summer lavender,
flowing red wine and undulating hills peaked by fairy tale
villages. Foodies, history buffs, and romantics are swept up
by the hypnotic allure of the rolling menu of seasonal home
cooked slow food, layer upon layer of history and, of course, the
shamelessly passionate Italians themselves.

For me, it was the combination of all those things. I wanted
to see myself, on my third espresso by 9:30am, gesticulating
wildly and shooting the breeze at my local bar in Italian.

The reality in paradise, however, is that speaking to people
in your mother tongue – even with folk you wouldn't necessarily
hang out with at home – is a pleasure beyond compare. When
you've been struggling all day to find Italian words for 'nail',
'blow dry' or 'petrol'. And even though you find yourself
surrounded by delicious aged cheese, hand milked from grass-fed
sheep, that rolls around the mouth and falls off the tongue with
names like 'pecorino di Pienza', most expats would kill for a
hunk of aged cheddar.

And such is the fickle heart of humanity.

The expats I encounter in Umbria are no exception. In the
main they are retired Brits that have come in search of some
place 'more'. More sunny, more relaxed, more bang for your
buck. And in Italy they find it. But they also find a whole
lot of stuff they had not foreseen – eye watering bureaucracy,
cynicism and a whole lot of face spite-ing nose cutting off by the
Italians (which is painful to watch).

Most of the expat folk I know have Italian friends. Most are warm kind and friendly. I don't know what any of them think about the south other than if they haven't already been, then they would like to go. The only memorable comment I have ever heard is from an Italian (from Bari) who said, 'The south ees not Italy, it ess like Argentina.'

Dee is of course, quite fluent in Italian even if she does have Kiwi vowel sounds. Dee can organise builders, decorators, and gardeners with aplomb. She is very at home in Italy and that is where her heart is.

Here is a story from Maureen which is more about Italian immersion and local life and a little cycling trip with her sister one afternoon and subsequent encounters with an old Italian man called Paolo.

Maureen:
'My sister and I were riding our bikes along a road near our house, we were just looking about being nosey, we waved to an old boy tending his land. Further along, the road the same man overtook us on his bike and stopped in front of us.

'Come and see my trullo?' he said.
'No,' we said.
And then a much repeated conversation took place.
'Do you want to buy my trullo?'
'No, thank you.'
'Of course, you do.'
'No, thank you.'
'Do you know someone who wants to buy my trullo?'
'No, we don't.'
'Of course, you do. Just come and look at my trullo, so you

can tell your friends how beautiful it is, then they will want to buy it, and they will be happy, and so will I.'

After a while, we agreed to go and have a look the following day. Not to buy we told him as we didn't need a trullo.

The following day we set off to visit Paolo, we arrived at his house, parked the bikes in his driveway and walked up to the house. In the garden, there were two white plastic chairs, on one of the sat a toilet seat. Being quicker than my sister I sat on the free seat and smiled sweetly at her.

'Sit down, sit down,' he said, and by this time I couldn't contain myself. My sister, on the other hand, was mortified. I can't sit on that she said, which only made me laugh more. In the end, she sat on the toilet seat chair.

Paolo then started to crack some almonds that he had picked from his trees, with his teeth. The only problem that I could see with this was, he only had two teeth, and they were not top and bottom or even near each other. I told Paolo that I couldn't eat the almonds that he was lovingly trying to crack open with his teeth as I was allergic to them, but my sister loved them. The look on her face when he eventually cracked one, not with his teeth, but with a stone, although it was one that he had sucked to death! He was on a roll now; the almonds were coming thick and fast and slightly wet and crushed. He was so pleased that she liked almonds that I had to keep encouraging her to eat up. Whilst Paolo was feeding my sister with the almonds I let my eye roam over the little trullo, what I saw was really strange. In the tree nearest the house, there was a wire rack with a mirror attached, on the rack, there was a razor, a comb some soap, a shaving brush and some cologne. Under it were a couple of blocks of stone with a bowl on it, the bathroom. On another tree, there was a coat hanging on a *coat hanger with a pair of shoes underneath and an umbrella hat and shirt on various branches, the wardrobe. On another tree, there was a plank of wood and on it were various pots, pans, plates, and glasses. On another shelf, there was a rusty tray with some cutlery on it. Close to this, there was a tree with a gas bottle hanging on a branch and a wire basket with some tins in it. The last tree there was a rust saw, hammer, axe, watering can and a tin which had a pencil and some other bits in it. Not sure what role the plastic chair with the toilet seat played as it didn't have a hole in it.*

It was now time to have a look inside his trullo. Inside there was a little storage area; he had a few bottles of homemade wine, some water, some biscuits and a bottle of beer. There were also the more expensive tools, a spade, a bigger axe, a broom, etc. There was a lovely little fireplace and hanging from the ceiling was a beautiful chandelier. Off in the alcove, there were two single beds complete with a blue candlewick bedspread and a blue teddy and the same in pink. He then told us that his wife had died four years before and that he missed her so much that he sometimes didn't want to go on. Out came the photos of his wife and then of him, then of the both of them on his wedding day, the photos of his children who all lived in the north of Italy. Tears were shed by all; then he cracked open a bottle of wine – thankfully not with his teeth. We toasted his wife and sat chatting and drinking until the bottle was empty. From somewhere he produced a bottle of limoncello which was about half full, homemade and very good.

As the sun went down we said our farewells and left; he said that he had had a wonderful afternoon with the crazy English women, and couldn't wait for us to visit again. I have to admit that we too had a great afternoon. I am not sure my sister will ever forgive me, but that's life in Puglia.

Paolo rode his bike from San Vito Dei Normanni to his land which is about four kilometres each way; twice a day come rain or shine.

If we saw him in the town, he would introduce us to his friends as the crazy English people who are so kind, but couldn't find a buyer for his trullo. He would always suggest a coffee or a beer in his local bar, where he would sit proudly announcing that we were his English friends.

When we arrived last year, I didn't see him out and about so asked our neighbours about him. They said he had died in December. He was ninety-three. Bless him.'

Maureen's story is a wonderful tale of the simple, bucolic life in Puglia. Not only is it about eccentricities, but it is also about love and mutual acceptance.

The Italians will invite you into their houses for drinks and food even if they have only just met you. In England, you can live on the same street for years and still have neighbours remain relative strangers. Us Brits tend to build walls, both physically and socially, keep everyone else at arm's-length mentality.

The yoga relaxation is now over, and I realise that I have half fallen asleep with my expat musings. I pick up my yoga mat and wonder if my head will always be fifty miles away from my knees when everyone else can hug their knees and practically kiss their toes.

I have sustained a slightly twisted knee during my

yoga exertions, and I hobble down the stairs with endorphins bathing my brain with lots of feel-good hormones. The instructor's words of, 'Bend your knees if you have tight hamstrings,' are echoing in my ears. My knees are always bent doing a swan dive forward as my hamstrings are as tight as Scrooge's pockets.

I can't speak for others who have come to this much admired and romanticised country, but at least I personally, feel willing to embrace my temporary Italian home in the heel of the boot – which is kind of a sexy stiletto – difficult to walk in but you feel good in them.

Chapter 14

❧

A Brief Jaunt Down to Sicily

'Were a man to spend only one day in Sicily and ask,
What must I see?' I would answer him without hesitation,
'Taormina.' It is only a landscape, but a landscape where you
find everything on earth that seems made to seduce the eyes, the
mind, and the imagination.'

Guy de Maupassant

'Sicily is more beautiful than any woman.'

Truman Capote

'Do you fancy going to Sicily?' my friend, Debs, asked
via Skype as thousands of miles separated us from
the Caribbean to Italy – Debs having an itinerant,
wandering, adventurous and wonderfully spontaneous
nature.

'Yes,' I said. And added, 'That would be lovely.'
As I always say everything will be, could be, can be
and is lovely. I realised that I really hadn't done much
travelling in my adopted country of Italy and had
always wanted to go to Sicily. Why not? By the end of
the afternoon, I had booked two tickets to Sicily from
Bari to Catania and chosen a little hotel on the Corso

Umberto in Taormina called The Hotel Victoria. Quaint I thought and with a history. Apparently, it was Oscar Wilde's favourite place to stay when he visited Italy in the 19th century. Easy for sightseeing and good access to the local restaurants. Perfect.

It would have been perfect if the hotel had been open when we arrived at 9 o'clock at night. My first clue to its non-opened status was the fact that the door was covered in brown paper – obviously so that you wouldn't be able to see the ghost of Oscar Wilde and his spirit entourage partying it up. I imagined the ghost of DH Lawrence at the bar with a whisky in one hand and a bottle of cough syrup in the other, quoting from *Lady Chatterley's Lover* – which I believe was once covered in brown paper, in order to disguise the fact that it was a book which was thought to be a bit 'rude' at the time of its publication (unlike Fifty Shades of Filthy which is read openly on the tube as a kind of badge of honour to mummy porn – how times have changed). And perhaps the ghost of Gustav Klimt is painting a mural. Taormina was always part of the Grand Tour and visited by the rich, famous, infamous and the posers. Or Truman Capote drinking an apple martini speaking in strange choking vowels and behaving with an air of self-entitlement – I can mix up the years and centuries here as they are ghosts. Maybe a ghost of a hotel receptionist or even a real one should've opened up and let us in.

A woman was closing her shop close by and I asked her in my emerging and hesitant Italian. 'Why is the hotel closed?' And imagined myself and Debs sleeping on a cold pavement somewhere – probably down a dark alley, a back passage or anywhere else that was unappealing – our suitcases being used as mattresses. Even Debs isn't that adventurous.

'It won't be open until the spring,' she said and then added a maybe, which added to my anxiety and alerted my cold but hopefully dry pavement seeking radar.

'How can this be?' I said. And she shrugged. Which could have been a depicting shrug of the Italian saying, *this is the life, or how the fuck should I know?* Being a similar Anglo-Saxon equivalent.

In these dire and emergency situations my ultimate self-medicating-go-to-place is prosecco, and so, I ordered two with snacks from a café which was thankfully still open to displaced British tourists. And rang my daughter to get hold of the internet travel company that should have ensured that Oscar and his mates weren't in the hotel and that someone actually in the 21st century was there to remove the brown paper from the front door and welcome us in.

I then ran in a panicked and rather an inelegant way up and down the Corso Umberto until I came across a boutique hotel called the Hotel Isabella; where I found a friendly receptionist who assured me that Debs and I wouldn't be sleeping on the pavement in the Piazza that night and that they had a room free for four nights. Relief oozed out of me like the sweat out of a tramp's sock.

'Lovely,' I said, and we dropped our bags into a double room and settled into two single beds that night. Debs sleeps on her stomach generally and with a mass of tight light brown curls, it was like sleeping in the same room with someone without a face or possibly Hagrid. Debs didn't snore, and I hoped that I didn't.

I have always had the mantra – and I have probably repeated it several times here to *paint a picture, write a book and climb a mountain*. Although the latter aspiration maybe a stretch too far as I have always been afraid of heights and once had a panic attack on the top of St Paul's Cathedral – at a time when it was still accessible, and you could get right to the top. Debs, on the other hand, has the daredevil gene and had only just six months before this little trip climbed Kilimanjaro in Tanzania with her husband, which is a huge challenge and quite a peak to climb. She suffered wet clothes, a sunburnt face that looked as though she had been in a fire and a tachycardia that under normal circumstances would require some hefty cardiac drugs. She is inspiring to me and a bit of a heroine of mine and is always encouraging me to be more spontaneous and in the moment. She accompanied me to Taormina without a clue of where she was going and thought nothing of it. *Do something that scares you every day*, they say, and I think that Deborah pretty much fulfils that life-stance. Whereas, my mantra would probably be, *Do something every day, anything without tripping or falling over…*

With this is mind, the next morning I was looking forward to seeing Mount Etna strutting majestically in the distance from the main Piazza IX Aprile which has an attractive black and white chequered floor – and is dominated by the beautiful church of San Giuseppe – only to find that Mount Etna was shrouded in cloud and fog and was nowhere to be seen.

Going to Taormina in March – spring – seemed to me to be a good idea. Fewer tourists and time to wander around without huge jostling crowds. But Taormina is on a rocky promontory and can often be shrouded in clouds in early spring and so was Mount Etna, hiding in plain sight. I soothed myself by listening to the murmur of the waves below and took some pictures of frothing surf before I dropped my camera and it jammed. Luckily I had already taken some pictures of the clouds and thought I might draw Etna in later with a felt-tip pen.

The Corso Umberto had a nice mixture of designer shops – if you want a Rolex *no thanks I already have one* – and more affordable shops. You can even buy a T-shirt with Al Pacino printed on the front – there was a huge Godfather thingy going on there and the theme music was blasted out of one of the shops as if to encourage you to go in a buy a T-shirt when in reality it just encourages you to walk on by.

I found it curious that in a shop selling almost everything, there were photos of nude young boys taken by Wilhelm Von Gloeden in the late 1800s, which were on postcards and displayed 'everything' and were to be found right next the children's toys. Italy is quite prudish – although Taormina is more gay-friendly than the rest of Italy. But I guess if it's art then it can be placed right next to Barbie and Buzz Lightyear. *'Mummy, is that a man's willy?'… 'No, dear it's art.'*

On every step and on every balcony there were these plant pots, Moorish ceramic heads depicting beautiful women and men with beards. These can be traced back to well over a thousand years ago to when the Moors or the Saracens occupied Sicily. The Greeks were here first in 750 BC just down the road from Taormina in a seaside town called Giardini Naxos. There is a wonderful Greek theatre in Taormina overlooking the sea which was built by the Greeks in the third-century BC and was partially rebuilt by the Romans. It also has a beautiful view of Mount Etna if the mountain isn't playing hide-and-seek amongst the clouds and fog. This is where Damian Rice was due to give a concert that August. The theatre is open from June-September for concerts, plays, and the cinema. The Romans, however, used the theatre for gladiator fights, and I imagined blood on the walls and the clashing of steel from all those centuries ago. And perhaps a few gladiators losing their heads…

There lies a story behind those heads – not the gladiator heads – the ceramic ones, which are used as plant pots. There is a legend about a young Sicilian girl who fell in love with a handsome moor many years ago, but he was a married man. On hearing that he already had a wife and children, she cut off his head in the middle of the night and made it into a vase and planted some basil in it – presumably so that she had something to put in her pasta every day. The story of these star-crossed lovers has been passed down through the ages and the colourfully painted ceramic heads, still in use today are a testament, to the story of the girl that fell in love with the wrong man and he, literally, lost his head.

A recurring motif which can be found on walls as plaques or painted on pottery is the three-legged woman known as the *triscele* – which funnily enough means three legs – a rough translation from Greek. This three-legged symbol has also been depicted in Greek and Roman coins and represents the moon and the sun. This three-legged symbol has also been on the Sicilian flag since 1946. Three legs and no body, curious. Both these iconic symbols seem to be emblematic of Sicily.

On exploring Taormina further, we found the Giardino Pubblico which is a public garden designed and developed by an English woman called Florence Trevelyn who found herself in Sicily after having an affair with Queen Victoria's son, the then Prince of Wales. The gardens were beautiful with lots of brick built follies, tropical plants and a later edition of a bronze statue with an angel leaning against another angel wearing a suit and with a suitcase. Presumably, this could have commemorated a young couple that died in the gardens whilst waiting or their hotel to open and had been immortalised in bronze in order to repay their patience and fortitude.

After visiting the gardens and en route to our hotel, I noticed that The Hotel Victoria had opened – two days later – and I rushed into the hotel reception, to rant about my reservation and the non-opened nature of my complaint. The receptionist (or it could have been the owner), looked not at a computer for my reservation, but at one of those basic calendars with the black and red squares on it and said that he couldn't see a reservation (there was actually nothing written on the calendar, and I wondered if it was actually in use). He was, however, very apologetic and I think that the problem was not with the hotel, but with the internet booking via a third party (I have stopped myself from naming the company here, but as Liam Neeson would say, 'If I find you, I will kill you.') If he had looked at the computer to check for my reservation I was half expecting him to say, *'The computer says no.'* Followed by a cough.

We stopped for a coffee to look at our itinerary and to decide where to go for lunch. I tried a *cannolo* (which means little tube). I thought that it tasted like come (or do I mean *cum*?) in a toilet roll, but then maybe I hadn't tasted a fresh one – no offence intended to the Sicilians here.

The Corso Umberto is dotted with plenty of reasonably priced restaurants and one restaurant in particular called Licchios. And for two ex-nurses we thought that this restaurant name choice was hysterical, *os meaning a hole or an opening, and well Lich* – maybe it was only funny because we kept drinking cocktails and continued laughing about the name of the restaurant, well after the initial joke had run out. I thought the manager was friendly, even flirty until I realised that he was like that with everyone, and I wasn't actually exuding any man-magnet power; *although if I had a super power that would be the one I would choose.* This lovely likeable and lick-able restaurant was where a lot of locals seem to eat at – which is always a good sign – also provided vegan food, for the newlyveganised Debs and gluten free for me, (although I do think that you shouldn't be too fussy in restaurants, or you might just end up with an empty plate). When Debs first told me she had become vegan, which means vegetarian, but also no dairy products, I panicked in the supermarket and bought potatoes and prunes. Normally not a good combination, but added carrots and lettuce into the mix to make a panic salad for supper one night, before we left for Sicily.

Later that night we drank some very expensive Aperol spritz cocktails, in glasses that said, 'Luck is an attitude' – 46 euros for four drinks luck was obviously an attitude for them, they must have seen us coming. Or perhaps the extortionate price of drinks would normally be justified with a view of Mount Etna. A piece of advice here, don't drink too many Aperol spritzes, as not only will you become poor, but it also turns your wee orange in the susceptible.

Back to Etna, the ever elusive Etna. 'Can we book a tour of Mount Etna?' I asked the very friendly and accommodating receptionist who had saved us from a cold pavement a couple of nights before.

'You can't go today; it's too cloudy. You won't be able to see anything,' she replied.

She then looked at the weather for the following day on the computer and said we might be able to go tomorrow as the weather was improving. With that piece of good news, I decided to book a tour for the next day.

We were picked up outside our hotel by a very tall young Italian called Ronaldo. As well as telling us about the local history (the tour guide bit), he also told us how he loved living with his mother. She fed him and did all his laundry. Now, I don't want to go into an Italian cliché-ridden-diatribe about single Italian men and their mothers, but the belief is that Italian men are spoilt, pampered and are not allowed to grow up until marriage. And then if the marriage breaks down, the Italian men go back to their mothers – as no one makes pasta like mama does, or so it seems.

On the way up to Etna, I noticed that all the dry stones walls were all made of lava, and I saw a couple of houses made out of black lava – obviously if you have an available resource lying around you should use it. In late March, the snow was still evident on the ground on the winding drive up and then we saw the magnificent (and previously elusive Etna) looming in the distance, snow-capped and magnificent.

Mount Etna is still active and erupted quite recently, belching out molten lava and volcanic ash, but when we went it was dormant thankfully. There are about 400-500 craters, and three are active – according to Ronaldo – we ended up at *Crateri Silvestri* at 6,000ft. The peak of the snow-capped Mount Etna was indeed visible and at almost 11,000ft is Europe's most active volcano. For the foolhardy, you can climb up there or for the timid and the lazy, you can cheat and use the cable car.

'No this does not count as a mountain, Elaine,' Debs told me. As I had aspired to tick off my 'climb a mountain' from my life-list. I had thought it had, *write a book, paint a picture and climb a mountain*… not far enough up the mountain then.

It was windy, and I daren't tell the well-travelled and hard-core climber, Debs, that I generally panic when the wind blows in my face and tried to quell the panic on this windy occasion. We walked around the edge of the crater and watched some Italian teenagers slide down icy crater walls, on sheets of what looked like green bin liners. It was bitterly cold and the wind was ferocious and I pushed my nose and mouth deep into my scarf to avoid having an, *Oh my God there is wind in my face*, panic attack. School children ran towards us without any notion of what Health and Safety is. It seemed as though they wouldn't mind being responsible for knocking off two English women off the mountain and to their deaths on the rocks below.

We survived the walk around the mouth of the crater and ordered two café *corretti* with Amaro Montenegro which helped warm up our red and wind-whipped cheeks. The fireplace in the café was made of lava. Predictably, as a souvenir, I bought an ashtray made of lava with 'Etna' inscribed on the inside as evidence that I had actually been there.

The next day we visited the city of Catania which had to be totally rebuilt after the Mount Etna eruption in 1669, and a lot of the Baroque buildings were built using lava – once it had cooled down, naturally. Apparently it took eight years to do this. Because a lot of the buildings were built using the lava, it gives the architecture a bit of a greyscale look and lacks the warmth of a lot of Italian Baroque style buildings.

There is a famous fish market in Catania – which took an hour to find – and every Sicilian I asked said that it was around the next corner. The market sells fish from its stalls in huge, great mounds. Large chunks of fresh tuna, swordfish, eels, lobster, shrimps and a fish with large teeth which looked like an alien and I wouldn't know whether to cook it and eat it, or clean its teeth. There was an overpowering smell of the stuff. The market stall holders all being Catanian were short, dark and swarthy looking and shouted out their wares in gruff Catanian dialect and I sensed that it had been the same for centuries.

They say that you should be wary in Catania because of pick-pockets, but I must say that I felt quite safe, and the bus ride from Taormina only cost 8.30 euros, and I think that it is a well worth a visit for a taste of Sicilian life.

On the last day, we visited a very small church off of the winding road that leads out of the main town called *La Chiesa di San Michele* – The Church of Saint Michael. It was a small, modest and unembellished church with half a dozen rows of simple wooden pews, without any of the grand ornateness of many Italian churches. There was, however, a large and impressive statue of Archangel Michael standing at the end of the church – probably made out of stucco – with his sword in his hand signifying being the Archangel of protecting warriors and armies. He would have struck me down with his sword in this little quaint church if he heard me say, 'Fuck!' As I tripped in flat shoes and then said, 'Oh fuck, sorry,

God, oh God fuck, I am so sorry.'

If there had been a priest present, I probably should have gone to confession, but being as there wasn't a priest in the vicinity and I am not a Catholic, I just made a hasty retreat whilst making the sign of the cross. I stopped at genuflecting, but maybe I should have done that as well.

A few months later I read about the film festival that occurs every mid-June in Taormina, and although Taormina is visited by the rich and famous, it is a surprising unpretentious place, in a beautiful setting and isn't as expensive as most tourist destinations. The people are also very friendly and are not 'tourist weary'. I would like a return visit to Taormina and stay at The Hotel Victoria, but the next time I will book directly with the hotel and cut out the middle man and have a tipple with Oscar Wilde's ghost.

And here is a little ditty to end with:

There was an English woman who lived in Italy
Who went for a trip to Sicily
The hotel was closed
So she wrote some prose
And hoped that she did that wittily

Chapter 15

ঙ৵৶

Easter, Tattoos, Dogs, and Guns

It is Easter Sunday, otherwise known as *Pasqua* in Italian – *Pasquetta*, being Easter Monday in English otherwise known as let's all go down the pub or stay at home watch the film, *The Robe*, on television and finish off all the Easter eggs. The symbol of the Easter egg signifying the empty tomb of Jesus – although I don't believe that anyone really thinks about the significance of the chocolate egg. Easter Monday is generally treated as yet another bank holiday, instead of celebrating the resurrection of the Son of God. Traditionally a lot of Brits get drunk during this long weekend and ended up talking to God on the great white telephone.

I'm rather partial to a Cadbury's Cream Egg myself. 1.5 million of them are produced every day from just after Christmas and until Easter when presumably all the factory workers have a lie-down and or go on a beach holiday to the Costa del Sol, if they feel absolutely egged-off. 80 million of these little eggs are sold every year in the UK and – in my opinion – the best way to eat them is to dunk the top into a hot drink, decapitate the little bugger and then lick out the contents.

There are no Cadbury's Cream Eggs in Italy –
although there are lots of delicious chocolate fondant
and praline sweets. Dozens of brightly wrapped
Easter eggs, some even in the shape of edible flowers
and *scarcella* which is a traditional plaited biscuit/
cake sometimes also made in the shape of a dove or
a doughnut. There are also animal figures made out
of almond paste, which is probably more traditional
in southern Italy along with the *scarcella*. The *scarcella*
signifies the eternity and the resurrection. A Brit
version would probably be a hot cross bun, best
toasted and with slavers of butter, but tends to be so
full of preservatives that everyone would be blowing
their own bum-trumpets by Easter Sunday.

I have arrived outside Lili's house in Carovigno
and can hear the distant drums and trumpets of an
Easter Sunday parade that I would be missing. The
Carovignese are even crafty enough to celebrate
another festival – which gives them another day
off on the Tuesday – the festival of *La Madonna di
Belvedere/Santa Maria di Belvedere*; an iconic religious
symbol of the Madonna whose image was placed in a
crypt – in the 8th century. This was a time when the
worship of sacred images was forbidden by Emperor
Leo the Isaurian. To celebrate the festival of La
Madonna, there is an annual procession in Carovigno,
with flag waving and tossing of The Nzegna a multi-
coloured flag. According to folklore and a small boy
discovered the image in a crypt and celebrated by
tying a multi-coloured handkerchief to a pole and
hence the multi-coloured flag.

Easter Sunday lunch is traditionally lamb and today is no exception. We are having homemade lasagne, followed by lamb as the *secondo piatto*. I have already been kissed on the cheek by Simona, Lili's daughter, who tells me that she has, *'Ho raffredore.'* I have a cold and blows her nose frequently. Before dessert, Simona with her new university grunge haircut and wearing Doctor Martens reveals a tattoo on her body, a butterfly. It is on her left shoulder, and it looks beautiful. Lili raises her eyes heavenward and shows her disgust.

I refrain from showing my butterfly on my left hip that was a gift to myself a few years ago. I am not sure why I wanted to ink my body with an image that would last a lifetime (apparently butterfly tattoos are now known as *tramp stamps*, lordy) but I guess that it felt a bit daring at the time and I thought that a butterfly tattoo would signify something; release and freedom for me personally.

I was in Bournemouth at the time of the prospective inking with a boyfriend on a Valentine's weekend in one of those seaside hotels that is just one step up from a Premier Inn, and after several gin and tonics managed to book an appointment at the very end of the day. An impulsive tattoo. The tattooists looked like the Big Fat Hairy Bikers. After my hairy tattooist finished my tattoo he said that having tattoos was addictive and that I would want another one. It wasn't for me, and I haven't. The tattoo will last a lifetime, and the relationship ended after another month and now I have a permanent tramp stamp!

After lunch we have *la dolce*, which consists of strawberries and cream and traditional Easter treats of *caralli e cupetta* – which I think are dialect words and *pasta di mandorle* made from almonds and the *scarcella*-like Easter biscuits with icing made by Mary, Lili's mum, who has gone temporarily deaf due to the end of a cotton bud that has been wedged in her ear and cannot be removed even by the most adept of doctors. She has nodded and smiled throughout the Easter lunch, without being able to follow any conversation.

I say treats or biscuits, or cakes because it's hard to define them. Now a British simnel cake is definitely a cake. A light fruit cake decorated with twelve marzipan balls to signify Jesus and the apostles, which was made popular at Easter by the Victorians. Although in our house it would never get eaten because we'd had fruit cake at Christmas and no one liked marzipan. A symbol of Easter that would lie in the biscuit tin until August Bank Holiday and thrown out to the birds, who would then gag on the balls. Does anyone like marzipan?

In our family, you were not allowed to eat your Easter egg until Easter Sunday. Which is torture for any kid who is not yet able to control impulsive behaviour and I was one of them. Not being able to wait until Easter Sunday, I worked out that if you ate the back of the chocolate egg and left the front untouched at the front of the box, then the deception was complete, and no one would know. I always dreaded being found out in case I was forced to eat simnel cake as a punishment.

After a heavy lunch, at Mary's, I go home with
another bottle of homemade red wine and a bag of
Easter treaty-things, that will probably remove all my
fillings.

Easter Monday is a family day for Italians and in
Santa Sabina, you can find them having a picnic in *la
pineta* – which is a small pine wood. Here the Italians
gather en masse; food is eaten, outdoor games are
played; children tread in dog poo, and the Italians
discard their plastic plates with carelessness, as though
the wood nymphs would pick them up for them. This
year I even saw a piece of roof felt, a picnic chair and
a sun umbrella discarded in the bushes. I wonder if
someone used the roof felt as a picnic blanket and
there was also a huge pile of discarded bread rolls.
Any discarded bits of food will be eaten by the stray
dogs – *i cani di randagi*.

I have become rather fond of the local stray dogs
and have even given them names. There seems to
be a group of blonde collies, Gimpy, Limpy, and
Crafty. Limpy is a dog with his right front foreleg
out at ninety degrees; he tends to lag a bit behind the
others. Crafty, who like his name, pretended to be a
domesticated dog one day and suddenly developed
puppy like qualities such as running around my legs
and nipping my calves as though he was trying to herd
me into my garden. I tried to out manoeuvre him and
thought that I had managed to get into the garden
without him slipping through. He was a persistent
bugger, and I felt relieved as I closed the gate behind
me. And there he was in the garden; he had slipped in

like Flynn. Maybe I should have named him Errol. I then booted him out (metaphorically speaking – don't report me to the RSPCA). He then rejoined the pack. The pack leader being a large beast that I named Brutus. Brutus being a handsome Heinz 57 with a bit of Rottweiler and Rhodesian Ridgeback perhaps. And being *testicularintacticus*, then he is probably the daddy of all the puppies.

I also came across some puppies on the edge of the woods back in March. The mum being another small blonde collie, whom I named Betty. Initially, Betty snarled, growled and I was once tempted to throw a rock just to scare her. Slowly I gained her trust, and she had two little pups, which looked as though they had come from the loin of Brutus. Imaginatively named, Spot and Fluff. I fed them for a week and soon found out that Betty wanted a stroke on the head more than she did food. She even started to come to me when I called her. Our relationship was short-lived, however, and once the locals Italians had picked up the pups for pets, she quickly went back to her feral state of nervousness skittishness and developed kind-English-lady amnesia and no longer came when I called her.

The Ferals and I have developed a polite tolerance and acceptance. Even the locals will feed any hungry pups although in general, the Italians aren't very tolerant of the *cani randagi* or even domesticated dogs. The Italians seem to have an attitude towards dogs rather like Marmite; they either love them, or they hate them. Dogs get abandoned on motorways and in fields. There is a huge stray dog problem from the top to the bottom of Italy. A few Brits have taken in strays, but in reality, there are simply too many dogs, and there is no sterilisation programme, so the ones that are left to roam then breed, and the problem worsens. In my street food is left out for them and they behave quite well on the whole and are non-aggressive (apart from Betty, who was only trying to protect her pups).

With Easter over I am at a friend's, Christine's for lunch. Christine and I had become friends since attending the previous year's creative writing course. Unlike me, she is a keen cook and has promised to cook me *parmigiana di melanzane* which is a traditional Calabrian dish, but is eaten all over Italy and is very popular and comprises of baked aubergines in a tomato sauce with mozzarella. Although Christine likes to add carrots to hers just to be a little different.

Christine lives in a renovated villa near Ostuni with about six acres of fruit trees, olive trees and a carefully tended garden with lavender bushes and beds of irises and a substantial vegetable plot. They have a large pool which is usually full of clean chlorinated water in the summer, but at the moment has 3ft of murky water and a few dead leaves floating in it.

Basil is exploring the garden, and I ignore the fact that he is doing a poo by the front gate during lunch. Christine has adopted a puppy. A caramel coloured mutt with aquamarine eyes and a lolling pink tongue, called Sepio. He squeals every time Basil approaches and Basil spends the whole afternoon dribbling saliva over his back.

During lunch, the conversation turns to security and personal safety. I have been a bit more wobbly about security since my neighbours were burgled in November and keep my shutters down at night and have a large Mag torch by my bed, that is so heavy and unwieldy that I probably wouldn't be able to hit a potential intruder with it anyway. Christine, on the other hand, has a more formidable form of security – she is currently in the house alone whilst her husband is in England – a Walther. Which to the uninitiated is a gun, a pistol – the same as James Bond's – which is loaded and ready to go and she keeps it under her tissue box. I wonder if she grabbed the gun instead of a tissue in the middle of the night she might end up blowing her nose off. Christine seems quite cavalier about the gun as though it is 'normal'. She also has a pop-gun – which I presume fires pellets – which she says she is willing to use to shoot up the arse of any stray dogs that might come onto the property. She is a crack shot and practises on cans in the garden, and I wonder if I am in the wild west and not in Puglia. My large Mag torch now seems like a feeble weapon. I don't like guns and wouldn't even let my son have a toy gun, although he would make one out of Lego bricks anyway and try and shoot me on the stairs.

After lunch, we go out for a walk with the dogs in the Puglian countryside. Despite Christine being in her seventies and with arthritic knees and hips she keeps fit by swimming in her pool in the summer and is always up for a walk. Long days spent seeing to her vast acreage also keeps her fit and spritely. It is late spring, and we are having one of the better days weatherwise. The weather has been awful with cold winds and rain.

There is no wind today. The dogs are off their leads and running about freely jumping through the tall grass which is dotted with red poppies. I never let Basil off the lead in Santa Sabina for several reasons. He is not particularly biddable and can develop selective deafness. He doesn't understand other dogs' body language and can't differentiate between a tail wag and a bum sniff from a snarling yapping dog. And because he will eat anything that is dead or discarded and will pick up anything from the beach and put it in his mouth from dead fish heads; to truffle shaped dog poo and sea sponges. Here in the countryside he is free to roam and run with his little short legs and has learnt to ascend and descend the dry stone walls and enjoys nosing his way through the wild irises, primroses, wild fennel and chicory. The olive trees lean towards the sun and nestle in the moist brown soil. Red poppies spring up in between the dry stone walls and on the outside of very old trullis, long since abandoned and yet to be renovated. Prickly pear plants *i fichi d'india* – grow in abundance. The prickly pear plants I am told, were planted by the Puglians as windbreaks and also for security. I imagine a sign that might say. 'Burglars beware of potential harm from pricks.' If you soak the pears the prickles can be rubbed off easily; sadly they taste of very little and the pips run through the entire fruit, so for me, eating them is a bit of a disappointment. I ate three or four in one sitting once and ended up with what looked like a plate of frog spawn after I had spat out all the pips. It's a lot of effort with very little at the end of it, a bit like sex really.

I take snapshots of the quintessential Puglian countryside, which seems unique and special to me. I am falling in love with my temporary home, truly, madly, deeply.

The boys are getting tired. Basil slows down a pace, and the pup needs a carry for the last half an hour. Christine slings him over her shoulder, and he dribbles down her tanned back. With a satisfied tiredness, we finally reach Christine's house and the boys flop on the cold stone kitchen floor exhausted.

Refreshed by a glass of cold *l'acqua frizzante* I drive home feeling a little blessed and also relieved that I don't have a pistol under my tissue box and knowing that I have a torch that could blind a potential intruder. I am comforted by the fact that Lili once said with a conspiratorial tone, 'We are protected.' And I don't think that she was referring to God or the pope.

Chapter 16

৯৵

Driving in Italy

The thought of driving in Italy, could and should, terrify most people. Although I must say that I have developed a keen eye for potential mishaps and think that risking life and limb on the Italian roads has probably made me a better driver. I am so used to the Italians taking liberties that I will laugh at their antics whilst my British passengers are gripping their seats in terror, grimacing and holding their breath. One particular time on the superstrada to Bari an elderly Italian man cut across my lane and was at right angles to my car, he was so close that I could see his gold tooth. He was smiling when he did it. My son, who was the passenger, was terrified, and when I laughed, he said, 'It's not funny, Mum.' Of course, he was right, but laughing nervously is far better than crapping your pants.

On my first trip to Italy, I hadn't even left the car park and had shunted the hire car into the car in front. I then proceeded to hit a foot high kerb on the way out of the car park. On arriving at the villa, I thought I had lost a hubcap – it turns out it had already been lost by a previous driver – and noticing a mark on the tyres I announced, 'Oh well nothing that a baby wipe and a felt-tip pen wouldn't sort out.' And it did. No extra charges on returning the car.

Today I am driving up to Carovigno a short distance away for a coffee in the old town with my son, Christian. Italian towns are quite often conflicted places. An attractive and alluring historical centre giving way to an urban sprawl, flats, and houses. Even the outskirts of Florence could be described as unattractive and unimaginative; predictable and a bit mundane. It is as though all the best architectural ideas have been left in the past and the modern Italian architects designing buildings that are soulless, rectangular cement blocks.

The actual town was described – rather unkindly I thought, by a visitor – as not being unlike Slough. And to those of you who do not know Slough, Sir John Betjeman wrote a stanza in a poem which began, 'Come friendly bombs and fall on Slough.' As presumably Sir John thought that it was an ugly town.

There are a lot of unfinished buildings with no windows – like the mouths of wardrobes with the doors open – the lack of windows I am told is to avoid paying tax on the unfinished dwellings. Unrendered breeze blocks are also a bit of an eyesore. At least the streets are clean; the pavements may be a bit uneven. The roads are full of potholes – as they are in Blighty. All of the old houses have an entrance doorway to the street and a larger doorway, which from the outside looks like a garage and these days are used as garages, but in the not too distant past in the 1960s pony and traps were the only form of transport

and the larger doorway was for the pony and the trap.
Presumably, in those days the pony would poop in the
pot holes, so that they weren't such a problem, once
they were filled in with horse shit.

The *centro storico* – historical centre in Carovigno
has a pretty piazza with a few cafés and restaurants,
and we even have a castle which dates back to the
14th century – even though it has been stripped bare
of any internal history by an errant heir who had
a gambling habit and had to sell off the gold taps
and tapestries (I would like to add here that a lot of
the castles in the south are a bit bare as though they
have been ransacked, and they probably have). On
the outside the castle is beautiful, *Il Castello Dentice di
Frasso* – and the courtyard looks like a Hollywood set
for Romeo and Juliet.

My son and I arrive on a warm and sunny morning
for a coffee at the Café Central. On arriving, a female
police officer dressed in the blue and white uniform
of the local *Polizia Municipale* also known as *Polizia
Comunale*, is directing traffic and seems to be helpfully
giving advice on the one-hour parking zone.

'Can I park here?' I say.

'Yes,' she says, 'for one hour.'

It's 11 am. I assume that she has seen me and
my car and will remember both me and the car. My
son dutifully turns the dial on the *Disco Orario* where
you can indicate your *ora di arrivo*, your arrival time.
An hour, we arrived at 11 am, the kindly community
police officer had observed us. We park on the right-
hand side of the street as is the law – no problem. All

is well for one hour, or so it seems.

Every Sunday in Carovigno the WW2 sirens sound at 12 to commemorate the Second World War. It is a loud and robust siren, and I wondered if we should look for the nearest air raid shelter. The first time I heard the siren, I nearly spat out my coffee. I warned my son about the siren, and our coffees stayed in our mouths.

When I first started driving in Italy, I would pull at my right shoulder thinking that the seatbelt would be there and regularly clip wing mirrors as I was not yet able to judge the distance on the right-hand side. I had no idea what *senso unico* sign, a one-way sign, meant. I kept seeing the signs and wondered whether it was the name of a face cream. Well, I did find myself going the wrong way up a face cream street much to the annoyance of my fellow Italian drivers.

Whilst driving in Italy you need to keep your wits about you. You should also always have a spare pair of glasses in the car; relevant documentation relating to the car; your identification card or passport; a reflective triangle in case you break down; a high viz jacket for the same reason and a big smile on your face to deal with the hand gestures – I once had a man place his two knuckles together which I assumed meant *kiss my arse*! And be prepared for the horn beeping! Although technically you are not supposed toot, beep, honk or thump your horn during daylight hours. Don't drink and drive. The driving alcohol limit is 0.05% which is minuscule. So you can lick out a glass of wine after someone has finished it, but that is all.

On asking a friend what he thought it was like driving in Italy, he said, 'It just flows.' Well, I suppose it does, it if you go with the flow, what possibly could go wrong?

The traffic does flow on the autostradas and superstradas the traffic files in from the right, and the left-hand lane is the fastest. There seems to be a rule by which the traffic entering the superstrada doesn't automatically join in but will wait for a gap. Bearing in mind that the fast lane traffic is usually going very fast and I generally only use it for overtaking. Stay too long and you will probably find a BMW or an Audi suddenly appearing behind you with flashing head lights giving you 0.5 seconds to pull over (maybe I should say a high-end car). Anyway, a high-end car may smash your back end if you don't pull over. *Pronto!*

On one particular day whilst driving to Lecce I was in the right-hand land and a car just joined suddenly 'without observing the unwritten rule' and I had to create a middle lane between the right and left-hand lanes. The insurgent driver had in fact created a third lane. Nerve-jangling-terrifying at least I created my own flow!

I always park at the airport or in the supermarket as far away from my fellow Italian drivers as possible – to avoid any dents and bumps – and generally this rule works for me. On leaving my local supermarket one day a car reversed into my car and I tooted my horn frantically to get the driver to stop – although it is illegal to toot your horn during day light hours except in an emergency. I leap out of my car ready for the 'What do you think you are doing speech.' I find that the Italian language has left me in a panic – this seems to happen sometimes the words are there and at other times the Italian lingua paralysis leaps in and this was one of those occasions – I think I was speechless.

Out of the perpetrator's car stepped a blue-eyed Italian who smelt really nice. '*Succede ogni giorno nel parcheggio.*' 'It happens every day in the car park,' he said, putting his hand on my shoulder in commiseration for my poor choice of parking space and as a congratulatory gesture in view of the fact that I could smell his marvellous odour. No exchange of numbers, I just watched him speed off into the sunset. I then realised that I had left all sense of logic in England...*boh!*

A lot of houses in towns have their front door opening onto the main street. And at night especially, you will see lots of Italian mothers and the odd man who can no longer walk to the café sitting on white plastic chairs outside their houses watching the world go by and sitting perilously close to the passing traffic, where they have a *quattro chiacchiere* four chats, which means gossip. They gossip about the weather; food and who cooks and can't cook; who's died, getting married or just on their way out. And then there is the *stranieri* – stranger's/foreigner's fodder. 'They come here they don't speak Italian.' 'They come from the next town, and they don't speak the dialect.' 'They come here, and they park their cars in the wrong place.' This, I fear, is to become a theme for me.

My Italian nemesis *incubo*, nightmare. Parking in the wrong place.

On a pleasant summer evening I parked down a beautiful side street in Ceglie Messapica, which has winding archaic narrow streets with pretty whitewashed houses. I parked in what I thought was in a non-hazardous way and went to a choir concert in the local church where a few of my English friends were singing in the choir. Ally an English girlfriend had joined me for the evening and we listened to renditions of 'Amazing Grace', 'Ave Maria', 'Since First I Saw your Face' with a finale of 'Volare' sung sweetly and melodically and finished the evening off with a glass of wine in a plastic cup which came out of a five-litre plastic bottle of supermarket special.

'Have some more,' the makeshift barman said encouragingly. 'We don't want to take this shit home.' Which I think is expat speak for – *We haven't given you the best wine that Italy can offer, and it really is shit.'*

On returning to the car Ally and I were greeted by a quartet of furious Italian mothers and grandmothers and one man. Which I assumed was the only man who couldn't make it to the café that night, or maybe he had been kidnapped by a posse of Italian women.

'Eccoli. Le donne!' – 'Here they are. The women!' I was suddenly made aware of a drama, a tragedy; an indiscretion; a faux-pas. That only 'The Women' as we were now known, could have managed to commit the ultimate crime.

'Ha parcheggiato di fronte alla casa e nessuno può entrare o uscire o andare giù per le scale,' 'You have parked in front

of the house and no one can get in or out or go down the stairs,' said one of women waving her arms up and down furiously.

At this point, all the women joined in with arm waving and with added Italian gesticulations – that I didn't quite understand, but I think they wanted to cut our throats. The man who didn't make it to the café is hanging at the back.

'*Scusa mia, mi dispiace.*' I smile and try to apologise. '*Scusa, scusa?*' One of the nonnas spits out as though she is trying to get rid of a fur ball whilst also spitting feathers. She was very irate. Spittle and feathers. I should have said *scusi* which is the formal way of saying excuse me, so she was further enraged by my 'familiar' use of *scusa*…

I can barely speak Italian, let alone argue in it and all I did was to hang my head in shame and tell my friend to get in the car 'Quick!' as though we have just performed a bank robbery. We sped off and left the nonnas and the man who didn't make it to the café to have four chats about the incident about 'The Women' for weeks, if not years, decades or centuries. You may hear stories about 'The Women' in the twenty-second century if you visit southern Italy and how they were hanged as witches for the non-moving traffic violation because they couldn't say sorry enough, politely enough or competently in Italian.

Before all this parking and driving drama, when I first arrived in Italy and after hiring a car expensively for a few months, I really needed to buy one. I was advised not to buy a green, white, or red one – the Italians apparently don't like these colours when

buying a second-hand car which is very perplexing
as these are the colours of the Italian flag – so that
leaves black, grey, blue.

I had always been fond of Fiats – I had been an
owner of a black one and yes, a red one – and as
I was in Italy then surely I would be being loyal to
my resident country to buy a Fiat. One evening I
was taken to see a 'Fiat' – although maybe this 'Fiat'
had retired some time ago – in a garage in town.
The owner had very kindly left the engine running
so that I could appreciate the blue and black smoke
that was emanating from the exhaust pipe. We could
have all died of carbon monoxide poisoning. Lili and
Mimo had very kindly arranged this appointment for
me. The car was blue – check, but other than that I
think that the poor Fiat Punto was in the terminal
throws of a blue and black throaty cough. It also had
125,000km on the clock and the asking price was
2,500 euros for a car that look as though it may not
have enough guts left in it to managed a gentle reverse
out of the garage.

The proud owner said that it used to be his wife's.
I tried to find some empathic response as I gazed as
the expiring and spluttering Fiat. All I could say was,
È troppo vecchio.' 'It's too old.' And I felt guilty saying
this as though I had just run over his cat. He seemed
offended and babbled away in dialect that I couldn't
understand, and then he pointed to his teeth and said,
'Deve parlare in l'italiano.' 'You must speak in Italian.' As
though his teeth had the entire Collins Italian/English
Dictionary printed on them. I thought that I was
speaking Italian, but I guess I was just not saying the

right words, 'Yes, I would love to buy your car that is going to choke to death very soon, thank you very much. *Grazie mille.* A thousand thank yous; it would be a privilege to be lumbered with a piece of junk, not!'

I didn't buy the car. But I did buy a little Aygo about a month later from a Toyota dealer in Brindisi after several trips and several calculations on bits of paper – why is it that the price isn't on the computer, but a satisfactory price can be obtained from a piece of paper?

I didn't buy my Aygo lightly. I did some research on YouTube and saw that the *Top Gear team'* had organised a five aside football game with Aygos, and I concluded that if you can play football with an Aygo, then you can negotiate narrow Italian streets with it.

Today, my little Aygo is parked in a 1-hour parking area on the right-hand side of the street with the arrival disc turned to 11:00 clearly indicating my time of arrival. In any case, I have been seen by a friendly and helpful female police officer who flashed me a smile. Satisfied that I had parked correctly at not at forty-five degrees like some Italians we leave for a latte macchiato and a cappuccino – always ask for a latte macchiato and not just for a latte, otherwise, you will be served a cup of hot milk. Lovely.

With great relief at no WW2 sirens going off we return to the little Aygo at 11:45am – forty-five minutes later.

On our return, there is a parking ticket stuck to the windscreen. Was I parked over the white lines? Had I been parked for over an hour? Actually no the *Ora di arrivo* had been turned to 18:00 and not 11:00 – my son told me afterwards that it looked like 11:00 from the inside of the car. *Tell it to the judge I am thinking.* Or maybe I could explain this accidental error to the helpful and friendly female police officer who was previously smiling.

I approach the aforementioned officer, and we have a conversation – in Italian not great but maybe passable with a few grammar errors.

'I have a parking ticket,' I say.

'Yes. You must pay,' is the reply. In a slightly huffy manner and her hands are on her hips.

'You saw me arrive at 11:00. You saw me and my car, and you spoke to me and said that I could park here for 1 hour. It is now only 11:45,' I plea.

No smile. 'Yes, I saw you arrive, and I spoke to you. But you still have to pay. The disc is wrong, and that is the law,' she says, calmly and officially, notebook now flapping in the air.

I try the ploy of it being my son's fault, and if I was more fluent in Italian I could have said that he was innumerate; he should have gone to Specsavers and get us all ha, ha and laughy, laughy. But I am still trying to pull the Italian words out of my mouth like handkerchiefs from a magician's mouth. I resort to phone a friend and try and get someone else to explain my situation, but to no avail. My friend on the phone says, 'She is just being a bitch.'

We walk up the police station – ooh fingerprints, handcuffs – I mumble and try and keep my body language humble and apologetic when I really want to scream that it is all just insane! Unfair! Fatuous! I am innocent! Or maybe that is going a bit too far.

The aforementioned police officer is still talking on the phone to my 'phone a friend' and tells him that I still have to pay, even though she has seen me and my time of arrival. Defeat and acquiescence begin to wash over me. Then my hope swells when she approaches and she talks to a group of indifferent police officers, who squash any signs of hope, who chorus in unison, 'She still has to pay.' Or they might have said, or we could put her in the stocks for a week.

Maybe I could speak to the commandant. I had met him previously when I applied for my residency and shook his hand. He blushed when he asked if I would write about him in my book. Very handsome, grey-haired man with a distinguished moustache and an elegant navy blue uniform with braids on the shoulders. Well, he is not here today, and I follow the aforementioned police officer into the police station. There is one other police officer present and drawers of filing cabinets – no paperless office in Italy yet. I expect to see an Imperial typewriter, but in this case a biro is the technology of the day.

My aforementioned female police officer asks for some ID, and I give her my residency card. 'Oh you are a resident,' she says with genuine surprise and repeats this to the other guy in the office, and they look at me with astonishment as though this is something they usually only do to tourists – slapping tickets on the unsuspecting-accidental-errorers.

I am proud of my residency; it makes me feel part of the community. The day I applied for my residency it felt as though I was bobbing in and out of endless non-paperless offices with 70s strip lighting and filling in forms on scraps of paper which I would then have to take to another office and fill in another form. The layers of bureaucracy in Italy keep a lot of people employed for life. Therefore, it is a commendable service.

There is no privacy in Italy – or this is my perception. A man who was at the front desk in the local government office and saw my height being measured – in two-inch heels and I am now two inches taller – and filled in my residency card also came into the office where all my personal details were being entered into a computer. Yes, a computer! He stood over the shoulder of the clerk and read all my personal details. Amazing. Absolute overt nosiness. It was so blatant that I actually wasn't offended. I have developed this weird acquiescence to most things in Italy, the driving, the bureaucracy, the nosiness, and I say to myself never mind aye… it's just the way it is. This, I think, helps with my tolerance levels in all quarters.

Back to the parking incident. She fills in my details from my residency card onto a form so that I can pay my 31 euro fine. I now feel that I didn't really commit a crime and that it is all a complete injustice. Where is my lawyer? All I did was make a numerical error on the disc. I clearly had no case for the defence, and no one was listening anyway.

Then suddenly I feel a bit more upright – no never mind aye in this situation – indignant even.

'What is your name?' I ask her.

'My name?' she says and I notice a slight flash of guilt across the once smiley face.

'Yes, your name?' I press. *Is it Ima Nolongersmileyface? I am thinking.*

'Why do you want to know my name?' she questions and clips me back.

'I am writing a book about living in Italy,' and I get out a piece of paper and a pen as if to demonstrate this and begin writing on it.

She visibly squirms in her own uncomfortableness. And I feel wrongly righteous and scribble something down in front of her as I just linger on the enjoyment of the moment, just a little. There would be no naming and subsequent shaming forthcoming.

'Mum, you shouldn't have said that,' my son says to admonish me. He seems slightly appalled and gives me a look that suggests I had just stolen a bag of sweets from a small child. He then adds philosophically, 'Well, at least you can say that you have given some money towards the community.'

The worst crime this morning was not the 45-degree angle parkers; the 3rd lane makers; the speeders; the stop and talk to a friend for five minuters; the nice smelling reversers. It was me, the-wrong-time-on-disc-thingyer.

Some months later and after post-Christmas festivities and a family reunion with my children, something strange happened. It snowed. Now, I am told that it only snows in Puglia every ten years, so this was a very rare occurrence. Nonetheless, it did snow and on a day that I was due to take everyone to Bari airport.

The flight was at 9 pm and so leaving at 5 pm seems reasonable to make it in time as the first snow flakes fell.

The flakes fell and then settled into two inches of snow within an hour. Before leaving Lili called and said that I couldn't possibly drive to the airport, and I wondered whether we should go by a winged unicorn instead. She said that she would call a taxi, and I thought okay that sounds good.

The taxi driver wanted 150 euros to drive the airport, 'because he might die'. And so we all piled into the car and joined the superstrada to find that the traffic had ground to halt. Once on the superstrada, it was difficult to get off even though the next exit was under 2 km away. The snow was continuing to fall, and the wind was blowing it horizontally, and bits of cardboard from fly-tippers were being scooped up from the side of the road and hitting the car. Everyone had their hazard warning lights on, and the traffic flow had trickled to 10 mph.

My son and my daughter's partner descended into caveman silence as they both had to work the next day. Whilst my daughter and I discussed ways of getting our of the predicament and how we should probably get off at the next exit.

I rang Lili and asked if they could get a train to Bari from Carovigno. She said yes, but we need to get there by 17:57, or we will miss the train. It was now 17:15. The snowfall was unabating, and we eventually managed a sluggish exit from the superstrada forty minutes later. I almost took a wrong turn and then had to drive down a snow covered incline to the station. The little Aygo swerved and juddered. 'Pump the brakes, pump the brakes,' my daughter shouted, and I did as I was instructed, but narrowly missed a wall. I quickly abandoned the car and ran to the station where thankfully an Italian man in a thick winter coat was standing on the platform and spoke English, and he said that the next train due to arrive was going to Bari. Suitcases were hurriedly dragged through the snow, and the three of them waited for the train, anxious and cold. The train arrived ninety seconds later. God, the angels or all them were looking after us that night.

I then had to get back up the hill and again asked for God's help. 'Please God, please get me home safely,' I kept saying to myself. My whole body was shaking with anxiety, and my right foot was doing a strange nervous twitching. And despite me not being particularly religious, he obliged, and I managed to get home without having an accident or freezing to death. Thank you, Mr Higher Power.

Six inches of snow fell that night, and a foot of the white stuff settled on higher ground in places like Alberobello and Martina Franca. No one was prepared for the poor weather conditions. There were no gritters or snow ploughs, and the roads were treacherous. It is also illegal in Italy to drive without tyre chains in snowy conditions and I didn't have any on my car that night and from what I could see neither did any of my fellow Puglians. It was such a rare occurrence and none of us had the proper equipment or maybe the sense to stay at home and wait out the bad weather.

By the next day, the snow had started to melt and gave way to the usual wet and windy and usually mild winter.

Driving in Italy can be a trial, but driving in Italy during a heavy snowfall can be deadly and nerve wracking. I don't think that my anal sphincter will ever be the same again.

Chapter 17

ی‌و

Different Journeys and Stories and Fioroni

I am at Anna's. I arranged to pick her up at six o'clock in the evening, to take her to a celebration in the local Puglian countryside to celebrate the *fioroni* – the newest and greenest of figs that arrive in June which are more succulent and larger than the ones that are harvested in July and August. As I have said before the Italians love to celebrate food and wine in the different months and seasons; grape harvesting in September, mushrooms, and chestnuts in October and November. All symbolic of the Italian epicurean pursuits. And I suppose that a shot of coffee is also celebrated every morning, as the Italian government keeps the price down deliberately because there is a national belief that it is an Italian right to have a morning coffee and is part of the Italian way of life.

I am sitting outside waiting in the garden. When I arrived, Anna was wrapped in a towel with wet hair, celebrating the Italian habit of tardiness. Nevertheless, this has given me the time to sit and contemplate my navel and watch the olive trees – some of which are 200 years old – and to watch the stones or are they watching me? Gentle gusts of breeze pass through the trees, and they seem to rustle in contentment. I let my thoughts breeze through my head and think about my own journeying.

Another year or so and I would be back in England. Somewhere desolate, remarkable perhaps, and without too many people. I have a fancy for Norfolk. I imagine myself wrapping up in several layers of clothes and a scarf protecting my face from the incoming cold easterly winds. A trip to a village pub with notepad in one hand and a glass of vintage port in the other. A crackling fire and Norfolk vowel sounds hitting my ears and perhaps missing the Italian musical tones. I shiver at the thought of the coldness; the wind and missing the Italian story that has been unfolding before me. Maybe I would have to drink a bottle of port to lessen the pain. Then I would become the local village drunk who falls out of the pub every night. With only the several layers of clothing saving me from serious injury, hopefully.

I don't want this journey, this wondrous episode of my life to end. Or am I clinging on to a comfort? Italy's warm embrace as I would a warm bath that is getting cold as I know that I have to get out of it, wanting to immerse myself even more, even though the cold chill of the bathroom air is chilling my skin which becomes prune-like-Mrs Tigglewinkle's fingers. I yearn to stay in my Italian bath a little longer, enjoying the waters not wanting to leave.

Recently, as I got ready for a trip back to England – for an MOT teeth, eyes and a trip to M&S – I found some English coins in a bag along with the house keys to my daughter's apartment and my key to my storage,

No 41 with all the things – *they are only things* – that are dusty and asleep in a 70ft rectangular box. The coins feel heavier than the Italian ones that I have become used to. England and its coins representing a colder, heavier and more restricted place.

'It will be nice to go home,' a friend said to me. But this place and its people feels more like home. 'Italy suits me,' I find myself saying. I am different here. My heart is here. Italy has done strange things to me. I feel freer; more open and less restricted; more in the moment. More me. Yes, Italy suits me, and I don't want the journey to end. The Welsh people have their own description for yearning for Wales and its essence; they call, *Hiraeth* and Italy has its own particular and unique essence and longing for me, which I would call *Bramosia*, which means a yearning in Italian.

I try not to concentrate on the potential losses that seem to be rolling in. And as the memories are stacking up I take pictures to capture my life here and write this book as a statement to my experiencing.

Anna has her own longing to stay in Italy. The country of her birth and in the house that she painstakingly renovated and the land that she has tended, which is now no longer possible because of her ill health. 'It's too remote for me.' I remember saying to her one day and the internet access is sporadic that it would be like living in a bucolic paradise, cut off from the outside world. Anna seems to enjoy the isolation, but to keep her company when I went back to England; she looked after Basil for me. She loves everything about him. His big fat paws; droopy ears and that sad look that he gives everyone even when he is happy.

'He has eyes like *occhio di buoi*, bulls' eyes. Like a soft-boiled egg,' she said.

I mentioned that I was going to the dentist in England, and I have until recently always managed to keep a healthy set of gnashers and avoided the Italian dentist experience. However, during a gum chewing session and archaic amalgam filling fell out. I explored the hole in my tooth which felt as deep as the channel tunnel and rang Lili to arrange an appointment at the dentist, pronto!

The problem is there is no appointment system at the dentist in Carovigno, and the system is like this. No appointment, you just turn up. One of the other patients lets you in via an intercom buzzer because there is no receptionist. You then sit and wait with thirty other people in a bare waiting room with plastic chairs and try and work out who is the next patient, and the wait can take hours. You then finally get your turn – even though in your head you thought of ways of a do it yourself filling, perhaps using some Polyfilla – not in my case though as I am allergic to it. The dentist's consulting room is a different affair from the waiting room and is gleamingly white and high-tech. The dentist as it turns out is your neighbour. He either knows your name telepathically – or someone has told him and he examines your mouth without taking a history. In my case, I hastily told him that I was allergic to white fillings and could die of anaphylactic shock. He filled my tooth with amalgam without examining the whole of my mouth and then said that I didn't need to pay. Job done.

Although, 'no payment' doesn't actually mean 'no payment' and it is an unwritten rule that you then have to buy a present to show your gratitude for the no fee. I then had to order a bag from England as a present for his wife; that had a ticket inside that said, 'Thank you for shopping at Harrods.' Job now definitely done.

My English dentist said that the filling was a job well done. Great and I paid him in the customary way.

Let's go back to Anna's and Basil's bull eyes.

This description would come in handy after he went missing one night when Anna was looking after him. I was having a lovely weekend in England and rang Anna to check on how things were.

'How is Basil?' I asked expecting a description of him lying contentedly on a cold tiled floor and his farts gently wafting out of his back end.

'Basil is not here,' she said. *What do you mean he is not there?*

'I let him out for a wee last night at 11 o'clock, and he didn't come back. I have been calling for him all day and all night. I am so distressed and so sorry. I am hoarse. I can't call for him anymore.' The little blighter had escaped or had he just got lost on a nose sniffing trail. Either way, he was missing.

Anna had sounded so distressed. I assured her that I would fly back early the next day and help her look for him. In shock myself, I couldn't speak for an hour.

The errant Basil had 'escaped' a few times when

we lived in England. He was pretty quick for a short-legged basset and would escape at every opportunity even if the front door was open for a few seconds. Usually, he would decamp to the local thicket. Run around in circles, get tired and then pal up with some other dogs and pretend that he didn't have a family of his own. Bassets aren't particularly loyal, and if they think that someone else will give them a biscuit, they will disown you. My daughter's partner, Dean, had to carry him home in his arms once after he refused to budge from the thicket and wouldn't come when his name was called as Dean wasn't carrying a biscuit. Basil's carrying carer, collapsed in a heap at the front door sweating and exhausted, and Basil had a satisfied look on his face that said, 'That was lovely, and I didn't even have to walk home.'

I knew that Basil wouldn't be scared and would go and look for people. Most likely the people that he thought would have biscuits and a bowl of water and maybe a bed. Later on, on that Basil worrying day, I received a mobile phone text message to say that Basil had been found in Cisternino 9 km away from Anna's house!

This is the story. A basset hound turns up in a bar in Cisternino after a very long walk and sits down with two Italian men and a black labrador. Basil is attracted by the cadence and the rhythm of their voices although he doesn't understand what is being said, he thinks that every time they say *buono*, they mean Bonio (a dog biscuit), and his looks up with bulls-eye expectation. As the evening goes on the men, start to feel tired and have thoughts of going home to bed. It is now 1 am.

The first Italian says to the second Italian as he looks down at Basil, 'Is your dog a boy or a girl?'

And the second Italian says, 'That is not my dog.' Basil looks up and if he could have had a speech bubble, would have said, 'Where's my Bonio? You have been talking about it all night, and I didn't walk 9 km for nothing.' *Boh!*

I would just like to add here that due to Basil's obvious pendulous-baubles, it wouldn't be difficult to ascertain that he is, indeed a fella, a boy, a bloke. On my daily walks, I often wait for the five secs post our passing clutches of Italians when the sniggering and the giggles start – as his baubles do hang quite low and on a hot day probably stretch down to his knees. *Do dogs have knees?* After passing by a couple of women on the sand dunes one morning, one of the women shouts after me, *'Enorme!'* which means enormous and I have often thought about putting them in a little-knitted bag for him to save him any future humiliation and ridicule.

Basil is chipped and has a silver tag on his collar that says, 'Basil' and underneath, *'Sono Inglese.'* 'I am English'. It should also have said, 'I am prone to running off in search of biscuits. Please call my mum.' And they did. Although the family that had looked after him for the night and given him bed and breakfast did say that they would have kept him if the owner hadn't been found. It was such a relief for Anna, and for me. Basil was unperturbed by his whole ordeal, but did bury his head in Anna's lap as if to say that he was sorry when she met the family at a nearby garage to pick him up.

Anna is no longer my Italian teacher – I leave
that now to the internet – and we have become firm
friends. There have been numerous times when
she has said, 'I made an apple cake for you, but I
fell asleep.' And there would be a blackened and
cremated apple cake on the windowsill waiting for
a decent burial. 'I bought a bottle of prosecco for
you, but friends came round, and we drunk it.' And
there would be an empty bottle of prosecco on the
windowsill.

She would be late getting ready, on my arrival for
airport pick-ups and she'd be wearing three layers
of clothing and a jumper tied around her waist (to
avoid excess baggage charges) and with large pieces
of Italian cheese in each pocket. On one particular
day, her suitcase was too heavy because it was full
of courgettes to take back to England. 'My daughter
loves them,' she said. The handle broke, and we had
to tie a piece of string about the suitcase in order to
pull it along, and I ruptured my abdominal oblique
muscle lifting it out of the boot of my car which took
three months to heal.

Another airport pick up time her case wouldn't
close because of bags of red and green chillis bulging
out of the sides, and so I suggested we leave the
chillis behind. She then ran out into the garden to
say that she was dying, and I told her that she wasn't
dying, but we would be late for the flight if we didn't
leave soon. I could also tell you about the time she
packed barely any clothes, but took 40 kg of bed linen
back to London, because, obviously, you can't buy

bed linen in England.

But I adore Anna and her eccentric ways. Where she lives near Pascorosa, it is so peaceful and quiet. A bucolic dream. She has a *lamia* (which refers to her house and not a child eating demon from Greek mythology), and her two little white trullis set in the Italian countryside with huge bushes of red geraniums and wild fennel in the garden that sway in the breeze. We share our wanting and yearning – *Hiraeth/Bramosia* and neither of us wants to leave. But leave we must, so I must try and live in the moment with it all.

I reflect on all of these things, happenings and experiences today, as the heat is dissipating after a hot June day and finally we drive to Cisternino along the Via Roma for an aperitivo. Via Roma is the road that Basil had travelled alone for 9 km – nose sniffing and tail wagging – in search of a bar and a Bonio biscuit. Since then, every time I drive down the same road, I wonder how he did it without being knocked down by a car as it is a busy road with all the speeding traffic.

Cisternino is another pretty Puglian whitewashed town that sits on a hilltop and has several attractive terraces where you can see the *belvedere*, beautiful view. Here you will find old Italian couples holding hands on benches, watching the setting sun dip behind green hills and reminiscing about their day. Bistros and restaurants are dotted liberally throughout the town, and they even have a vegan restaurant, but for the carnivores, you can buy a two-inch thick steak from a butcher's adjacent to the restaurant and eat it in the restaurant where they will cook it for you, or take it home to cook. In Cisternino they have moved away from the more traditional Puglian cuisine of seafood and meat is more prominent on the menu, such as ragu sauce made out of *cinghiale*, wild boar with *orecchiette*, pasta.

We arrive aperitivo time, which is around 6 o'clock in Italy and usually comprises of snacks, an Aperol or Campari Spritz or a prosecco. Anna and I have a prosecco each and drink them on a terrace with a panoramic view of the countryside and watch the orange sun dipping lower in the sky.

We then drive to *Pezze di Greco*, which translates into Pieces of Greek, in Fasano for the sagra and the celebration of the *fioroni*, the first figs.

In a beautiful and quintessentially Puglian setting of olive groves, we park the car and follow the sound of the folk music and find the small grottos which have been carved out of the soft limestone. These little grottos literally served as a butcher's, a baker's and maybe even a candlestick maker. These little hobbit-like dwellings were lived in from medieval times and maybe even earlier. We are told that the *frantoio*, olive press, in one of the larger grottos was where the olive oil was produced, dates back to the 900s. The olives would have been sent down from the roof after being collected from the olive groves, down channels in the side of the grotto to be crushed and then pressed.

This press is activated and turns every Christmas where a 'live nativity' is portrayed which I suppose makes a change from being in a makeshift stable and if performed in England in a damp and draughty village hall.

The limestone walls have the appearance of burnt popcorn. I touch them. 'They are damp,' I say, and Anna adds that it would have been warm inside once the fires were going. A piece of lace is stuck in one of the walls; a reminder of when cotton was produced in the area, and I can't help but think that it has been strategically placed in order to give some antique 'authenticity'. I shudder at the thought of whole families living in such sparse conditions in the damp and the cold. The smoke from the fire invading their lungs and also trying to eke out a difficult existence from the surrounding land.

Large stainless steel bowls are full of olive oil and on calor gas burners heating up feverishly for the *pettole*, dough balls that will be cooked soon. Nearby and sitting in jugs is the dark sauce, *vincotto*, which is made from reduced fermented wine with the addition of figs, as it is fig season. This sauce has been popular in certain parts of Italy since Roman times. An Italian woman wearing an apron with sweat pouring off her brow and a florid complexion sweeps up the batter, and her hands move at great speed as she flips them into the boiling and pungent olive oil, and the cooking of the *pettole* begins at a fast and furious pace.

Outside the music continues and crowds are gathering. Children are pulling at their parent's outstretched hands, and dogs are on leads – probably hoping to eat a scrap of discarded meat, or to find a 500 hundred-year-old olive tree to pee up. The Italians tend to have an ambivalent relationship with dogs. If they love their dogs – as some of them do – they tend to take them everywhere supermarkets, shops and even into airports. These loved dogs are enjoying the spectacle, the party.

The figs are laid out in large trays and adorned with the deep orange pomegranate flowers. The orange in stark contrast to the dense green of the figs. A woman that I had seen arrive earlier – rather speedily on a red moped – is eating one of the artisanal fig ice creams that are for sale and is clothed head to toe in orange – the same dense orange of the pomegranate flowers. I can't stop looking at her and then realise that rather than being rude, I have just developed the Italian habit of staring at people – if I am interested of course. This is in contrast to the repressed downcast look of Englishness, or maybe it is just a bit of shyness that I am shedding. I am becoming less English and more Italian, it just seems to be happening in an unconscious way.

We pay 5 euros for a ticket which enables us to have a slice of bread with speck or prosciutto with two figs and a rather large bowl *pettole* covered in the *vincotto*, together with a small plastic cup of the local white wine. Not a great meal for two people that are wheat intolerant. I leave the bread. Anna takes back a fig in disgust and says that it is too ripe. Once satisfied with her second fig, we open them, and they reveal the sweet and succulent fruit inside. Anna eats the skin as well, and I nibble at mine like an English woman who is yet to become used to messy eating. And in truth, if you munch on them in an animalistic way it really is too much like front bottom sex for me, a bit of fig porn.

With no light pollution, the sky seems densely black; a jet black clear night sky sprinkled with stars. The people, the music, the chatter and the setting in amongst the ancient olive trees that are emblematic of Puglia.

We enter a grotto where a talk is taking place about figs and olive cultivation. The presentation is projected on to a large screen. The speech is far too rapidly delivered for me to understand. Although I manage to understand something about protecting the virgin olive oil production for future generations (but I am not sure how), and the fact that the fig trees do not need bees to pollinate them – and considering that the world bee population is dwindling, this is probably a good thing. Apparently, wasps burrow into the figs and on leaving manage to cross-pollinate. There are rumours that there are dead wasps in figs, but that is most likely just a 'hairy hand story' otherwise known as an urban myth.

Understanding only a few sentences, I instead concentrate on watching a piece of spittle pop in and out of one of the speaker's mouth and resist the temptation to jump up and wipe his mouth with a tissue and say, 'Now that's better. Carry on.' I also notice that he is wearing socks and sandals which is a definite, no no.

Thyme with purple heads and pungent leaves grows along the walls of the grottos. Also, huge bushes of rosemary and much smaller caper plants sprouting in the steps. All the plants seem wild and in gay abandon – *in these days of politic correctness 'uninhibited enthusiasm' is preferable, but it doesn't have the same ring to it.* The grottos are lit with small garlands of lights like little fairy caves in the nocturnal light. A magical place where I expected Gandalf with his staff in his hand to turn up at any minute. A fairy tale which is Italy, but in this case Puglia with its rustic-simplistic charm and hidden treasures.

As DH Lawrence once said, 'Can you give me something for this cough?' He probably didn't say that but what he did say was, *'For us to go to Italy and to penetrate into Italy is like a most fascinating act of self-discovery.'*

I find myself still loving and discovering Italy with gay abandon!

The next day, Mimo hands me a plate of fioroni from the countryside, which I quickly install into the fridge as they spoil so easily in the heat of the day. Later, I will enjoy them in a messy-eating way and may even eat the skins. As long as no one is looking.

Chapter 18

৯৵

From the Heel to the Tuscan and Umbrian Hills

During my second summer in Italy I decided to travel up north to see a friend in Umbria and also hoped to explore the nearby region of Tuscany; different places, landscapes, and a more diverse Italian culture perhaps? And wondered what differences – if at all – I would find between the north and the south.

I never thought that I would complain about endless sunshine and hot, fiery sunny days, but I am just about to. Being English I shouldn't. An English summer can consist of an hour of sunshine at 2 pm – probably on a Wednesday – on a day in July, and the rest of the time you really shouldn't go out without a coat and an umbrella. If you happen to get a ticket to Glastonbury for the summer music festival, then along with your She-Wee, you will also need a Kagool, wellies, and prophylactic tetanus shot. You should also get pre-festival lessons on how to swim in a muddy quagmire.

The heat in Puglia can be heavy and oppressive in the summer months. Especially in August when the Sirocco wind, hot and humid, can blow into the house through an open door like a hairdryer on the highest heat. At night the heat can be intolerable, a wet warm veil strangling the breath. I have even found myself lying upside down in the bed in search of a cool spot. Every brain cell is feeling as though it has been fried in olive oil. Days can be spent just on the task of rehydration and trying to stop yourself slipping off of plastic chairs like an invertebrate due to the continuous outpouring of perspiration. I am tempted to write here women glisten, but no, in the heat of the day you sweat like a steeplechase horse.

With a temperature of 40c in the hot heel, I was looking forward to a drop of 15c down to 25c and some relief and a cooler and more temperate climate with a forthcoming trip to Tuscany and Umbria, to visit Dee.

The south isn't termed *Il Mezzogiorno* – the Midday – for nothing. Being baked in the midday sun means that you could literally fry an egg on your thigh. Italian heat escapees bathe to the neck up in a still and dormant Adriatic, and you can still find bathers in the sea at 9 pm unable to face a wet, damp and sleepless night as the temperature sometimes only drops to 25c overnight. If you have an air conditioner that is currently working then there is some relief; mine does not, unfortunately. It makes a humming sound then belches out a faint breath; that is warm; it's about a useful as the arms on a T-Rex.

The harbour is busy at night with meals still being served at 11 pm. Holidaying frenzied crowds buying things they don't need from market stalls set up at the far end of the bay. Mosquito rackets to swat the daily and nightly invaders; perfumed chalks in the shape of shells and a myriad of handbags and sundresses.

The fishing boats bob up and down on an almost glass-like sea in the cloying night air. The fishing nets sleeping like giant cobwebs awaiting a morning's unfurling and a catch of fish. The octopus and squid are usually caught by men in wetsuits, or less adventurous fishermen in green waders, venturing not far from the shore with smaller nets and harpoons. I have had the unsavoury privilege of watching Squiddly-Diddly being bludgeoned to death against the rocks – this is normal practice – which is not a pleasant sight, but this is the reality. The octopus on your plate having suffered a murderous death.

Tired children squawk and whine in baby buggies. Shirtless young Italians whizz in and out of the evening walkers on their Vespas and the old men in short shirt sleeves drink grappa and play cards. Music blares out from the bars making a cacophony of noise. Young couples wrap themselves around each other on every corner and in every bar, and such public displays of affection are not unusual in Italy. The boys and girls have probably known each other since childhood and are probably going to marry. The girls are treated like precious and exotic objects; something to be desired and these little coquettish mating rituals are played out publicly, but to me, don't seem overtly sexual, but more like a dance – a seated tango.

Cocktails are drunk; crepes and *gelati* are consumed, and no one seems to want to go to bed and face the nightly *incubo*.

The night before I left for much cooler climes I wrote in my journal, 'No sleep.'

If there no sleep available to me, then I walk and at 5 am, on one August dawn morning, I was greeted by teenagers with sandy feet and wet hair – never having been to bed themselves. A woman lying face down outside the Cliff bar that sits at the water's edge on the rocks – presumably she had consumed an excessive amount of alcohol. I could see several pitched tents on the beach and signs of wee on the sand dunes. And as I completed my walk there was a raucous volleyball game being played by tanned Italian lads with thin and athletic bodies, at 6 am on the Mezzaluna beach. You can have fun when you are young. When you are older like me, walking is the better option even if it is with a sluggish zombie-like stride. At least I can observe the summer theatre, in the south, where they know how to live and to live in the moment.

It has been said, that the north produces so that the south can live. Which is probably an unfair assumption. It would be like saying that the south provides the pasta and olive oil (it is estimated that the south provides at least 80% of Italy's pasta) so that the north can eat. These divisions and prejudices have been around for years. The northerners are perceived as being laconic and detached and the southerners, lazy and passionate. But it seems to me, as Italy drowns in its own bureaucratic nightmare and inept and successive corrupt governments, govern like a

slumbering dinosaur; but some of 'the blame' maybe
a lack of unity and nationalistic pride amongst the
Italian people which enables the north/south divide
to develop into a much wider chasm. A united Italy
is a relative baby – in historical terms – having only
been a unified country since 1861. Before unification,
the south was part of the Kingdom of the Two
Sicilies which stretched from Sicily right up to Rome.
Rome and the middle of Italy formed the Papal
States, and the north was further divided into regions
of the Kingdom of Sardinia and the Kingdom of
Lombardia and Venetia. The north-eastern part of
Italy was part of the Austrian Empire.

Italy, as a whole, has an intoxicating lure for most
us, Johnny Foreigners, from the food, the wine, the
art, opera and the theatre or the 'show', which mirrors
Italian life. Italy has become almost a parody of itself.
The apparent histrionics, the passion, the innate and
strong family values, the stunning vistas; high fashion
and culture. If you put it in a blender and mix it all
together then this is the 'Italian product' and it has
been this way for centuries. Italy is a romantic, poetic,
charming and transformative beast. It is almost as
though Italy over the centuries has written its own
novel so that we, the rest of the world (who probably
perceive ourselves as leading more mundane, boring
and less romantic lives), all get sucked into this
maelstrom of Italian cultural delights. In modern
times, we eagerly read the pages of the Italian 'novel'
and hop on planes to sample the Italian 'product'.
Having said all this, Italy does, in fact, deliver. The
Italian dream, the romantic 'novel' and notion does

not disappoint.

Italy provides escapism from the humdrum and if you want a simpler and less harried life and can ignore all the background noise of an inefficiently run country, then this is the place to be.

A Florentine Kiwi expat has allowed me to share his view on living in Italy and Italian life and he said, *'It took me five years to realise that I was not part of the 'Show' that is Italy. I am part of the audience. So, I now just sit back and laugh or weep with them, but I don't think that I will ever leave the theatre.'*

When I arrived in Florence, it was already feeling cooler and if I had planned things a little better – and also if I had realised that the Firenze Santa Maria Novella (SMN) was so near the tourist attractions – I may have dipped into Florence's luxurious and textured history. Instead on my planes, trains and automobiles journey, I stepped out of a taxi at Florence railway station with my unwieldy bag and headed straight for the train concourse. I had one of those holdall-thingy-on-wheels that is like a supermarket trolley with a wonky wheel and as you drag it behind you, it twists your arm almost 360 degrees and as it has probably seen another holdall thingy-on-wheels that it fancies and doesn't want to go in the same direction as you.

In the station concourse I observed my fellow train travellers. There was a hubbub of sweaty tourists with maps pinned to their faces, and many of them were drinking mineral water out of 500ml plastic bottles looking lost, stressed, anxious and fatigued.

Me and the holdall-thingy, on the other hand, felt refreshed and dare I say, a bit chilly in the now much lower 25c temp – ooh just like a spring day in southern Italy.

I moved towards the ticket office window where there was a man sitting behind the glass – whom I thought would be able to tell me how to get to Chiusi – he instead waved at a basket of tickets in front of him and picked one up and showed it to me and I realised my error. I was supposed to pick up a white ticket in order to enter the queueing system. I wondered why I was given some disconcerting and angry looks when I just strolled up to the window. An absence of a queue should have told me that something was amiss. The stressed hububby-travellers all had white tickets in their hands. Realising my mistake I took a ticket from the lip of a plastic dispenser and became aware that I was number 349 and that I probably wouldn't get any words of wisdom from the mouth of the man behind the glass until the next pope dies, or as the Italians say, *ogni morte di papa*, which doesn't quite translate into 'When hell freezes over' or 'When the Queen cracks a smile' this all meant that I probably wouldn't get served for a very long time…

Using my superior observational skills, I noticed the self-service ticket machine that accepted bank cards. Problem solved. I looked up at the illuminated train timetable, and it told me that the train to Chiusi would be leaving in the next ten minutes. A woman in front of me with twelve fingers also attempted to use the automatic ticket machine. She then proceeded to punch in too many combinations of numbers into the machine, sighing, saying something incomprehensible to her daughter, and the repeated the whole process all over again. Now my ten minutes was dwindling down to five and then to three. I class myself as being a non-violent person, but it is times like these when the adrenaline flows, and the stomach tightens, that I could easily have pushed her out of the way and held her down whilst I obtained my ticket. Fortunately, she eventually solved the puzzle, and I made it to my train on time, without resorting to violence and a possible criminal record.

I hoped that I was on the right train and settle down with the holdall-thingy, which was now feeling even more unwieldy and it was like trying to manoeuvre a dead person that had been wrapped in a Persian carpet. Just to make sure that I was on the right train, I texted Dee, 'Is it Trenitalia?' Which is a stupid question really, because it obviously wasn't Trenindia and I wouldn't end up in Calcutta. No reply came, and I decided to have some faith. I rested my head back and listened to the well-enunciated tones of my Italian travelling companions and found that I could almost understand most of what they said without the slurring and vowel changes of my southern dwellers. No 'sh' sound in *questa* – which sounds more like a soft drink rather than meaning, this.

And so my holdall-thingy was my only companion until a young Italian chap asked, *'Questa la tua valigia? Posso togliere la roba?'* – Is this your suitcase? Can I put your things away.' *'Sì grazie.'* And he levered my holdall-thingy onto the rack above us.

You have to validate your train ticket prior to boarding the train. Otherwise, you can incur a 100 euro fine. I had forgotten to do this in my mad dash to what I hoped was the right train. *Il Controllere* – the train conductor, in a smart dark blue uniform moved down the train carriage and dutifully punched a hole in my ticket. No fine, phew! It's quite astounding how cheap train travel is in Italy, 12.90 euros for 111km journey, much cheaper than the 25 euros for a taxi drive from Florence airport to the train station. The trains in Italy are clean as well as being more economical than their British counterparts. Although you might need a pole vault to step up into them. Short legs – like mine, and a heavy bag are not conducive to a lady-like boarding or alighting for that matter.

My holdall-thingy aloft reminded me of previous high days and holidays and my father's suitcase and my fears of what would lie in it.

I always worried about the contents of my dad's suitcase. I couldn't pry, because he would be offended. He came very, reluctantly on a couple of holidays with us when my children were small. He lived alone, and I don't think that he did much washing. Thoughts of not enough clean pants would rush through my head, and I would also imagine what it would be like if airport security opened the bloody thing and dared to have looked at its contents. *'Yes, he did pack it himself. And no, he wasn't carrying anything for anyone else and yes, they are his dirty underpants.'*

His suitcase was old. A relic of the 60s, tan-brown,

with hard bashed edges with a musty, 'been under the bed for too long smell'.

I imagine unwashed socks; folded but not clean. His light blue safari suit lying on top of the unwashed socks. Would there be shorts? Oh dear God, what if he hasn't packed any swimming trunks?

On a holiday to Spain when I was eleven years old, the lack of swimming trunks became apparent. Eleven is an age when you first start to notice boys and realise that not all boys smell like hay, sweat, and grass and can actually smell of Ambre Solaire and chlorine. I had hoped that a boy might notice me in my bikini and my newly tanned skin. My sister and I had been playing with some boys of the same age in the pool, which consisted of being splashed in the face or my head being shoved under the water. Boys at eleven may smell nicer, but really haven't yet gotten into puberty and you, a girl, is something that can be played around with and possibly drowned in the process.

My dad had decided to join in on the near-drowning fun and started to walk on a wall next to the pool, from where he was going to dive into the pool from; which was embarrassing enough in itself. He was in full view of everyone in the pool or at the poolside, and the lack of swimming trunks was obvious to everyone.

I became acutely embarrassed by all the boys in the hotel pool saying, 'Why is your dad going to go swimming in his underpants?'

I clipped back, abashed and affronted, 'No he's not!'

'Then why does it say Y-Fronts on the waistband.'
They all chirped in unison and not being able to stifle
their collective sniggering.

Deeply ashamed by the Y-Front incident I did a
slow breast stroke to the other end of the pool. My
like for boys quickly turned to dislike again, simply
because they pointed out the bleeding obvious.

Horrible. I shivered at the thought of another
Y-Front replay embarrassment. *'If God can hear me'* – I
would say to myself – *'let there be trunks.'*

Dad would always pack an array of oddities. Pills
for constipation, which were called, 'Carter's Little
Liver Pills', promising a cure for a torpid liver; a
sallow complexion and a bilious headache – although
I couldn't imagine what a 'bilious headache' might be.
Fungal toenail ointment, Vitalis hair lotion – which
he always smelt of. Surgical Spirit, a cure-all for
everything, if the little liver pills didn't do the trick.
And ten-year-old flip-flops.

I would repeat my plea to God, *'Please God let there
be trunks under his squashed Panama hat!'*

In my train compartment, an Italian family were
busily chatting about what they were going to do
for *Ferragosto* – an Italian national holiday which is
celebrated on the 15th of August every year, which
was introduced by Emperor Augustus in 18 BC,
presumably as a celebration to himself. Unlike August
Bank Holiday in Britain, where precipitation is likely,
in Italy, a national holiday in August comes with a
guarantee of good weather. The British Bank Holiday
paradoxically, a British scene of children crying with

the cold, their cheeks red from the oncoming wind
and rain on a pier probably in a place like Margate or
Skegness. Squirming and whining under an umbrella
that would ultimately invert and more sobbing
because of boredom. Still, there is always fish and
chips and cherryade to cheer up any hypothermic
kiddy.

An Italian Ferragosto on the other hand; brown
bodies, gelato, games of bocce, volleyball and football
played on white sands against the backdrop of a clear
blue-green inviting sea that is as warm as a bath.

I remember a particular British holiday in Margate
when I was about six or seven when it was actually
foggy. You couldn't even see the sea, and yet we
still made sandcastles and our homemade woollen
cardigans covering our swim suits – which could also
have been knitted. Only the Brits would put their
children through such torture. *'Soggy jam sandwiches
anyone?'*

And then there is also the British preoccupation
with camping. A small tent with a leak, then you get
wet; children in close proximity to each other get
nits. Two days of nit combing and three days of rain.
Camping heaven!

After having invested in a six man tent – even
though there were only four of us and a golden
retriever. I would torture my children two or three
times a year with 'camping heaven'. I would bribe
them with promises of fun-filled weekends in the
country, usually in the New Forest. The car would list
with all the camping equipment, and a trailer would be
full too. It was never fun-filled. And as for the 'I love

camping' delusionists – it is, in fact, a horror story.

In the New Forest, the horses would eat the children's cereal out of their breakfast bowls and squirrels would eat through bags of food that had been left in the tent. There would be interminable queues for showers and loos, towels and toilet rolls stuffed under everyone's armpits; plastic wash bags swinging in anticipation of a luke warm shower. We even woke up one morning to find that the ground sheet was moving under a swell of water that had collected after a night of heavy rain. It always seemed to rain when we went camping and no parent wants to see their children crying because they have grass and bits of twig in their sandwiches and their socks are permanently wet.

Being not so responsible parents and in order to anaesthetise ourselves from the camping misery my husband and I drank a bottle of sloe gin one miserable camp night. We obviously became so tasty – gradually being embalmed in sloe gin – that the midges fed off of our faces, and we emerged in the morning looking as though we have some sort of contagious disease, covered in red spots. I also noticed that my son had thrown up during the night, and there was a flock of seagulls outside the tent doing a clean-up. The dog had also done a poop outside the neighbouring tent. Time to go home.

If you have to drink yourself senseless whilst in charge of two children, a golden retriever and a framed tent that requires a degree in pure mathematics to put up, then it is probably time to give up the fun-filled camping!

My Ferragosto would be spent at the Tuscany and Umbrian border with a friend whom I had never met – although we had been in contact cyberly – and I hoped that her two boys would be house-trained.

I looked out the window and drunk in the changing landscape. Fields of corn and sunflowers, neat rows of vines, distant mountains and hilltop towns. Solar panels, chicken runs and some alpine looking houses painted yellow – not really what I was expecting to see. The Tuscan pastoral scene was also very green, and I wondered, *does it rain a lot?* Strange names of towns, *Compiobi, Sieci, Pontesieve, S.Euero, Rignano, Incisa* and the curiously and strangely named *Figline* – where at the station in Figline, there was a lone woman waiting beside the train track, presumably for a fig.

The Tuscan hills unrolled and unfurled with the ubiquitous cypress trees – a Tuscan portrait which everyone expects to see. And I hoped that I was heading in the right direction.

Finally, a text from Dee, *'Can you get off at Castiglione del Lago?'* After looking at the timetable, the reply was no, although I could have been heading for Key Lago for all I knew. The timetable promised another three stops until Chiusi. I retrieved the holdall-thingy counted the stops and jumped off from a great height at the third stop and found myself in Key Lago – Castiglione del Lago. I sent an embarrassing text. Dee had to do a turnaround as she was now at Chiusi station and whilst I was waiting for my kind host, I ordered my first Umbrian prosecco and watched an

English man fall off of his chair and noticed that my seat was wet and so greeted Dee, after about half an hour, with a wet bum and profuse apologies for getting off at Key Lago.

Dee took me to a bar along the shoreline of Lake Trasimeno where I was greeted by a plethora of American and Australian expat women. Some of whom were looking gorgeous in bikinis. I, myself, haven't looked good in a bikini since 1975 and was quite grateful to be fully clothed with no wobbly bits on show. The bikini-cladders and my new host went off on pedalos for a trip on the lake, and I turned to some English expats rather than look at my shoes – or whatever else you do when you find yourself transported to an unfamiliar place. And I struck up a conversation with a retired couple in their sixties called Caroline and Ken

Caroline and Ken were Brits and almost talked in unison and nodded agreeably with one another at the end of every sentence. 'Lake Trasimeno has its own bio-climate,' Ken informed me. And I wasn't quite sure what he meant. A different weather system from the surrounding area perhaps?

They seemed to agree on the sentence, 'We love it here and wouldn't live anywhere else.' It certainly is stunning, 128 sq km of blue, cool lake surrounded by serrated looming mountains, hills, and medieval towns. A timeless place.

I felt bonded by our common language, although I was a little bit concerned about their consumption of large beers and even larger packets of crisps and wondered about the health of their livers and arteries.

But if you are retired and live near a huge lake with a temperate climate that seemed more like a beach resort, then surely this is the good life? Caroline proceeded to tell me that she loved living in Italy and that the only thing that she missed was Marks and Spencer – well we all do, don't we? Where else would you buy your knickers? She also added that she missed kippers. 'You can't buy kippers here,' she lamented. A strange thing to miss. I thought about my mum's love of eating kippers for breakfast and stinking out the whole house. I always thought that eating kippers was like eating a chewy, fishy shoe filled with bones.

As they continued munching on their calorie-laden crisps, I asked about how good the health care was in Italy – and wondered if they might have to use the health care system sooner, rather than later.

'Oh, it's good,' replied Ken and added, 'but you have to bring your own towel and food, plus your own knife and fork and someone to give you a bed bath.' All the nursing care done by the relatives then, I thought. Now that is a way to run a health care system.

As a nurse in the UK, I had experienced people being admitted and not supplying their own pyjamas or even a bar of soap. No wonder the NHS was in such a mess. And if a nurse had asked a patient's relative to bring in food, then there would be an uproar. Although I always hated it when old ladies would bring in their old unwashed flannels announcing that one was for their bottom and the other for their face and I was always terrified of mixing them up! As they were usually old and grey, the original colours long faded and so stiff that they could stand up by themselves.

With the crisps eaten and the beer drunk, I thanked my fellow Brits for their company and hoped that the bikini-cladders returned soon, before I got a bit too inebriated after a prosecco and a spritz.

Dee has a three storey, red-bricked Italian villa with fantastic views over the Umbrian hills where the sunsets can be admired and savoured. Her green lawn dips down at the bottom, and she has a small olive grove with about twenty-five olive trees and access to a large vegetable plot where Roberto, her gardener, grows seasonal vegetables. Roberto tends to Dee's garden lovingly and tells her the best time to pick the fruit and vegetables. He used to run marathons and now in his seventies still nips around the garden like an athlete, hacking away at various trees.

After sunset, it was a lot chillier than I was used to and resorted to sleeping in bed socks and a track suit when only the night before I had just slept in a vest top and knickers. *That's why you haven't got a boyfriend I thought to myself. Although every time I belch and fart I say the same thing. It has become a sort of affirmation.*

I have also developed a deep voice first thing in the morning and sound like Ray Winston and want to say, *'You slag or shut it!'* Or am I confusing Ray with The Sweeney? Either way not an attractive trait. Sometimes I cough like Dylan Thomas in damp Boathouse. I could recite 'Death hath no Dominion.' With alternating stanzas al la Ray and Dylan. *That's why you haven't got a boyfriend!*

At a barbecue one night a Scotsman bemoaned the fact that is rained too much in Umbria and that he may as well have stayed in Scotland. There was a throng of guests that I didn't know and decided just to become an observer. I dipped in and out of conversation, and my pronunciation of quinoa was corrected, 'It's pronounced *keen-wah*,' an American woman informed me, and I wasn't quite sure whether I was being patronised. She also told me that she was allergic to practically every food group. Pity she wasn't allergic to *keen-wah*. Another American woman was so voluble that I thought my head might spontaneously combust – I would like to point out here that I have nothing against American women, there just happened to have been a couple of them in the room with particular foibles and characteristics. At that moment I was beginning to wish that I had drunk more alcohol and went in search of wine. I also thought about munching my way through a bowl of *'keen-wah'*. A good source of protein apparently, even though I can't pronounce it properly.

Dee, who was a great host, and an embodiment of graciousness and calmness, told me a story about when she went to interview Francesco Illy's grandson at a vineyard for a magazine article on the 100% organic wine which was being produced called Amore e Magia, from the Francesco Illy family vineyards. His grandfather had invented the automated coffee machine and coffee bearing the Illy name can be brought anywhere in the world – you can see the Illy name everywhere in Italy on signs outside cafés.

Dee was offered a glass of Amore e Magia

and asked by Senore Illy what she thought of the wine. 'Describe it,' he asked probably expecting something like *It has a good nose. Peppery, with flowery and blackcurrant notes on the back of the tongue.'* Instead, she was so awestruck by being in Franceso Illy's grandson's presence, she said in a panic, 'It tastes really good.' And then backed up her statement by saying, 'I am not a wine writer. I'm a travel writer.' Presumably, she should have explained how the wine travelled up and down her tongue and around her mouth.

Wine lubricates the mind and loosens the tongue. I bought a bottle Brunello Montalcino, which is a famous and much-revered wine produced in Montalcino, in Tuscany. It is a wonderful wine, but expensive, expect to pay about 18 euros for a bottle. Which I would describe as a bit chunky, peppery and stains your teeth. I am not a wine writer; I just drink it.

Dee and I drank Brunello one night with pecorino cheese (from Cortona *Nero Pecorino Stagionato*) and Cadbury's Dairy Milk and odd, but winning, combination. We were joined by Lucca, an Italian estate agent one evening. He wore slip-on loafers with no socks and yes, a jumper wrapped around his shoulders, and he bore a gift of Desiderio a red wine from Cortona – Merlot grapes – which tasted like fermented blackberries, dense and fruity. I don't know if it was the wine, but Lucca seemed to speak in philosophical and poetic tones all night.

'Words are a raft and feeling the wind, and you don't where it is going.' Even though he was speaking in English, I really didn't know what he was talking about and after the line, 'You have to prepare your soul for your desires,' I realised that maybe it was time to go to bed, especially after he said to Dee, 'She doesn't speak Italian.' And the answer would probably have been no, not quite or maybe not at all, just a little, she tries (but he in fact was talking complete bollocks). By the time I had thought of a response in Italian the conversation had moved on. I am convinced that you can not be fluent in another language until you are confident. Speaking a foreign language – or attempting to – can be like a relay race. Once you start to overthink it, you pass the baton on to the person with more fluidity or in my case to Dee – I very quickly acquiesced and passed the baton on to her fluency on almost every occasion.

The next morning there was a knock at the front door. I trotted down the marble winding staircase and opened the creaky oak door. The caller was a woman who announced that she was from the *Polizia* or so I misheard. She was actually announcing that she was from *le donne di pulizie* and had come to clean the house rather than to arrest me for conspiracy to strangle the Italian language which is probably punishable by death.

In the north, the views are amazingly spectacular. In Tuscany and Umbria, there are wonderful bucolic vistas, the greenest of hills with apricot villas emerging like cleats in the landscape. Cypress trees reaching their spikes towards a clear blue sky and acres of sunflowers with dipping heads adding to the rich Tuscan and Umbrian palette. The hilltop towns are pristine but somewhat alike in their impossible attractiveness. Cortona is spotless, not even a sweet wrapper on the streets. You probably won't see Frances Mayes buying her groceries, but you will see a poster of Diane Lane in shop windows. And also be warned most of these hilltop towns have a bit of a climb to get up them. Cortona has multiple steps and an escalator and, therefore, not easily accessible in a wheelchair. Although there is access by car, parking may be difficult. Whatever the struggle to get to Cortona the views are breathtaking. Lake Trasemino dips deep into the valley, and your eyes are drawn to the mountains that are so distant that they appear to be blue – *blue remembered hills*.

Italy lends itself to the afternoon light. The Renaissance buildings being bleached out of colour in the bright sunshine of midday come to life in the fading light, 'the golden hour' and then take on a honeyed hue and shadows emerge and dance across the buildings and darkening the narrow alleyways. Dee captures all of these scenes with her professional Canon DSLR camera (I think that it's the Hokey Cokey 2,000 model with all the knobs, bells, and whistles). She snaps away looking like Frida Kahlo – but without the monobrow – in a long skirt and with flowers in her hair. Painting her own pictures through her camera lens of the ridiculously beautiful and sublime Italy. She keeps her spare lenses under a pile of beach towels in the back of the car. The boys getting bored by our adventures took pictures of the back of our heads from the passenger seat, and I bought them a football to prevent them from doing

continuous reels of play fighting throughout our
village journeying.

I realise that I am seeing Italy through my own lens.
The Greek-like south with bleached white buildings
and aquamarine seas and the artistic, historical and
beautiful north with its undulating and mountainous
landscape; each town drawing you into its secret
corners and heritage. Etruscan tombs dotted
throughout Tuscany, built 5,000 years ago long
before the Roman Empire. The south has Matera, in
Basilicata which dates back to Neolithic times 9,000
years ago and maybe the oldest settlement in Europe.
Matera's hill tops are sprinkled with Neolithic caves
that were still inhabited in 1950s. The abject poverty
was highlighted by the writer, Carlo Levi, who wrote
about the extreme poverty and hunger suffered by
the inhabitants of Matera in his book, *Christ Stopped at
Eboli*:

*'In these dark holes, I saw a few pieces of miserable furniture,
beds and some ragged clothes hanging up to dry. On the floor
lay dogs, sheep, goats, and pigs… Children appeared from
everywhere, in the dust and heat, stark naked or in rags,
eyelids red and swollen… and with the wizened faces of old
men, yellow and worn with malaria, their bodies reduced by
starvation to skeletons… I have never in all my life seen such a
picture of poverty.'*

Italy was shamed into doing something about it, and
now boutique hotels and fashionable B&Bs reside in
the caves where there was once poverty, squalor, and

death. Matera has an ancient and biblical look, and the Sassi has been used as a location site for many films, including the *Passion of Christ*, in 2004.

I have visited Matera and not only is it riveting and jaw slackening to look at it, but it didn't enlighten me. Instead, I felt a deep sorrow and tenseness that seemed to pour out of the ancient buildings and into me. I felt the same way when I visited Catania, as though previous tragedies suffered by these cities resonated within me, in a more visceral way. A deep, dark, sorrow.

Italy's previous shame is now going to be the city of culture in 2019.

It feels like a luxury, a privilege and completely self-indulgent to do what I am doing right now. Living my life in an almost totally amorphous way. If magic really does happen outside your own personal comfort zone, then I was way outside of mine and the magic was definitely beginning to happen.

The following saying, says it all (or maybe some of it, not all of it, part of it):

Life is like a camera,
Focus on what's important,
Capture the good times,
Develop from the negatives,
And if things don't turn out,
Take another shot.
Anon

It was becoming a joy to reframe my life. To

experience things more fully and to realise that I really could take another shot at life. Write a book; paint a picture and climb a mountain. Or conversely take some notes; draw a stick man and climb some stairs. The former being more challenging. I have written about my trip to Mount Etna, but it was by car. I was told quite properly, that it didn't count as no actual 'real' climbing was involved. I still have my three life challenges.

In the summer in Italy, each Italian region and town celebrates its local food and history in food festivals called *sagras*. One night Dee, her two sons and myself, went to Cortona in Tuscany to attend the local *sagra*. A Cortonian *sagra* comprised of huge steaks cooked by at least ten men and at 28 euros a head, it wasn't a cheap experience. The musical entertainment comprised of an enthusiastic organist who murdered all the songs from the past thirty years of pop music and the Italian audience seemed appreciative.

In stark contrast, another *sagra* that we attended in Pouzoula was not only cheaper and seemed simpler and more authentic, and was held in a field. Luckily for us, also minus the enthusiastic organist. The Pouzoulian *sagra* charged only 5 euros as an entrance fee and another 10 euros for food and wine. We had simple cold cuts and cheeses washed down with the local wine. The locals danced the waltz to an 'Oompah', in stiff circles, no swirling Dervish energetic dancing of the Puglian folk dancing. No hair was let down, and the Puozoulian dancers danced closely together, probably in an attempt to keep any possible moves of superfluity under control and to keep warm. No passion in the dance, just a stiff waltz. In the south, the music is vibrant with a Greek influence that makes you want to attempt to dance the Pizzica and dance until your feet ache. Scarves are raised, and skirts lifted to expose quickening of the feet to an ever increasing beat with the tapping of tambourines, throbbing drums; strumming of guitars and the playing of penny whistles; a frenzied dance that builds into a crescendo. I once danced the Pizzica until 2 am one night during a street party outside of my house which was only stopped due to complaints from the neighbours. A reasonable request because of the hour. Our gay abandonment only thwarted by the needs of those who had to get up for work the next morning. I really did dance like no one was watching…

The northerners are more laconic, and the shop assistants immediately lose interest as soon as you don't want to buy anything. A Brit who was at the barbecue (she had come to Italy to sell a boat some years before and had never returned to Blighty), told me on the way to the village shop to buy some water, *'That everyone is Umbria is miserable.'* This seemed to be in evidence as the young guy at the local shop was pale and unsmiling and wearing a white doctor's coat. He looked as though he was about to perform surgery on the vegetables in front of him instead of loading them into a plastic bag; all whilst unsmiling. In the south, everyone says *Ciao* – even if you have never met them before. Here in the north, it seemed a more formal *Salve* followed by an exiting *Arrivederci* was more common place. Small words, creating an even greater distance, between you and them; a bit of northern detachment perhaps?

In the north, the meals tend to be more meat based, sausages, game, veal, beef and of course, *cinghiale*, wild boar that run around freely in the countryside and are culled and shot during the shooting season. Umbria is the only Italian region that doesn't have access to the sea and therefore seafood is not largely featured on menus. We had a reasonably priced lunch at a Michelin star restaurant, called *La Porta* in Montecchielo. And ordered a *Melanzane Parmigiana*, baked aubergines, and parmesan cheese, served in the shape of a tower or *Tagliata di manzo con crema di rucola e parmigiana e pomodroino ripieno* – in other words sliced beef with a creamy rocket and parmesan sauce with stuffed tomatoes all for 18 euros per person with high-end food. All washed down with a Merlot Trasimeno 2012 doc.

At another restaurant, I think it was called The Mona Lisa; I had veal that was served in the shape of a rose on the plate. Dee calls the north, Salami Land, which is fine if you like a lot of cured sausage offered at every meal. No woman wants an Italian man with a miserable, cold sausage in his hand.

I wonder if all the meat eating and saturated fats in the blood and furring up the arteries makes the northerners less affable or is it the cold winters that makes the northerners more miserable and distant? They say that further south you go and the more hot-blooded and passionate the Italians become.

In medieval times, Italy, in its non-unified state was made up of city-states; each state warring with one another. Each town was fortified with their virtually impenetrable walls to protect them from marauding invaders in those ancient times. In modern times, these towns now open their gates to the present day insurgencies from the touristic culture, and they act as though they don't like it. By this I mean, be polite to the tourists and a bit more welcoming, they are, after all, adding to your GDP.

Invasions were so common in medieval times and the names of the towns were changed after invasion and I am guessing that they ran out of suitable names. Post battle, two towns were called *Becati Questo* and *Becati Quello* – roughly translated at Becati This one and Becati That one (one town being in Perugia and the other in Sienna). I can imagine the leaders of the Perugian and Sienese military one night getting drunk on *vino rosso* and saying, 'Sod it. You have this one, and I'll have that one. I just can't be bothered.'

The 20th and 21st century invaders have set up homes and created small colonies of Brits, Belgians, Dutch, and Americans. Some villages, I am told, cater totally for the wealthier expats and the whole village can be run like a giant cruise ship in dry dock where people can pay 79 euros for a bottle of water. The face of the fake and inauthentic Tuscany that has been invaded by the oligarchs, purchasing and 'idealised' version of Italy.

No wonder some of the locals are pissed off, increasing the GDP or not it must be like delivering a

Disney version of Italy.

In the south, it feels more authentic, to me anyway, but then I am probably biased because I live here. They are small pockets of expats, but not many. We have more rubbish that is discarded and not collected; we have more potholes; less meat, more fish, and definitely more smiles. In the south, a whole family will come out of their house to help you with directions, when you are lost. You can find yourself arm in arm with someone that you met two minutes previously – also whilst asking for directions – and they then invite you to pop in for coffee anytime.

The north, I believe, feeds the head, the eyes, and the palate and the south feeds the heart, the soul, and is passionate.

I prefer the latter although I appreciate the differences as I do in Britain. Where the reverse seems to be true. The northerners tend to be warmer and more hospitable and the southerners more cold and detached. A cultural mentality probably doesn't have anything to do with the weather then, as it gets bloody cold in northern Blighty!

Chapter 19

୭ஃ౿

The Glorious and Sublime Italian Language and What Am I 'Sì, Sìying' To?

On another and recent trip to Umbria, Dee and I discussed the wiggly corridors of the Italian language. Dee, being a Kiwi, clips all the English vowels into obscurity, but in Italian, she enunciates and flows.

Fluency, it seems, for me, for now, remains elusive. Before moving to Italy, for two solid years, I spent hours listening to the Linguaphone in the car whilst driving through English rain splattered streets. At home, whilst dusting the odd shelf or throwing something in the microwave for dinner. Occasionally, I would open the oven door and put something in there too hoping that it would return resembling something edible.

I remember Mr P, my Italian teacher here in Italy, walking away after I had given up on my seventh lesson of Italian; his head bowed as if in defeat when in fact I was the defeated one. I had let go, if only momentarily, of the struggle.

When I landed in Italy to step out into a new and unchartered life, I demonstrated quite proficiently the delusion of competence in a foreign language. *I*

thought I can order a coffee in Italian and count to a hundred
– no problem… I was, of course, demonstrating the
first pitfall of learning which is being unconsciously
incompetent (you are a fuckwit, but just don't know
it). I quote Wikipedia regarding The Four Stages
of Competence – Noel Burch 'It suggests that
individuals are unaware of how little they know.' I
couldn't recognise my own language skill deficit until
I reached Stage 2 'conscious incompetence' with Mr
P the Italian teacher and reached the bottom of the
I-am-never-going-to-be-able-to-do-this-well-of-despair. I felt
the same way about trying to do hospital corners
and nearly gave up my nurse training in the first
two weeks of Introductory Block. But I persevered
and succeeded. Maybe I should treat the many
corners of the Italian language in the same way, with
perseverance and not give up.

I confessed to Dee something that I do out
of desperation when I am trying to converse in
Italian during that visit to Umbria. We chatted on
her balcony on an unseasonably warm November
evening and under a glorious blanket of stars and
sipped glasses of chilled prosecco. And I said to her
that I say, 'Sì, sì,' when I have lost the gist of the
conversation in Italian, and she admitted that she does
the same. It kind of a default position of language-
learning-newbies.

'They might be asking,' she said, 'am I disturbing
you?'

And I say, 'Sì, sì.' This obviously leads to an
embarrassment on both sides. With the sì-sìying we
can agree or disagree to anything, out of fear, panic,

and lack of fluency.

At the beginning of my Italian language journey
mixing up my personal pronouns was a weakness
of mine and still is. To this day, I continue to
introduce my daughter's partner as *Il tuo compagno*,
your partner rather than *il suo compagno*, her partner.
In my quivering fear, I would sometimes just repeat
what was being said, which I suppose was better than
saying nothing at all.

I have peppered my fridge with Post-it notes
covered in verb conjugations, imperatives, nouns,
useful sentences; particles and antonyms – what are
they? The words that glue each sentence together, up,
down, around and over. These come in handy when
you are speaking a different language, and you want
to explain, that you don't know whether you are on
your arse or on your elbow. This idiom in the English
language explains beautifully how I feel about trying
to speak Italian.

The Italian language is also full of Italian idioms
that make little sense. Having said this I have used,
'aqua in bocca,' which means, 'Mum's the word'. If you
have water in your mouth you can't spill the beans as
it were.

Here's an example of me using *acqua in bocca*, when
I was being interrogated one day by my immediate
neighbour. She speaks no English and takes great
delight in correcting my Italian:

'When are you going to finish your book?'

'Soon, by the end of the year.'

'How long is it going to be?'

Mumble from me, 'I don't know I have finished it yet.'

'Are you going to publish it in Italian? I would like to read it.'

'No, I am not. Well, perhaps.'

'Do you have English and Italian friends?'

'Yes, I do have Italian friends.'

'How many and where do they live?'

Fuck me, did she think that I was lying? I tell her, whilst pointing with my finger in several directions, as if to indicate my far-flung friends.

'Do you like it here? How much rent do you pay?'

And there was the final bullet, the ultimate nosey question and to stop the interrogation (her husband was now pulling apologetic faces over her shoulder).

I said, 'Acqua in bocca.' And gestured an imaginary zip closing my mouth and hoped, that she would soon close hers and terminate her Italian phishing expedition.

She really did want to know the ins and outs of a duck's arse!

When Italians have had too much to drink, they are, *'Ubriaco come una scimmia'*, 'Drunk as a monkey.' Which is as weird as saying, 'Pissed as a fart' in English and makes me wonder how a fart ever gets pissed and how that idiom ever became part of the English language.

My favourite idiom has to be, *'Oca giuliva'* merry goose, which means that someone is not the sharpest tool in the box.

The Italians are also fond of using the words *cavolo*, which means cabbage to be used for damn and *cazzo*, meaning fuck – put it all together *'Non me ne frega un cavolo, cazzo.'* I don't give a damn, fuck'. This could come in handy…

In England, we have some funny and strange street and place names, such as Back Passage, which apparently is a street in London or Boggy Bottom, which is a village in Abbots Langley. There are also some strange place names in Italy. *Troia*, which means Slut is a town in Foggia, Puglia. There is also a *Belsedere*, a Cute or Nice Bum, a village just outside of Sienna and *Orgia*, Orgy which is just down the road from the cute bum, which indicates a little bit of orgiastic naughtiness maybe and I am glad that there isn't a village called *Hugeschlong*…

One afternoon I made one my favourite faux-pas around the difficult question of what do you say around five o'clock in the afternoon? What is the correct greeting? I was walking with Basil and met a local on my daily walk around the harbour, and as he was approaching me I had a huge struggle in my head about what time of day it was and should I say, *buongiorno* or *buonasera*? The man and I eventually crossed paths on a corner, and he said, *'Buonasera.'* I had not yet completed my internal thought process about what the correct response would be, and I said, *'Bonjela.'* Which was verbal-hybrid of buongiorno and bounasera – Bonjela is, of course, a trade name for a mouth ulcer treatment and is not a greeting.

The Writer said that I should sleep with the lingo and not having had any Italian offers, sleeping with the lingo to improve my Italian language skills seemed a very remote possibility. Dee said the same, 'Find an Italian boyfriend.' Lordy, there must be a better way.

As I have said before Anna has become a friend and so we no longer conjugate the verbs together, and so the internet has been my main source of learning – 59% fluency it tells me. But I still feel as though I am at Base Camp Italia, with a long way to go to reach the summit height of fluency. I always say that when I am with Italians. *'Sono sola sempre. Non parlo italiano ogni giorno dunque, non parlo italiano va bene ancora.'* I am always alone every day, and therefore I do not speak Italian well yet.

I consider myself articulate in my own language and not being able to flex my articulateness in another language is frustrating and at times embarrassing. Language is a bridge to emotions, and I can only express the very basics in Italian. To complicate matters, the Italians are bonded with each other, by their own local dialect which is their first language and is spoken in the home in preference Italian. Even today, these local dialects thrive.

Dialects can vary from town to town. Older generations may only be fluent in dialect and not in Italian. Although the main dialects and their derivatives in Puglia are Barese, Salentino and Grecia-Salentina – which would include more Greek words. In other parts of the country, the Italian dialects would have their roots in French, German, Croatian, Slovenian languages. Faertar, is a rare French/Franco-Provencal dialect that is spoken in two villages in Foggia, Puglia.

The Carovignese dialect has adopted English

words due to the close proximity of an American military base thirty-odd years ago. The words, *gum, drink,* and *dick* have assimilated into the local dialect.

According to *italicissima.com* due to mass emigration to the USA, especially by the Southern Italians – who may not have been exposed to standard Italian. The strange hybrid of *Italiese*, an odd mixture of Italian and English evolved. *Pinabarra*, peanut butter; *cipe*, cheap and I kid you not, *tencsalotto*, thanks a lot. The best has to be *aiscrima*, ice cream. Which makes me want to say, or sing, 'Aiscrima, you scream, everybody scream.' Which is what we used to say as kids in Middlesex and that was the closest we ever got to speaking Italian.

As Tony Soprano would say, *'Fuhgeddaboutit!'*

The Italian language was developed from the Tuscan dialect and was written down by Dante in *Divina Commedia*, the Divine Comedy, which has over 14,000 lines of poetry and details a soul journey in the realms of Hell, Purgatory, and Paradise. Latin was the language of the upper classes, and the Italian language developed from the Tuscan vernacular, but there was a need for a more common and accessible language. To this day, the Divine Comedy is read and quoted from by proud Italians. Much like Chaucer, who wrote in the English language, perhaps English would have died out if it were not widely spoken and read in the Middle Ages, as English at the time was thought to be the peasants' language. I also ponder on the what ifs. If the Spanish Armada hadn't sunk, we would all probably be speaking Spanish. If the French

had won the Battle of Waterloo (even though French
was spoken in Parliament until the mid-1200s because
of the Norman conquest), we would be speaking
French. And if Hitler had won World War II then we
would probably all be speaking a Germanic language.
English has evolved as the world language, and Italian
is a language that everyone fantasises about speaking.

The English Channel has kept us separate from
Europe and disconnected us from speaking a second
language (or even seeing it as a necessity), and the
Americans have probably led to the world domination
of the English language, the common language.
Air traffic controllers speak aviation English, as the
commonly shared international language, to ensure
that planes don't crash into each other. No one
expects the guys in the tower to speak the world's
6,500 languages.

The Italian language had to evolve and become
more widely spoken because the Italians were finding
it difficult to trade with each other due to the lack
of a common language. Many dialects, I am told, are
unintelligible between each other. A few miles up the
road and the dialect is like a different language.

I once worked with an Italian nurse and after
recently being on holiday in Venice she said, 'I
couldn't understand what the *fook* they were saying'
because they spoke to her in Venetian dialect, instead
of standard Italian. Slight changes in intonation can
leave Italians perplexed if the accent is unfamiliar. I
find some solace in this.

As I have said before, Italy is a relatively newly
unified country, since 1861 and at that time, the

Italian writer and politician Massimo d'Azeglio said, *'Fatta l'Italia, facciamo gli Italiani,'* 'We have made Italy, let's make the Italians.' In other words, *Let's all speak the same language.*

In 1868 'Italian Standard' language was forced on the Italian people and the dialects – although still in existence today – were relegated to second languages. Dialects have morphically blended with standard Italian to become regional dialects.

If the Italian language was meant to glue together a nation, then the prevalent use of dialects is probably divisive. A secret and private language that excludes others. Imagine if each county in England spoke a unique language – because these Italian dialects are very much like separate languages with their own nouns and verbs – it would be very schismatic, alienating us from one another; creating an, 'us and them culture' and this is how it is in Italy. Anyone who is from out of town and doesn't speak the local dialect is a stranger or a foreigner.

Italian dialects, although widely spoken and are the common language of most Italian families, are not written down but passed down from generation to generation verbally. With two languages on the go, there is little motivation to learn other languages and particularly in southern Italy; where English is not widely understood or spoken.

John Hooper who recently published the book, *The Italians* wrote:

'By the 1980s less than 30 percent of the population spoke only, or predominantly, the national language. Since then the

figure has risen steadily, largely because of television. A study published recently by Istat in 2007 found that it had reached 47 percent.'

Therefore, with an apparent lack of 100 per cent of Italians actually speaking standard Italian, it is then, of little wonder that learning English is not seen as a necessity. I attempted to rectify this situation – of learning the English language – by giving English lessons to two very motivated students and realised that I had to reacquaint myself with English grammar in order to be able to teach the English language properly. One delightful Italian teenager who was going to go to school in Dublin amazed me at her eagerness to learn and her quick grasp of the English language.

One morning I was positioning a book around various parts of my body, and I would say, 'Where is the book?' And it would be under my arm for instance.

She answered all the questions correctly until I sat on the book and said, 'Where is the book?' Thinking that she would say, you are sitting on it, and she replied.

'It's under your arse.' Which was not incorrect, but not quite the answer that I was looking for at the time.

Italy is ranked twenty-seventh out of sixty-three countries in proficiency in speaking English – according to *www.local.it* – and is also twentieth out of twenty-four in the European ranking. The Danes, the Dutch and the Swedish are the best. Probably because no one speaks Danish, Dutch or Swedish outside of their own countries. I had noticed whilst watching the Swedish version of *The Girl with the Dragon Tattoo* that in Swedish *'Far jag komma in'* sounds just like, 'May I come in.' Or maybe it was just my imagination.

My Italian is continually corrected by the Italians and rightly so. Although I would like to perfect this sentence as a way of a rebuttal. *'Faccio degli errori quando parlo italiano perche parlo due lingue. Fai tu?'* – I make errors when I speak Italian because I speak two languages. Do you? Of course, this would be rude, but I would like to say it. As it is their expectation that I should be fluent.

Lina, my neighbour, will always say to other neighbours, 'Speak slowly so that she will understand.' And then she will translate whatever I say because she is used to my accent. No matter how hard I try, the English tones always slip through. I always think that I speak Italian as though I have pebbles in my mouth, and I know when I am not being understood, when the person that I am talking to knits their brow in puzzlement, smiles and then gives up. Patience is not an Italian virtue.

When I looked back at my notes I read, *'Spent the day speaking Italian'* – and I thought – *fuck how the hell did I manage that?* Most days it is poorly constructed grammar and spluttered words. Although it may not have been such a successful day as I offered Mimo a *tavolino* – a little table to dry his hands on after working in the garden rather than a *tovagliolo* – a serviette!

I am not alone in these Italian language mishaps.
Here are a couple of amusing stories from a friend
who has lived in Italy in various cities for many years:

*'My husband, went shopping for some figs in Rome, the small
fruit shop was run by a big busted woman, like a fisher-woman.
There were lots of old dears in the shop. I told my husband
to get me, un chilo di fichi (pronounced 'fiki'), he asked for a
kilo of 'fica' which means fanny, and the Roman shopkeeper
answered gesturing with her fingers, ' La fica qui non si vende'
– 'sorry mate don't sell fannies here!' He never wanted to go
shopping again.*

*When I was a kid my aunt sent me to get a salami roll – I
didn't speak much Italian then – I asked for 'un pannolino di
salami" a salami nappy!'*

It has been my experience that if I am attempting
to have a conversation with an Italian, they start
off slowly and then speed up maniacally – once
they think I have the gist of the conversation – like
a Formula 1 car off of the starting grid. *'Capito?'*
'Understand?' 'No actually, I would like to say you left
me on the starting grid, and I am still trying to put my
helmet on, and I've probably put it on back to front.'
The conversation has roared away from me with the
burning and smoking of rubber tyres, disappearing
into the distance.

I can give you an example of this. The other day,
I went to my local *frutta e verdura*, fruit and veg stall in
Carovigno. I began by asking for two avocados – no
problem there – and some apricots. So far, so good
until I came to the strawberries, *fragole*. And somehow

managed to ask for a kilo of the buggers, and I didn't have the lingo to say it was too many – to be quite honest, I was also bit embarrassed – and I just looked at them heaving on the scales and wondered how I was going to get through them in the coming week. Strawberries at every meal probably. *'Che paese?'* 'What country?' the grocer enquired without including, 'where', or, 'do you come from', for that matter, (I seek some satisfaction in the fact that sometimes the Italians don't even speak their own language correctly and miss out the odd verb here and there). I told him that I was English, and he enquired whereabouts. I wanted to say near London and then changed my mind and wanted to say near Windsor. All he heard from my stumbling words was *Regina*, Queen (this was before I had the chance to say near where the Queen lives), he sped along in Italian and said, *'Piacere, Regina,'* 'Pleased to meet you, Regina.' Subsequently, I am now known as, Regina. Dear God and God Save the Queen!

I remember a young guy I used to work with saying how he thought that Italian was quite easy. He really couldn't speak Italian; I might add – and that a lot of the words sound familiar. Yes, *preservativo* can mean jam, but more commonly it means a latex contraceptive, a condom. I think he was also a bit deluded a *delusione*, in Italian means a disappointment. *Eventualmente*, means possibly not eventually. There are dozens of 'false friends' or words that seem to mean the same but don't and I think that due to his delusion he could have quite possibly ended up with condoms on his toast instead of jam.

I am actually giggling to myself as I write this as I have found an article on Italian proverbs. At a wedding, if it is raining, it can be a common thing to say *'Sposa bagnata, sposa fortunata,'* wet bride, lucky bride. The English equivalent would be, 'Rain on your wedding day is lucky.' But if Giuseppe went to an English wedding on a rainy day and used the direct translation from Italian to English – thinking that he was paying the happy couple a compliment – 'You know what they say, wet bride lucky bride.' Then there could be an ensuing fight and the throwing of wedding cake and Giuseppe ending up with a black eye after a misinterpreted compliment.

My greatest non-achievement in the Italian language (a now infamous faux-pas), was the day that Mimo was trying on some clothes in Italian designer shop – Ralph Lauren and the like. He put on a smart shirt and jacket for a forthcoming wedding, and I commented. *'Come Michele Corleone.'* – 'like' Michael Corleone, to imply, 'You look like Michael Corleone – smart and Italian. It was intended as a compliment, but backfired because of my accent, and I failed to roll the 'r', so it sounded like *'Come coglione.'* Like a testicle – I think – a pink hairy ball. I couldn't have been further away from a compliment.

Lili became excited and a bit agitated and said Madonna – more than a few times whilst shaking her hands as if to dispel something wicked.

'What did you just say? You said that Mimo looked like the end of a man's penis.'

I was obviously blushing profusely in

embarrassment and had a look of horror on my face, at this point.

Initially, I thought she meant 'bell end', but she meant ball it was just her description that was lacking. I hung my head in shame… and it wouldn't be the last.

This story was regurgitated endlessly to my continuous embarrassment throughout the summer at every supper table.

I have read that being bilingual is beneficial for your brain; it may even stave off Alzheimer's disease. In an article from Mercola.com, it states,

Bilingual brains have more grey matter, which includes neurons that function in cognition and high-order cognitive processes.' Other articles on language learning assure me that it is never too late to learn a new language – let's hope not.

Fluency is when you can speak and understand a language effortlessly. Occasionally, I have thrown out the odd sentence here and there from a deep unconscious and hidden place within myself, but this is a rarity. Apparently, if you can dream in your second language, you have cracked it as well. I dream, about dreaming in a second language.

Anna wrote to me recently from England and said, *'I wish I was there and going over it with you! It is grandioso! Keep writing and keep speaking the romantic, musical and wonderful Italian language, regardless of mistakes… do not worry, you will win, you will conquer the Italian language and the Italians!'*

I wish I could share her confidence and

enthusiasm.

In my mind, it feels like cerebral gymnastics trying to speak Italian; it's difficult, and it doesn't flow. My perception of getting the words from the brain to the tongue feels like milliseconds, but in reality, I am doing cerebral Tai Chi, and it all happens in slow motion, and my tongue swells in my mouth like a giant sponge and something difficult to comprehend and untranslatable flops out.

I seek comfort in the fact that the Italians who can speak English often confuse chicken and kitchen; and hungry and angry. I imagine a possible mixed up sentence could be, 'I am going in the chicken because I am feeling angry.' Poor chicken.

Fluency and articulacy in a foreign language are hard to measure, but if I were to measure mine, I would say that it is ten inches short of a foot.

Chapter 20

ๆๅ

A Tale of Dogs and Cats

I have come to the conclusion that I couldn't write a book about my personal journeying and experiences in Italy without writing a bit more about Basil; who is the only man in my life and whom I love unconditionally despite the constant drooling, baggy balls and farts that are so strong that they can burn off nasal hair. Only this morning, as I was squatting down on the jetty at the harbour in order to take a picture of the sunrise when I noticed that Basil was wiggling on the lead suspiciously beside me. There was a pungent smell of fish, and I knew that I didn't have a urinary tract infection and turned round to see Basil wolfing down his breakfast consisting of a stolen raw fish as its tail quickly disappeared into his mouth, and I hoped that he wouldn't vomit up his sushi meal later.

He sleeps a lot, snores, and farts with impunity. But I have to say that I wouldn't have been able to do any of this without him. I am constantly reassured by his presence and sleep soundly knowing that he would bark at any potential intruder, even though his bark is definitely worse than his bite, and would probably forget about my safety and guarding his house, if he was offered a biscuit, followed by a tummy rub.

Considering that Basil can take himself on a 9 km walk and spent the night with complete strangers, he actually doesn't like being left alone. I have to put his bed under the garden table if he stays outside when I am out – obviously, a plastic table will protect him from unknown monsters – and he is even more anxious if I leave him in the house, and he moves his bed into the bathroom; because obviously, this is the safest place and monsters don't use the bathroom. In his defence, shortly after we moved to Italy there was a spate of terrific thunderstorms. One particular storm lasted for about eight hours, and Basil spent the whole time trying to sit on my lap which I wasn't too enamoured with because of the unfortunate teabag placement. Since then he shakes and dribbles when I leave him alone and often tries to bury himself in the garden. Freud would have had a field day.

Basil can be sensitive and after one particular friend said that Basil smelt, this was the following conversation:

Me: 'Why the long face?'

B: 'Very funny, my face always looks like this.'

Me: 'Okay, what's up?'

B: 'Well you know that bloke that came over with coffee today, who calls me Dawg…'

Me: 'Yes.'

B: 'He kept smelling his hands and said that I smelt… when we were alone he kept smelling his hands.'

Me: 'So, you lick your willy and your balls every

five minutes. But I don't say anything…'

B: 'Good point. But do I smell?'

Me: 'Well you smell like a dog to me. But after 10,000 years of dog domestication, us humans, kind of flare our nostrils at the 'dog smell'.'

B: 'What do I smell of?'

Me: 'I guess you just smell different to dogs of other nationalities. Italian dogs smell of garlic, tomatoes and a hint of oregano. American dogs smell of baseball catcher's mitts and cookies, and you smell of damp tweed and mothballs.'

B: 'I have never worn tweed and do moths have balls, really?'

Me: 'It's a stereotype, Basil, and no moths don't have balls…'

Ten minutes later after a bath and several coat shakes.

B: 'What do I smell of now?'

Me: 'A gay man who has had bath in dog disinfectant and then covered himself in ten-year-old aftershave…'

Hangdog expression.

Me: 'Why the long face?'

B: 'Bloody hell, don't start that again… can I roll in horse shit?'

Me: 'No!'

Basil has had his quota of health problems. He slipped a disc whilst jumping out of the back of the Aygo – probably because the boot is the size of an envelope – and now travels on the back seat breathing his beautifully scented breath over my shoulder.

Everyone knows that bassets really shouldn't climb
or jump because of their long backs, however, back
in England I used to have a stairgate to prevent him
from climbing the stairs. Now, bassets are reported
not to be very bright. I personally think that they hide
their intelligence under a cloak of stubbornness and
unbiddableness (Basil was five years old before he
would come back after being let off the lead and he
would also run after joggers and cyclists, he can run
surprisingly fast despite his little legs). To demonstrate
his carefully disguised intelligence, Basil would nudge
the stairgate open with his nose and then run upstairs,
terrorise the cats, eat the cat poo in the litter tray and
then mark his territory by pissing up the valance on
my bed. Delightful. Bean bags and boxes placed on
the stairs wouldn't stop him, and family members
would curse and fall over the obstacles, whilst Basil
would continue his daily ritual of galloping up the
stairs undeterred to mark his territory and create
more valance graffiti.

When he was a puppy he ate about £800 pounds
worth of glasses, stole money from my daughter's
purse and hid it under his bed (I think he wanted
to go travelling), stole various cakes from kitchen
worktops (a vertical basset is much taller than a
horizontal one), and once dragged a Christmas turkey
across the kitchen floor. We still ate it. And he has
also buried various items in the garden including
biscuits, sweets, and an old shoe.

On our first night in Italy, my daughter woke me up
in an anxious state after listening to a dog bark for

what seemed like hours. Basil must have been the culprit as we thought he was residing in the local hotel. It wasn't Basil he was in another town having a B&B experience with Dave Greenfield. It was Basil's night time howling that nearly got us evicted from my sister's house before coming here. Bassets can make a lot of noise when they want to.

Having said all this, I do love him dearly, and here in Italy I have no stairs, and there is no new territory to conquer and mark, so he doesn't piss in the house here. Maybe he was just telling me that I should get rid of the valance, as they haven't been in fashion since the 1990s.

As a child in my amalgamated family we had a chocolate poodle called Coco and a Chihuahua called Pepe. Coco always seemed hungry and once ate a bin full of discarded corn on the cobs – a treat for us in those days – and spent the next two days splayed out on the lawn like a starfish and getting up intermittently to dispel them from his body. Pepe was a vicious little thug who would run out when the postman came and hang off of trouser legs, and the postman would try and shake him off and then run down the path scattering the letters. Pepe was also a bit hypersexual and would get enormous erections – I swear that they were bigger than the actual dog – and I would shout to my mum, 'Pepe has got his willy out again.' And Mum would run it under a cold tap until it disappeared and Pepe would always have a surprised look on his face.

My eldest sister once took him to take part in a catwalk fashion show at her college in Chiswick, where she was studying fashion and design. She dyed him pink, or was it purple? He trotted smartly down the catwalk, looking all pretty in pink, and then in a retaliatory gesture, he pissed up the fake flowers on the runway.

My sister Stella and I would spend most weekends at my dad's at the Georgian house that he was renovating in order to turn it into Fawlty Towers (no joke as a guest once put a sign up saying, 'Fawlty Towers' to cover up the real sign of the hotel, probably because my dad was a bit eccentric). And by eccentric I mean he would arrive home with a goat in the back of his estate car and have chickens on the front seat. I never even realised that he had a shotgun. But as legend has it, when a teenage girl came for an interview as a receptionist he was wearing a white coat spattered with blood and laid a freshly shot goose over the kitchen cabinet and said, 'Take that home to your mother.' The soon-would-be-receptionist was so impressed that she took the job.

The house had gardens of about three acres and the biggest and lushest lawn that I have ever seen. It was like a big spongey-carpet. We had 70ft long rhododendron bushes and a beautiful collection of azaleas. Chickens ran around freely, and goats and geese occupied the apple orchard. Most of all, it was a great place to have dogs, and my dad loved greyhounds. And before the stables were converted into hotel bedrooms he bred a litter of greyhounds and kept them there. My sister and I would give the pups extra milk from bottles and watch them nurse, snuffle and snuggle and then fall asleep. There were six pups in all, and they quickly grew into gangly and bounding adults. We would call their names from the garden – once they were allowed outside – and loose legged adolescent canines would run towards us at 30mph and knock us down like ninepins and then lick our faces and proceed to run around in circles, great training for the racetrack. Once they were old enough they were sold or sent off to dog training boarding school.

My sister and I spent many a windy and cold afternoon at a dog track in Loudwater, Buckinghamshire whilst my dad raced his dogs. We would loyally and raucously shout for Pinto, Beauty or Quarry Mount Joy and jump up and down if they won. The car rides home were a bit of an experience. We would sit in the back of Dad's battered estate car and be dribbled on by at least three greyhounds. With all the dribbling and drooling and being knocked over in the mud and also probably not washing at weekends, I must have really smelt as a kid.

Dogs have always been part of my life.

Before I had Basil, I had a golden retriever called Tessa who swam like a fish, was as biddable as a butler and always came back when she was off of the lead. She was a wonderful family pet whose nose was put out of joint when Basil arrived. She ignored him for two weeks and then decided that he was probably going to stay and tolerated him up to a point. Basil was inseparable from Tessa and would howl if she went to the vets without him. I once had to ask the

mobile dog groomer to take Basil into the van whilst
Tessa had a wash and brush up, and he spent the
whole time dangling his ears in the water and paddling
through puddles of water. When Tessa died at the
ripe old age of sixteen Basil howled for two weeks,
I even let him in my bedroom for a bit of comfort
– and to avoid complaints from the neighbours – as
long as he kept away from the valance.

Since then Basil has been the only dog. He is
pretty undemanding but wilful and stubborn at times.
Sometimes I have to physically drag him off the
beach because he doesn't want to leave – wanting
more sunbathing and paddling time probably – and
he will only come when I promise him a biscuit.
There was also a day when he dropped a few logs
on the beach and horrified (the beach was full at the
time) at his sudden evacuation; I searched for a poo
bag in my beach bag, and there was none. An Italian
woman made a sign of a 'T' at me which I can only
assume meant, *terribile*, terrible or it could have been
T for turd, and I anxiously tore some pages out of my
journal that I had just been writing in and scooped
up the offending logs and then wrapped them in a
beach towel. I really didn't want little children making
sandcastles with poo turrets.

One night here in Italy Basil became ill and had
difficulty in breathing. It was a worrying episode and
with Lili's help, I took him to see a vet in Bari for a
health check and a heart scan. By the time we arrived
at the vets (a couple of days after his breathless
episode), Basil was in fine fettle and let the vet

examine him and then jumped three foot off of the examination table to demonstrate his strength and stamina. He had a thorough examination and was given a clean bill of health.

This is how it went:

A case history.

Seven and a half year male canine, approx. fifty-four years in human terms. Mainly sedentary lifestyle. Occasionally lies on the bed even though he is not supposed to. Walks six miles a day.

History: two hours of paradoxical breathing, peripherally shut down. No blood pressure recorded due to lack of a sphyg (blood pressure monitoring equipment). Owner unable to count respirations due to a lack of a second hand on her watch. Although the owner still had a certified Advanced Life Support provider course in date, she felt out of her depth and incompetent.

On examination: Hangdog look due to breed. Pink lolling tongue and excessive salivation. 'Nurse, please pass me a tissue.' Knows only a few Italian words and wags tail to, 'Who's a good boy then.' Heart sounds normal.

Echocardiogram: Mildy hypertrophic left ventricle. No motion wall abnormality. Valves normal.

Lost patient briefly between echo and chest x-ray due to exploration of available exits. Dogs tend to do this when they are in a state of panic.

Blood gases: essentially normal with carbon dioxide levels down due to hyperventilation and possible panic attack. No brown paper bag available.

'Nurse, can I have another tissue.'

Chest X-ray and ECG normal with a bit of T wave inversion, which is usually associated with canines and in sinus rhythm (normal rhythm). Patient very obliging during ECG as he was having his tummy tickled at the time. Heart rate fluctuating depending on the state of panic, or the rapidity of tummy tickling.

Diagnosis: Fit as a butcher's dog. Differential diagnosis may have a floppy soft palate causing previous airway obstruction. Possible tummy tickling fetish.

Treatment: A pat on the head, a dog biscuit, and a long walk. Hypertrophic (thickened) left ventricle (pumping chamber of the heart), due to a very fit and active dog; when he is not asleep.

Summary: All investigations completed within minutes. A southern Italian veterinary service being more superior and efficient to the current NHS service for humankind in the UK.

I have a litre plastic jug full of cat food with the intention of feeding the feral cats. Although one or two of them are really friendly, especially a little mackerel tabby which I have named Tigger – unimaginative I know – and a male tabby with an attractive, angular head who is so handsome I have named him Terence, after Terence Stamp. Tigger's kittens often frolic and play in the afternoon sun and jump through holes in the brick walls and chase after leaves. They are completely untouchable little-cute-feral-fancies.

So I have bought a huge elephant ball size bag of cat food and will probably become the mad cat lady of Via Claudia. I tickle Tigger's ears when she lets me and stroke Terence's back, which he arches with contentment. Tigger is looking like she has another belly full of kittens and wonder if Terence is the culprit. None of the cats here are neutered or spayed.

It's a beautiful late November evening with streaks of pink across the sky at dusk. I fill up two bowls that have been left by an Italian cat lover. These are quite often full of leftover rice and pasta which the cats seem to eat as it saves time catching birds, lizards or anything else that might be edible.

I walk up to a piece of wasteland where no one seems to want to build a house and where a man plants tomatoes every year and can be seen watering the thirsty plants during the long and very hot summer months. One day he stood by his wall berating me for feeding the cats that then stayed around and pissed on his tomato plants. He told me that I shouldn't feed them because as long as I fed them then they would stay around. I have actually seen the Italian cat lover who comes daily with pasta and rice for the cats being verbally abused by the locals. Undeterred she still visits daily, and the cats don't go hungry, and yes, they stick around.

Two dogs are approaching. One is walking along the wall as though he has been trained to do so and I realise that it is Scruffy – now be patient with me it's difficult to name all of these animals – and walking confidently alongside him but on the pavement is a labrador cross. A handsome, tall cream dog which has some Italian herding dog in him.

Scruffy lands on the pavement and sits at my feet. An adorable long haired terrier with matted fur and toenails that are so long they look like spurs. I stroke his head and he flashes his little white teeth in a smile. The unnamed dog I shall call, Bob. So, Bob and Scruffy get a handful of cat food pebbles. They seem hungry.

As I have mentioned before, we have an abandoned dog problem here in Santa Sabina.

And not all of them are friendly. One large cream-coloured Italian herding dog that I named Paul has charged me at least three times whilst I have been out walking Basil. Baring his teeth, barking in threat and his hackles standing up on his neck and shoulders as though they have been electrified. He seems to have taken to leading a group of stray dogs and when he charges the others follow. I turn my body into a star shape, wave my arms and a big stick (this has replaced the tartan umbrella as a weapon of choice) and shout in a deep tone. *'Vai,'* go away. Obviously, not all of these dogs are pettable and in a pack they can be quite dangerous, and I am not naïve enough to think that they wouldn't attack me with even the slight provocation. Basil is still unable to read any signs of aggression and will wag his tail as though he could go off for a merry run with them.

I return home and think about Scruffy and wonder who abandoned this friendly little dog. He has been around for about two years and used to keep guard on the beach when Betty had her pups. He would bark an alert if anyone passed too near and Betty would appear snarling and growling, but she was just protecting her pups, and Scruffy was happy to be on sentry duty for her.

I am sorely tempted to kidnap scruffy, clip his claws and give him a bath. I wonder if he would let me.

Tigger comes when I call her now and lets me pet her of a fashion. She swats me with her paw if I am overdoing it. I think her tabby kitten may have died, and I didn't see it this morning. I noticed that it had a wet tail the other day. Its head was as small as a bird's, and it was weak and wobbly on its feet.

The other day I picked up an injured cat from the road and took it into the woods thinking that it would quickly succumb to its injuries. I looked down at the injured cat and couldn't bear to think of it dying alone, so I wrapped it in an old pillow case and took her home. She was obviously in pain and seemed to be paralysed from the waist down. She died two hours later lying in the warm sun and with me gently stroking her head. I buried her in the fields opposite where I live in the same pillow case that I had carried her from the woods in. Two of the feral cats followed me into the field and watched me bury her and then followed me back home. I can't really explain why they followed me and stayed for the cat burial, maybe it was just instinctual. I found it comforting.

Staying with the cat theme. Here are a few honourable mentions.

Olive and Pasta. Two tiny tabby kittens that were

washed out of a neighbour's garden with a garden
hose (he obviously was not a cat lover). I found
them shivering underneath a car and soaked to the
skin. One of them had a bloody nose from the
water pressure. They couldn't have been more than
four or five weeks old. I took them home and dried
them off with a towel and placed them in a shoe box
lined with cotton wool to keep them warm. I bought
two syringes from the local supermarket and fed
them baby milk for twenty-four hours. I did some
research on the internet, and it said that you should
burp kittens like babies if you are artificially feeding
them. I thought that this could possibly be true, and I
extended their chins after a syringe full of baby milk,
and sure enough they burped! I knew that I probably
couldn't keep them and hoped that their mum would
come to find them. They hissed at me in unison
from inside the shoe box. I put the shoe box in the
garden the following afternoon and sat and waited.
I could hear their mother calling them and the two
young kittens tottered unsteadily to the garden wall
and disappeared behind the water tank. The mother
scooped them up one by one, and that was the last
that I saw of them.

Visitors to my garden have included Boy and Ted
who were male tabbies and would come to sleep on
the swing seat and wait around for a handful of cat
food and have since disappeared.

And lastly, Kitty who is my skinny-cat-love and has
been a daily and constant visitor. Whilst other cats
have died or have just moved territory; Kitty has been

a regular for over three years. Initially, I couldn't touch her and now she loves a stroke and a belly tickle and will even rub noses with Basil. She is what the Italians called *furbo*, crafty and she is crafty enough to steal fish out of Lili's pond and Lili has threatened to kill her on several occasions. And I guess that's why she has survived because she is *furbo*.

It would be easy for me to get over involved with the dogs and cats in the area, but just like me, they are just visiting. And eventually, I will move on too.

But what if one of them decides that it not just visiting and wants to move in.

This year I have lost both my English cats Polly and Lizzy. Polly being a part British blue and Lizzy a Persian, they both reached the great of seventeen. Lizzy fell out of a tree when she was three years old and banged her head (she always had unequal pupils) and damaged the radial nerve supply in her right leg and as a consequence ended up with a flaccid foreleg which then contracted up into being a little chicken-wing-leg. The vet told us to take her home because she would probably die over the next few days, but heroically she lived for another fourteen years, hardly impeded by only have three legs in use; although she never climbed a tree again.

Polly was a robust and vocal cat who was a keen hunter when she was young and fit. However, it wasn't just birds and mice that she would bring home. Quite often she would emerge through the catflap in the kitchen door with someone's fillet steak or chicken leg that they had left on the kitchen top for their supper. Or regurgitate a partially eaten Koi Karp on the front door mat. I often wondered if she would be caught in the act of stealing other people's food or shot by an annoyed Koi Karp owner. She must have been quick as well as sneaky as she survived the kitchen and pond robbing episodes.

The other day, I discovered that I am not the only cat lady that occasional feeds the local ferals (notice that I left out the 'mad' part). There is an Italian woman (a different one who usually provides the pasta and rice, perhaps she has been driven away by the non-cat lovers). She wears a jacket with a pastel flower pattern that Mary Berry would be proud of and has two baskets on her bike; one for water and one for a large plastic box of leftover pasta and some cat biscuits. The cats all swarm towards her like bees and she chats away to them in Italian and fills plastic plates for them to feed. For the moment they are all fat and happy and seem to breeding like rabbits.

I think I will leave her to it as she seems to be doing a sterling job.

Chapter 21

৩৩

Writing and Not Writing

This book is as much about living in Italy and writing, as it is about my own restoration and healing. Getting rid of the burnout and stressed self that yearned to lead a more fulfilling and meaningful life. My journey back to me and learning just simply how to be. It is also about my struggle between wanting intimacy – yes at times I still want this – whilst enjoying the solitude, although to be honest there isn't enough room in my bed for intimacy as I sleep with two vertical pillows in the bed, and there isn't any room for anyone else. In any case, why would I spoil the enjoyment of my little piece of heaven experience with the presence and possible contamination of my personal space? They say that there is a lid for every pot and instead of looking for someone else's lid for my pots, I now look for my own lids. I am developing my own personal philosophy: 'You must always love yourself more than you love someone else and in that way you will never be alone.' Not because of a selfish and narcissistic bent on life, but because loving someone else is more of an external experience which has to start with the internal experience of loving yourself first. Once you start to enjoy your own company, then you will never be truly alone. All relationships end in division or death, but the relationship with yourself will be the one that in reality, the long-lasting and the one relationship that you have the most control of.

Although on my three personal quests of writing a book, painting a picture and climbing a mountain, the second quest is yet unrealised. My paints and coloured pencils remain untouched – I have yet to release that part of me. Or maybe my painting block is like having haemorrhoids; you know that they are there, but you just can't see them.

Time has its own elasticity here. It lengthens and contracts, but I am not bound by any rules of time. I choose when to go to bed and when to wake up; when to eat; when to read and when to write. I enjoy the huge gift of the present and embrace it, as it is all that we have this present moment. I wrote to the Writer one day, 'Life is a gift, unwrap it.' I may as well have said, 'Life is a box of chocolates, you never know what you are going to get.' As his caustic reply was, 'For most people life is like an envelope of anthrax.' Different views on this life. A beautiful gift or an envelope of poison.

The late Terry Pratchett once said, *'Inside every old person is a young person wondering what happened?'*

Not wanting to have a 'what happened?' moment, but rather seeking, 'Shit I am glad all of that happened,' moment of reflection. I have come to realise that everyone has a path to take and experiences to make and savour. Write your own story and take the more convoluted and interesting path rather than the straight road from the carrycot to the coffin.

Perhaps part of my restoration and reinvention is my writerly quest. Book writing, for me, is far more difficult than writing poetry. The poetry pops up in my head like a pop-up cookie, and I have to write it down straight away before it disappears into the void. The book writing is a more laborious and uphill struggle; like pulling a selfie-stick away from a narcissist or trying to perform a card trick, whilst having nothing up my sleeve, and I wonder if I am ever going to pull off the trick, tah dah!

Writing can also involve avoidance of actually writing something. Writing is like a muscle, and they say the muscle should be exercised every day. Or the counter argument is, only write when you have something to say. But like most people I sometimes avoid the writerly muscle exercising by doing housework; answering emails or surfing the net for yet another kitten that looks funny in a glass jar. Writing can be lonely and despairing. 'All writers are miserable,' the Writer once said, 'Apart from Anthony Burgess' who, apparently, according to the Writer was quite jolly and fond of a pint, which is surprising as he wrote such a dark and disturbing novel. Perhaps all of his dark stuff went onto the page instead of being internalised into the self.

Stephen King said, *'You must not come lightly to the page.'*

I guess he means that to be a writer you have to be

'serious' about writing, committed to the task and art of writing. And for the past three years, I think that I have been more in the camp of writing *when I have something to say* and the *writing every da*y, has come with the rewrites.

The main thing that I have learnt is, write the bloody thought or sentence down, as memory is about as reliable as the English football team and if you don't write it down then, there will be a lot of running around and very little in the back of the net/ on the page.

I wanted to write from an early age, and I suppose as a child I was introverted and maybe a little 'geeky'. I remember when I was about nine years of age writing two sentences on an old Imperial typewriter and thinking to myself, 'Well that's a start.' It didn't go any further, probably because I was nine and had the attention span of a goldfish and probably was more interested in playing in the garden.

I spent a lot of time on my own mainly because my sister – even though she was only eighteen months older than me – saw me as a nuisance and an unwanted appendage. Someone who was always two steps behind her and perhaps a little whiny. A parental perennial question always being, 'Where's Elaine? Why isn't she with you?' or 'Don't forget to take Elaine with you.'

No wonder she would try to kill me at every opportunity, or that is how it seemed. She would often promise to meet me at the park, and I would find myself standing alone, waiting for a sibling that wouldn't be turning up. Although on days when we were flung together – probably because it was raining – we would read in silence. It was as though the reading of books and the ensuing silence was our arbitrator. And at times when cabin fever set in we would fight in a very physical way usually by trying to pull as much hair out of each other's heads whenever and wherever possible. I am surprised that we weren't both bald by the time we were teenagers. My mum would always threaten to bang our heads together as if to knock some sense into us and stop our perpetual catfighting.

Reading was an escape and a gateway into my imagination, a door in which I could lose myself in someone else's world. At secondary school, I would spend my lunchtimes in the library eating peanut butter sandwiches and reading books from the shelves, which no doubt, to this day, probably still have peanut butter smears on them. My little greasy fingerprint and reading journeys.

The teacher who ran the library asked me to help tidy up the books– as long as I washed my hands first – which I would do with relish, caressing the spines; flicking open the books and smelling the pages and reading first pages and putting them back. He rewarded my diligence and love of books by handing me a book as a present when he left the school for another job – this was a new book and not nicked from the library, *The Faber Book of Twentieth Century Verse* and inscribed on the inside cover he wrote, 'Enjoy now and in the future.' Peter Gordon. I would read the poems over and again, but alas to this day I cannot recite a whole poem, *I sent a letter to my love – in a something, something.*

My parents favourite poem was *The Highwayman*, by Alfred Noyes, and there was once an old tape recording of my birth mother reciting this poem, and I imagine her north London inflection as she delivered it: *The wind was a torrent of darkness among the gusty trees / The moon was a ghostly galleon tossed upon cloudy seas / The road was a river of moonlight over the purple moor / And the highwayman came riding —/ Riding — riding —/ The highwayman came riding, up to the old inn-door.* The tape is long lost, and so is she.

Years later, my dad told us a spurious story about how Dick Turpin came and stayed at his rattly and old Georgian house. And I imagined the Highwayman riding up to our front door. The story was completely untrue, but I believed it for years – *the highwayman never came riding up to our front door.* Mainly because dear old Dick had been executed some seventy years before the house had been built.

When I was eight I wrote a story about the death of Martin Luther King Junior, I can't remember it now, but I do remember my teacher being 'impressed' and sent me to the headmaster for him to congratulate me on my story telling. I spoilt the occasion by picking up a piece of chewing gum from the stairwell – chewing gum was banned in the school – and handed the offending piece of rule breaking chewing gum to the headmaster on entering his office. He, therefore, shook my hand with congratulations on a good writing piece and received a gum-filled handshake.

I read stories with unquenchable thirst and became eager to write my own stories. But I didn't really start writing until after my children were born and as they grew older I would write them stories and poems – usually on scraps of paper – which I have kept and saved. I have since saved them more permanently on a hard drive. One day I might resurrect them for my grandchildren. I would love to be like Judith Kerr, still writing in my nineties and able to nip up a few flights of stairs without getting short of breath. She wrote all of the lovely Mog the Cat stories and illustrated them herself. Judith says, *'I like to go to bed knowing that I have written something. I can always rewrite it tomorrow.'* A good philosophy. There is also a saying, *'First drafts don't have to be perfect, they just have to be written.'* This saying is on a Post-it note on my fridge to remind to write something, anything...

Once getting over the fear of the empty page, a sentence can build up to an outpouring of thoughts. Judith Cameron, who wrote, *'The Artists Way'* advocates writing three A4 pages per day to get the creative flow going and maintaining it whilst getting rid of the inner critic. I am not sure whether writing morning pages are meant to deliver threads of gold – *a writer's alchemy* – and perhaps the threads turning into bars of gold, in order for the hungry writer to put food in his/her mouth. But writing three pages of literally anything, without self-criticising, seems to help in unblocking my writer's S bend and allowing the flush and flow of ideas.

Dee once introduced me to her friend, as a writer and this title I am not at all comfortable with, and I certainly don't feel worthy of the title. Perhaps I am more apt title is would-be-writer, writer-newbie or occasional-jotter. At the moment I feel like the latter, no pressure, just jot and see what happens.

Life is like a corridor with many doors. You can either walk slowly down towards the end of the corridor, without noticing or opening any of the doors and live in a safe and predicted straight line. Or you can pause, stop and take a risk of opening a new door. Perhaps it will involve a career change; a change of place; a change of heart; a change of people that will touch your life. Be open to the change and the experiencing of the new room behind the door and begin living your life more fully and openly.

Here's a poem, tah dah!

Things change
People and circumstances change
Losses and gains
Refocus and reframe
Things are different and not the same
Life happens
Embrace the change

Being here in Italy and doing just this, talking to you. Is like giving myself permission to have my best days. And to make sure that I actually live my life more fully, openly, honestly and creatively before I die.

For fourteen years I lugged a black leather suitcase full of papers and notes – I never tidied my briefcase, and there was literally years of detritus in there – to Buckinghamshire to work as a volunteer counsellor at a local mental health charity and sat down every Thursday morning in Room 1, where I would always ask my clients, 'Where would you like to start?' This all now seems like an age away. I can now spend the whole day counselling myself pretty much and ask myself. 'Where would you like to start and what would you really like to do today?'

I might go to Ostuni and wander around the *centro storico* – meander down the narrow whitewashed alleyways and buy a wooden spoon from Giuseppe, who is only seventy-four, but looks ninety-four because of his daily toil and spends all his time making wooden cooking implements in a dimly lit workshop. He thinks I am German even though I tell him that I am not and he sometimes gives me a handful of almonds or dried figs that he produces from behind a curtain at the back of his workshop. He presents these little goods like a magician producing a rabbit out of a hat, and I am always effusive and appreciative of him producing something from behind the curtain. His kitchen tools are wonderfully crafted, a bit on the expensive side, but I make sure that I take my friends down to see him, in the hope that they might buy something from him and to enable him to carry on his craft and to keep him in a steady supply of almond and figs.

I might also just look at the view from the

terrace in Ostuni and appreciate the view of the
vast expanse of olive trees that give this region its
green and pungent elixir, olive oil. The olive oil that
accompanies and enhances every recipe and can be
found perched on every dinner table here. A man
could be playing a violin and another man a guitar
and the sweet sounds could follow me on my journey
down the narrow alleyways without me having any
particular destination. I allow myself these simple and
small pleasures. The hiss of a coffee machine or the
pop-pop sound of a passing *Ape*, pronounced ar-pay,
(the small three-wheeled trucks), may accompany my
stroll. The *Ape's* are built for one but inevitably have
an old man at the wheel accompanied by his wife,
with pieces of string tying the door handle closed to
stop his wife from falling out; the weekly shopping,
and a large calor gas bottle and two barking dogs in
the back; pop-pop and it is out of sight.

The fresh smell of the sea and its bounty
emanating from the *Pescharia*, fish shop, selling the
morning catch of fish and the smell of garlic and
tomatoes wafting from the restaurants. I could be
tempted to sit down at a restaurant, to have *Peppate
di cozze*, mussels cooked in a pepper and garlic sauce,
washed down with a cold glass of white wine, the
glass dripping with condensation and the sun glinting
off of the stem. The hum of my fellow diners, the
clattering of cutlery on plates and the grease of the
mussels leaving its mark on my lips, wiping my mouth
slowly and languorously with a napkin, knowing that I
can do this, because I chose a different life.

One of the most wonderful sights here in Italy is
the magnificent murmuration of birds at dusk in
the autumn and early winter. Thousands of *tordi* or
storni, thrushes or starlings – depending on who you
are talking to, some say either or – first fly over the
house dropping purple shit on the patio after they
have been munching their way through the olives in
the olive groves; they then fly upwards and form huge
spirals and swoop down creating magical shapes in
the sky. Late one December afternoon whilst walking
at the beach and along the water's edge I saw a huge
murmuration of *tordi* form a serpent-like image and
shape – including the tail – and then in formation,
they dipped down and almost touched the sea and
disappeared into the distance. No wonder in ancient
times people believed in giant serpents and dragons.
An absolutely unforgettable and stunning sight. My
jaw slackened in astonishment.

Sometimes I get up at 4 am just to photograph
the sunrise and wait for the cold colours of the night
to give way to burnished oranges and sears of yellow
as the sun lips the horizon and rises above the sea
in all its majestic glory. I do this because I want to
and because I can. And most of all because it is awe-
inspiring to watch the day break and I am excited
every time I watch the birth of the morning sun,
knowing that the majority of people are still in bed
and have yet to waken.

I am happy to sit in a café and watch the world go
by with a cappuccino in my hand – I have one at any
time of day, no matter what the Italian protocol is –

and not mind if I have a frothy moustache and don't care if anyone notices.

Not Writing and a Wet January and a Three Year Anniversary
ふや

As I write this, it is cold, wet and dark and has started to rain. The winters here seem to be like this, and it is a constant battle, not the let the *muffa*, mould take hold on the walls, and I spray them with bleach regularly. Packets of desiccator are also in every corner. I don't think that any Italian house is built with proper damp course, and this seems to me to be a national problem. So, I battle with the *muffa* on a daily basis – much like I do with the *zanzara* in the summer.

On January 26th I would have lived in Italy for three years. In three years, the swing seat has rusted and shortened its legs daily and will eventually rust into oblivion much like the rusting hulk of the Titanic on the North Atlantic floor.

I am struggling with my rusty writing habit. The three pages have stopped for now as I re-read many pages that seemed to be repetitious and I really can't write, *'I can't seem to write anymore, anymore.'* I blame the author of the *Artist's Way* Julia for this, as she recommends that you, the writer needs to complete three pages – on A4 paper – even if you do repeat nonsense sentences, such as; I can't write anymore. I realise that I need to find a solid and disciplined writing habit.

As PD James once said, *'What do you mean I need to write another book, because the roof on the house needs replacing…'* Obviously, she probably never said that but what she did say was, *'If you keep sitting at the bus stop on a bench and watching the bus with LIFE written on the side of the bus pass you by, then you are not living your life or going anywhere. Keep away from and ignore the distractions at the bus stop.'* In other words, get on with it Mrs Slacker.

Apparently, people like me who want to write, do get distracted at the bus stop. I avoid writing at times, and because of this, my house is spotlessly clean. My dog is at fit as Usain Bolt as I keep dragging him out for walks, even if he doesn't want to go. I have taught myself how to read Tarot and Lenormand cards and can have a go at Palmistry. I can divine my own future by scrying the contents of the bottom of a cappuccino cup that usually says, *'You need to get on with it today you work-shy-procrastinator.'* I have developed an interest in photography and can while away a few hours taking pictures of the clouds, birds flying across the clouds, people pointing at clouds – more distractions at the bus stop.

We do this, us writerly folk, so that we can say – as the writer's deepest fear is rejection – *'Oh it wasn't my best work, because I was distracted at the bus stop rather than getting on the bus.'*

'The mind has to be quiet in order to write.' I read this in an article this morning. Well, mine is quiet most of the time, but when a writing block comes it is difficult to get over it, under it or around it. A folder in my computer, entitled *Random Bits of Writing for the Book*, allows me to be more free flowing – because I tell myself it is random and doesn't really matter – as I try to discard my inner writing critic and flex my writing muscle, otherwise it will wither and die, rather than be exercised and grow as strong as Dwayne Johnson's thigh… dear Lord now I am really distracted.

Because I am not working solidly for something or someone, I have realised that it is all too easy to become preoccupied with the mundane things in life. Such as, when am I going to do the washing – or more importantly – when and how will it get dry? When will I wash my hair; change my sheets; go food shopping; finish reading that pile of books on my bedside table; go for a walk – the obstacles to walking, maybe the rain or the fact that it gets dark at four thirty in the afternoon? When will the sun come out – I live in southern Italy, where the fuck is it? As I need to go for a walk and inevitably get the washing dry. When shall I ring my mother? As she is eighty-eight and spent hours knitting me a scarf with her arthritic hands and I have yet to thank her. When will I conquer the Italian language as the future perfect has me stumped?

When will I stop making excuses for filling my time or not filling my time with all the above?

When will my prince come? Well, I should be aiming for kings now I am older and life isn't a fairy tale and living alone isn't all that bad. It's better to live alone than to live with the wrong person. Besides I am content living with the farting basset, who seems to sleep most of the time and has appalling table manners and can fling huge strings of slobbery-saliva great distances with a shake of his head. The slobbery-gib cleaning also keeps me busy wiping down white walls – if they don't have *muffa* on them, then they are covered in slivers of gib.

I can worry about my stiff neck which prevents me from fully appreciating the murals on the ceilings of almost every church and cathedral here and also worry about my clumsiness which enabled me to set fire to my scarf one night whilst making a cup of tea. I paused for two seconds and said to myself, 'Is my scarf on fire?' Then proceeded to put it out. Obviously delayed reaction has also come with age and some brain shrinkage.

As you get older – and this happens to most women I think – random hairs grow on your chin which happen to be black. And I wonder if at times, I am going to metamorphosise into Hagrid. These random buggers seem to grow overnight like asparagus. This is a really unfair phenomenon that happens to womankind. If you ever see a middle-aged woman distracted at a traffic light then she is probably playing with a random chin hair. Pubic hair growing on your face, lovely and then the pubic hairs in your lady garden become sparser and I wonder why nature invented this translocation.

I dread the day when I wake up from a wee-interrupted sleep to find that there are a couple of teeth on the pillow that should have been in my mouth and wonder if I will ever be able to afford dental implants as I don't want to wake up with my teeth in a glass on my bed table. Or maybe I shouldn't really worry about it and take up gurning if that dreadful toothless day ever comes.

Periods are a nuisance of the past and long since forgotten. I long for the day when the hot flushes will leave me. I hate planning when I have my last cup of coffee before a day out and have to plan my toilet journey. A weak bladder is a curse and a nuisance. I squeeze my kegels at every opportunity in order to prolong my need for a loo visit. Maybe I should practise with ping pong balls and aim to shoot one out to 20ft then I know that I can hold cup of coffee in my bladder for more than half an hour.

It's almost impossible now for me to go through the night without getting up for a wee – even my dog doesn't do this.

Although I can perform a 'tree' posture in yoga, which you would think indicates that I have a fine sense of balance and control. I am not absolutely sure that this is the correct term, it could be plant posture or hold-this-difficult-posture, posture. Despite this yoga balancing triumph, I have any uncanny knack of falling over – even on level ground – or hitting my head on tree branches at almost any given opportunity.

I will now regale you with some funny stories about falling over and hitting my head on tree branches – as it is raining, I have just washed my hair, and I can't think about doing the washing again or how I am going to be able to dry it.

Lamp posts were always in my way as a child, and I would regularly almost crack my head open on them – mainly because I used to walk along looking at my shoes. My mum didn't recognise me unless I always sported a huge egg-like lump on my head, which was most of the time. And so my head bumping is not a mid-life phenomenon but something I have been developing the art of over several years. Since living here, I have nearly knocked myself out in the woods at least three times, as the branches of the trees are not large enough for me to see or am I still walking with my head down and not looking at what is in front of me?

I have also stubbed my toe on a root of a tree whilst wearing flip-flops which resulted in a gash which bled profusely. I hobbled back to Lili's house to find that she was almost prostrated by the sight of my blood, and I had to stay with her for ten minutes to make sure that she wouldn't actually pass out on the floor. I stuffed a tissue on the injury and hoped that I wouldn't need stitches. Luckily, I found some steri-strips and fixed the problem for myself.

I have fallen on the rocks whilst trying to wash my hands in the sea and split my shorts. Unfortunately, no one told me about the split in the said shorts until the next day, and so I had my pants on display for a good twenty-four hours.

I have tripped whilst carrying a plate full of food at a lunch date with some expat friends. I landed – rather unceremoniously – face down on floor tiles, legs akimbo and spent the rest of the time eating with one hand whilst holding an ice block on my face to reduce the swelling. I vowed then that I was too old for platform wedges as even flats with an inch of rubber sole didn't seem to prevent me from slipping, tripping or falling over. Perhaps I should always go barefoot and cover myself in bubble wrap.

I had an unfortunate fall outside the pet store one day and again found myself face down, on the tarmac this time. I like to vary the surfaces that I fall down on. How did it happen? A 25kg basset pulled me in the opposite direction – obviously because he didn't want to go in and have his claws clipped – and I lost my centre of gravity and fell like a tree that had been cut down in a forest. I gashed my knee and scraped my hand in some gravel.

With holes in my cropped leggings and feeling a bit embarrassed, I hobbled into the pet store and explained to the girl who was serving – whilst oozing blood over the newly washed floor – that I had just fallen over.

'What a shame, you are not having a very good day,' she said whilst shooting iodine over my hand and knee. After she had ushered me in to the back where Basil usually had his claws clipped and alsatians and poodles have coat trims and a bath.

I wanted to say that my mum would usually put weakened Dettol on my wounds, followed by some Germolene, but I didn't want to interrupt her mission with the iodine, and wondering whether I could actually be allergic to it.

I looked for a tissue and found that my pen had
exploded in my bag with the impact! Now I was
covered in black ink and blood. She shook her head
and led me to the dog sink where they washed the
dogs and now for a bit of variation, falling women
and invited me to wash my hands. Which I duly did,
but this just resulted in me smearing more black over
my hands. Basil eventually had his claws clipped and
followed by a dog biscuit. He wagged his tail, and I
hobbled out, wanting my mum and some Germolene.
And feeling like a bit of a numpty.

On another mishap-day, I was enjoying a lovely walk
and after about an hour into my walk, I noticed
that something was amiss. It was a sunny day with a
clear blue sky, and as I watched my own shadow cast
against the sand dunes, I saw something extra hanging
out of the back of my shadow-bum like a dragon's
tail and whatever it was, was wafting quite happily in
the light breeze. I had five sheets of toilet roll hanging
out of the back of my shorts – unused I might add –
I was horrified. What a *brutta figura*, ugliness or
creating a bad impression! I laughed to myself and
wondered if the Italians had thought I had some emergency stock of loo roll just in case I got caught short.

Years ago, I also hit my head on a bookshelf, when
my son was about three. I hit the bookshelf with such
force that I put my teeth through my bottom lip and
was in agony. I then tried to explain to my young son
what had happened whilst blowing bubbles of blood
out of my mouth, he seemed unconcerned as he
was watching *Thomas the Tank Engine* at the time and

Percy was in trouble. Besides, three-year-olds have difficulty in conveying empathy. So, I trotted off to the bathroom and filled my mouth with tissue to stem the flow of blood; kept calm and carried on.

In the camping days, when we still thought it would be fun to camp in a damp field somewhere, I broke a finger on a tent peg that catapulted out of the ground. It was probably broken and throbbed with intensity. I fixed the problem myself – or so I thought – by immobilising the injured finger with a lolly stick and taping it to the adjacent finger. The finger never healed properly. I now have an ugly bent finger years later which is as knobbled as a witch's finger. And because I have brought up the subject of witches – and it is still raining – this brings me nicely to the custom or tradition that is celebrated in Italy at this time of year, La Befana who is an old woman and most likely a witch, who delivers presents on Epiphany Eve and not surprisingly only to the 'good' children.

La Befana and the celebration of on Epiphany Eve was probably invented by a greedy kid that realised he could get two lots of presents from Babo Natale on Christmas Day and also from La Befana on January 5th. Befana is a witch who is always covered in soot as she comes down the chimneys to visit Italian children and either leave sweets and gifts in their shoes or stockings or coal if they have been naughty. She drinks wine that is left for her and will thump anyone in the back with a stick if they see her. She must not be seen because she is ugly and dirty and needs to use some face wipes or soap. She may also clean the house of all the problems from the previous year. A scary thought really, an ugly-back-thumping-cleaner who rides a broom. I have seen effigies of La Befana hanging from wires across Italian streets, a hanging, and frightening ugliness. Luckily she didn't visit me. Maybe she was afraid of my own crooked finger. If my kids were still small, I am sure that they would be scared shitless by the thought of a Befana visitation.

But then in England, we have Morris Men that can be quite scary and they are out during the day in English pubs during the summer. The first Morris dance was recorded in 1448 and was probably invented by a drunkard called Morris, who thought it would be fun to tie bells to his shins and wave a tasseled tambourine, whilst brandishing a wooden stick. Other inn dwellers probably joined in with him, thinking perhaps that it was a new religion. In my opinion, men should only dance in tights and have sculpted strong and muscular thighs, preferably at a ballet performance. Which bring my thoughts back to Dwayne Johnson, I wonder if he would look good in tights?

I am obviously still distracted and writing nonsense, and it is still raining. Basil has been leaving muddy paw prints across the white and grey tiles like little signatures, every time he comes in from the garden. I have also just read an article that says, 'Most writers can write 1,000 words in an hour.' Good Lord, I had better up my game then. Firstly, I have to mop the floor. I can feel cabin fever descending…

Chapter 22

ം∾ം

Being Alone and Not Lonely

'Aloneness is a presence, fullness, aliveness, joy of being, overflowing love. You are complete. Nobody is needed, you are enough.'

Huffpost, Aug 2015.

What does a quest reveal about you? When I decided to leave absolutely everything that I knew, my job, my home, my family, and friends and live a completely different life in a foreign land, what does that reveal about me? Or how others perceive me? There is the old adage, *'To be is to be perceived'*.

I have been called brave and courageous by many people who would never contemplate leaving what they 'know'. Far from thinking that I had a brave and passionate heart, I just knew that I couldn't go on doing what I was doing: on autopilot and feeling unfulfilled and exhausted for most of the time. I began looking for an escape from the mundaneness of my life. My life had become pedestrian in every sense of the word.

I worked as much as I could, fearing my days off like a wall of ice. Even on my annual leave, I would find excuses to work. The constant working

– I thought – allowed me to function, even at some low level. Being a professional, I could hide behind the role, of being a nurse. Being alone with just me, seemed repellent and something that I needed to run away from. Work, eat and sleep was a comfortable 'uncomfortable zone'. The repetition in itself was comforting, but I wasn't allowing myself to face my demons, the fear of solitude and loneliness. Being alone and loneliness had merged into an unfathomable murkiness for me, a dark tunnel with no light at the end. Keeping busy, I thought, will enable me to survive. An existential crisis seemed to be looming. Low moods would appear from unknown sources. I had become easily irritable and impatient. When the night fell, I was relieved that another day was over. I was existing, but not living and I certainly wasn't happy with my way of being.

We are, us human beings, generally social animals. We need to have a sense of belonging in a group, in a family and to be acknowledged and accepted. The American psychologist Abraham Maslow said that fundamentally all human beings need to progress and have a hierarchy of needs met in order to reach, *'Self-actualisation'*, or your full potential as a human being, *'Morality, creativity, spontaneity, acceptance, experience, purpose, meaning and inner potential.'* Maslow said, *'What a man can be, he must be.' This need we can call self-actualisation'*. In other words, be the person you want to become.

After physiological needs and safety and security needs, Maslow thought that love and belonging was also essential in order to work up towards self-actualisation. Whilst I agree that everyone needs to be loved or to feel love in some form, I wonder about the belonging bit. Do I need to feel that 'I belong' in order to survive?

I think that needing a sense of belonging can be stultifying and 'not for growth'. We feel awkward in public if we don't know anyone and feel self-conscious. I remember running away from a children's party because I felt that I didn't 'belong' and wasn't part of the 'group' and so I chose to leave; which was a bit frightening for my mum as I was only about six years old at the time, having made the executive decision that the party wasn't for me. At such a young age, I felt as though I didn't belong there.

And because, as an adult, I chose to live on my own in Italy (where I literally did not know anyone), I gave away that sense of belonging or wanting to belong to a group and decided to belong to myself. This in itself, can be enormously freeing and enables you to wander around towns and do a bit of sightseeing without feeling self-conscious. I can sit with a group of people and because I see myself as being there to 'observe', I don't strive to fit in. I don't worry what people might think and whether they think I am either brave or odd, or both.

Ridding myself of the cloak of 'needing to belong' enabled me to live alone and also to function in groups without feeling like an outsider.

We 'connected beings' also find it difficult to be and live alone. In the past, I have felt totally disconnected from myself when I was alone and felt almost fragmented. I felt envious of others, the world 'out there' that seemed vastly different to my own. A DVD and packet of Maltesers sometimes just wouldn't always do the trick on a Saturday night, and I would walk to the local supermarket with my head dipped down almost sighing on my way to get a screw-top five quid bottle of wine and imagined the rest of the world clinking classes and laughing about something amusing. I didn't feel that I belonged to anything on those lonely Saturday nights. Therefore, it is a question expectation as well as envy. Envying others and having the expectation of myself that I should be doing something interesting and preferably with other people. I felt lonely because that is the way that I chose to see myself.

Being alone is a physical state, but it's our thoughts and emotions that lead to the path of loneliness. If you can become comfortable and accepting of yourself, then the cold hand of loneliness can't creep up and tap you on the shoulder. I have often felt lonely in a house full of people. Feeling lonely can be due to a lack of a sense of belonging to yourself and to others. At parties, I would feel like a sackcloth-and-ashes outcast – outcast from the coupledom and then being seen as a threat to others' coupledom as I was unattached. A woman alone; I would often imagine the hosts wanting to put the 'lone woman' in the understairs cupboard, passing small items of food in the gap underneath the door, until the party was over and then ushering out discretely the 'lone woman' saying, 'It was lovely to have you. Wasn't it Neville?' Then swiftly shutting the front door behind me.

Stephanie Dowrick describes very eruditely in her book, *Intimacy and Solitude* just what solitude is: *'You and I share a drive toward connection. We probably also share a hope that at least some of our connections will be loving. But, as you have already discovered, your connections with others can only be as rewarding as the connection you have with the only 'someone' with whom you live every moment of your life: your own self.* She goes on to say: *'One of the greatest pleasures of solitude is that it gives you a chance to take a rest from seeing yourself through other people's eyes...'* In other words, being alone can allow yourself to be yourself, to be authentic and to appreciate who you are and where you are going, without worrying about what other people think of you.

I couldn't go from a head-down-lonely-foot-shuffle to the supermarket on a Saturday night to upping-sticks and living in Italy, so I started with small steps.

Going for a coffee on my own with a book and finally reached the heady heights of travelling to London by myself and watching a friend in a play (it was lucky I was there truth be known, as there were only about three other people in the audience). And no one can hear the sound of one hand clapping.

We are, as part of the human race, connected beings. Connected beings that find it difficult to be alone. In order to tolerate the aloneness, I believe that there is fundamental requirement to like yourself – a bit of self – love and empathy – and to feel comfortable with yourself. One of the ways forward, I believe, it to stop thinking as being alone as a disadvantage or an encumbrance, but to see the freedom and potential openings that being alone can offer you.

There is no one to fall out with when you live alone. No one to argue with – apart from your own internal conflicts that just have to be ridden out and processed – when you are living a solitary existence. No one to have a dispute with about who takes out the recycling bins or who does the washing up. No one to say, 'But I thought I asked you to do it.' No one raising their eyebrows or sucking their teeth with dismissiveness or disdain. No one to invalidate you. No one being passive-aggressive and giving you the cold shoulder and thus creating a tension-filled and unbearable silence. No one to give you an automated touch that doesn't touch anything within you anymore. No one to reject you. No one to call you 'Darling' instead of your name, so that they don't confuse you with someone else. No one to lie to you, even if it is just by omission. No one to fart under the duvet and then try and put your head under the covers.

The post-divorced me has tried relationships. Four flings and a relationship, which all ended up in funerals. For me, there is nothing worse than a man suddenly looking at you differently. It is as though the shutters have come down and you know that it is over or it never really started. Funny things that you used to say suddenly become irritating to them. Some men behave so badly that they force an ending that is initiated by the woman, in order not to have to do the deed themselves.

I guess the best thing now, about being single is

that I no longer look at my phone for a text message every five minutes. I don't plan my life around anyone else which can create a huge amount of space and opens the doors of total freedom. Or the best thing of all, I don't have to shave and pluck. I have gone native. I wear plain bras, and knickers, and the big bag of lacy-teeny-weeny undergarments that were still lurking at the bottom of the wardrobe have now been given away – ninety-five pairs of knickers! Ridiculous, what was I thinking? Big comfy pants are the only way forward.

Here's a quote which encompasses a lot of what I have just said:

'I like to show women who exist in solitude but do not suffer. Rather, they are safe, existing in the sense of enjoying the company of just herself.' Idalia Candelas, Illustrator

I used to look in the mirror, and although a much younger face stared back at me, I was unsure who I was in the reflection. A wife, a mother, a daughter, a sister, a nurse, a counsellor, these are all positions in a family and roles. But who was I? Because I had been a part of a couple, when the coupledom destruction came, I found myself struggling with my identity and sense of self because I had melded into a 'relationship-self'. The 'me', who I fundamentally was, a person, the whole 'me' had been lost. It has taken me years to find out who the 'me' is and what I want and what is important to me. The initial feelings of isolation shifted when I realised that I had my own identity and didn't have to be part of another in order to exist. I don't have to be in a relationship with another person, and this may sound like an eye-rolling-cliché, but you really do have to have a relationship with yourself first, before you can ever be truly available to another person in a relationship. Also, I believe that the constant yearning for a relationship ostensibly undermines a person's self-development and the ability to sit within themselves in that room which is the 'self'. Whatever that room looks like.

'I used to think that the worst thing in life was to end up alone. It's not. The worst thing in life is to end up with people who make you feel alone.' Robin Williams

Loneliness, to me, is about losing your personal power and giving it over to the fear of being alone. Loneliness is allowing yourself to inhabit a cold dark place deep within your soul and treading water, rather than accepting the freedom of a more liberating and personal space. Time alone – or even the thought of being alone – can be filled with fear, boredom and seen as dead time. Or it can be filled with simple and small pleasures.

'Small pleasures, Elaine,' my sister once said to me. At the time I didn't understand what she meant. Time on my own back then really was dead time, time to be killed rather than to be enjoyed. Today, I can say to myself, 'What is it that you really want to do today?' Time is a pleasure and a joy, it is moving a bit more swiftly than I would like, but I treasure it. What would you really like to do today? I urge you to move away from the vacuum of the black rectangular thing on the wall, move away from Jeremy Kyle and channel hopping. Take your face out of your smartphone and stop playing Candy Crush and ask yourself, what would you really like to do?

My small pleasures: ordering a Jenga pile of books and realising that I would never get through Homer's *Odyssey*. Getting lost on internet trails that would lead me to learning how to read Tarot cards. Twisting my body, into places that they had never been before, in learning a gentle style of Hatha yoga. Going on long walks with the wall-sniffing basset and watching sunrises, sunsets, choppy seas and calm mirror-like seas. Watching the dark, twisting bodies of the trees in the small pine wood and noticing the light changing through the leaves and dappling onto the bark. Imagining faces in the ancient olive trees, the deities the Green Man and the Green Woman (although I should probably look for Jupiter and Juno instead). Taking Basil across the rocks along the shore and discovering little Lilliputian-like coves with gently lapping shorelines. Burping, flapping, crashing waves with spitting sea spray on stormier days. A cup of mint tea and a hot water bottle; a new pen, a new blanket, a sideboard filled with a blaze of candles and nag champa incense lit and smouldering; a new day and a new experience.

On another small and simple pleasured day, I went for a bracing walk by the sea. I always do the same walk; a figure of eight around Santa Sabina through the small pine wood, down past shuttered up residences until the gaiety of June and down past the

Scoglio di Cavallo, the horseshoe beach. I gazed out to sea – and was not really thinking about anything in particular, which is indeed a small pleasure – when I was nearly blown off my feet by a strong *Tramontana*, the north wind, which was blowing gustily off of the sea and I could taste the sea salt and feel the gritty sand on my lips.

I find it strange here, that every Italian I meet – if they talk about the weather – will always tell me where the wind is coming from and without licking their finger and holding it up against the wind. The *Tramontana* is cold and dry. The *Grecale*, is a north-easterly wind. The *Levante* is from the east and the *Scirocco*, the south-easterly wind that blows in from the African continent and is responsible for the hot and humid conditions in the summer. The *Ostro*, which comes directly in from the south. The south-westerly *Libreccio* and westerly *Pomente* and lastly, the *Maestrale* from the north-west. I think that these winds have quite musical names and sound more like operatic arias than winds. A bit more romantic than listening to the shipping forecast in Britain, *Hebrides Bailey, south-westerly veering north-westerly seven to severe gale nine…* I have heard that people have recorded the shipping forecast and fallen asleep to it because it is so soothing and it is such necessary information when you are in a semi-detached house in Ruislip and nowhere near the North Sea.

On this particular day, I wasn't alone but accompanied by the blustery *Tramontana*. The sea was whipping up whites and frothy greys. I was wrapped up in an oversized padded jacket and wearing two pairs of socks and two scarves. I revelled in a solitary walk, battling against the elements. Basil's ears were being held aloft as we battled against the wind. The sea spray splattered my glasses; my nose dripped with the cold – probably not the most attractive sight.

One of my neighbours was sitting in his car with the heater on and also admiring the turbulent sea, through a steamed-up car window. He wound his window down and asked me if I wanted some lemons, (he always speaks to me in French, which is odd as I always speak to him in Italian and say that I am English. Despite nodding his head, as if in agreement, he carries on speaking to me in French as though he hasn't heard me. Maybe he just likes to speak French). He gave me half a dozen lemons from a bag on the passenger seat. I stuffed the lemons in my pocket and thought about them, sliced in a gin and tonic. Although in all honesty, the gin in Italy is not the best – you could probably unblock a sink with it.

Although I live alone, I also meet people, the Italians every day. Even in the winter when the population is minimal, there is always someone to have a two-minute conversation with. I have been offered all sorts of things on my walks. A handful of fresh peas, a big bunch of sorrel – which apparently is good for sauces, (but then how would I know), bunches of *rosmarino*, rosemary, bags of black olives and fresh mushrooms picked from the woods. It is almost as though the whole community is willing me to become a culinary genius or at least make more effort in the kitchen. You can't blame the Italians for believing in miracles.

The Pursuit of Writing and Creativity
‍ ‍

The American psychologist Carl Rogers said, *'The good life is a process, not a state of being. It is a direction, not a destination.'*

Creativity, even the smallest of creative pursuits, needs to come from a calmer and quieter place both externally – external peace, quietness or perhaps silence – and from within oneself, that can answer the question, 'What is it I really would like to do today?' Choices and decisions if not acted upon and the energy transformed, is similar to having a compass in a labyrinth. You know where you want to go, but you can get there, and you may just end up in the same spot.

Many writers need peace and tranquillity in order to write, although some may be able to write in noisy cafés or on tube trains. My writing only takes place when there is stillness and library-hushed quietness. The stillness required for the necessary creative unravelling of the mind. For me, the end of summer mayhem was longed for. The pin-dropping silence yearned for.

I expect the noise and the hubbub of the summer. Every child seems to scream in the heat of the day, and the cicadas make a noise that sounds like a thousand manual typewriters, both are annoying – yes, I am a grumpy woman that now wears big knickers. And there is nothing to do but to wait until the summer ends and peace is restored.

Recently that longed for quiet time, was shattered by two-way yelling and screaming from an Italian family that have become my new neighbours who arrived within two weeks of the last noisy-makers leaving. A rollover of noise, how lovely.

I like nothing more than to sit in the garden even when it is a cold and damp morning and listen to nothing but my own thoughts. Or hear the odd cat fight as they fight for territory on an adjacent wall. God's thunder and lightning is not an intrusion, but the human voices at full pelt is like a thorn, that develops into a sword into my side. Digging into the flesh. There is obviously a huge dramatisation here by me, and I am obviously becoming Italian. Instead of the English 'ah well or never mind aye', I have become completely histrionic, reactive and emotionally-Italian about this. However, if I wanted Italian theatre that was audible from my back garden, I would have bought a ticket.

When Dee came to visit recently, we had dinner at my favourite restaurant in Carovigno, *La Loggia*. La Loggia is a very romantic restaurant with themed areas, glass tables with leather chairs or sumptuous fake zebra striped seats; soft lighting and stellar seating and a beautiful fairy-tale-garden with twinkling lights for al fresco dining. I have to say that the food in this restaurant is exceptional and whilst you can have your pasta with a Pugliese theme – which usually involves seafood – I ordered my usual fillet steak to bump up my iron levels. Dee ordered fresh tuna that was barely seared and could have still been moving on the plate.

We had a post-prandial chocolate liqueur that was so delicious we had to stick our fingers deep into the bottom of the glass and sucked the liqueur off our fingers, like Nigella Lawson having oral sex with a chocolate pudding.

Sufficiently satiated we stepped out of the restaurant under a gibbous moon and heard a screaming melodrama from an upstairs window. The shouting escalated into high-pitched screaming, accompanied by the smashing of plates, mirroring a black and white film, a Felliniesque Italian melodrama. The Italian opera was right there occurring just above our heads and in the interest of observing the human condition and Italian culture we tried to record the scene – just the audio I might add. We enjoyed that little piece of Italian drama. Because it wasn't observable or audible from my own back garden.

Of course, anyone can live here (by here I mean in close proximity to me), I have just become the grouchy woman who lives alone and whose expectations are exceeding the reality of normal life. In reality, my new neighbours are probably not that noisy. In all likelihood I have just become hypersensitive and hypervigilant. Although it doesn't feel quite the same in my little Italian world. Nothing ever does stay the same, and it feels like the start of the ending of my time here. And with the recent Brexit decision I might get turfed out on my ear anyway, a true alien, non-EU, interloping-grumpy-big-knicker-wearing-Brit.

Being alone and feeling comfortable with it, can be like a reward for slaying the dragon of isolation and fear. Solitude is not something to be denigrated but celebrated.

As I am writing this, I confess – due to the fact that this is my last year – that I spend 90% of my time, completely alone. To get this book written I have to sit on my faux-leather beige office chair every afternoon and organise the words that become sentences, then paragraphs that then metamorphosise into a book – I hope. I have found bits of writing on Post-it notes, train tickets, menus and bits of torn up serviette – apparently if you are posh you say, 'Napkin.' I am not posh and so I'll stick with serviette. The remnants of my writing cluttering my desk like large pieces of wedding confetti. If I had always carried a notebook as advised by seasoned writers, then I wouldn't have this detritus to muddle through. It sometimes feels like ingredients to a huge recipe, and I have no idea what I am making or how it is going to turn out.

In my solitary afternoons, I have found out that my spelling is appalling and how one writes has nothing to do with how one speaks – I am feeling a bit posh here using the personal pronoun 'one' – maybe I will advance to saying napkin. The verbal shortcuts that we take in everyday speech do not, on the whole, transfer to the page.

Although as a distraction – writers tend to distract themselves from whatever they are meant to or supposed to be doing – I have opened an Instagram account. The steroidal media can connect us to millions of people or in my case about twenty-five. I also have not a clue about #hashtags and in my virginal #hashtag post, I hashtagged what I thought was an apt description of my picture – which was of the harbour and some heavy and leadened clouds – *#belchingclouds*. Not realising that there isn't a hashtag for 'belchingclouds' – probably because no one else has thought of describing them as such – and my pic went to a hashtag for belching, literally short videos of people belching. I also have sent photos to #instapuc instead of #instapic because obviously I have fat fingers, and the 'U' is too near the 'I'. Also left a comment below someone's photo saying, 'Great shit!' instead of 'Great shot!' (although for all I know, they could have had a great shit that morning and they just put a picture of a glorious sunrise just to celebrate the fact). I fear that technology has yet to keep up with us fat-fingered-folk.

If I am not being distracted like a fruit fly that doesn't have long to live, then I do this – tap and write – and my words end up here on the page. When I write, I feel as though I am talking to and writing to someone. Maybe even to myself, to bear witness to how I am experiencing things and how I am much more in touch with being in the moment in my everyday life and how grateful I am just to be

able to do this and 'to be'. And if no one chooses to
read this, then the pages will help to fan the flames
around my coffin in the crematorium. My preferable
exit would be on a Viking long ship launched off of
the north-west coast of Scotland with a fit young man
firing a flaming arrow into the boat to ignite the only
two copies of my book that were ever published, that
surround my body and probably a couple of barbecue
cubes under my bum to really get the flames going.
Although if I am still wearing huge knickers by then, I
should whoof up in bursting flames, a treat.

I have managed to get over my *writing fright* – after
reading a quote from Saint Francis of Assisi, *'Start by
doing what is necessary, then do what is possible and suddenly
you are doing the impossible.'*

Just by doing a little bit every day, I can see something
building. It's the fear that is paralysing. Fear of not
be a good enough writer; fear of not being accepted
and the worst one of all fear of fear, that can stop us
all from doing almost anything. Apparently – and this
probably isn't a real statistic – seven people die a year
by putting their socks on in the morning. Would that
really put most people off getting out of bed, fearing
a sock-putting-on death due to a fall? Imaginary fears
lead to the darkest nights of the soul. The ball of
worries that can sometimes hang around – probably
because they have nothing else better to do. I think
that it is true, as the saying goes, *'Today, is the tomorrow
that you worried about yesterday.'*

Why worry about anything? Because it is part of the human condition to worry about any perceived threat either physically, emotionally or materially. Worrying leads to stress. Worrying usually involves ruminative thoughts about things that haven't actually happened yet or situations that you feel you have no control over.

Although acute stress can be good for us. It helps us get through an exam, pass a driving test or pay a bill on time. The primal reason for acute stress was nature ingenious design to enable us to harness adrenaline and run away from a sabre-toothed tiger. Chronic stress, however, is emotionally and physically debilitating. It is the sort of stress that we feel we can do nothing about. Being in a job that you may hate. Being in a relationship that is going nowhere or is invalidating. Being in any situation that seems to have no ending or escape route.

Confronting fears is about sorting out what is 'real' and what is just a ruminative worry. I always ask myself now, 'What can I do about this situation?' Rather than running away or procrastinating, I faced my darkest fears about being alone and prioritised what was important. I may have escaped to a different country, but I have tried not to escape myself and have tried to pull all the different parts of myself into a whole. A more integrated and self-aware me.

The silence is there, but it is all mine and can be yours. Embrace the silence and inhabit the space of being alone. Just at this moment, the silence is only broken by the tapping of the computer keys, a 30mph wind that is ripping through the palm trees and the gentle hum of the stove. The loudest internal sound are my thoughts that I am transferring to the page. I am owning the silence and owning my thoughts.

Being alone allows you to take stock of your life and find out what is really important, without getting caught up in what is more important for another person. If it is not important or irrelevant, then let it go.

The strange thing is that in Italian, being alone and being lonely are the same. *Sono sola*, I am alone, I am lonely. Clearly, the differences have been lost in translation. Or maybe it is because the Italians are rarely alone and are, in general, surrounded by a loving family. Or at the very least part of a community where someone will be looking out for you; a bridge and a connection. But this doesn't answer the question, how some of us have felt entirely alone in a room of people. Whether it is about the need to belong or the lack of self-connection; lack of self-love and acceptance, or a combination of all of these things.

As a child, I spent a lot of time in the back of wardrobes waiting and hoping for a secret world to open up to me. As an adult and after stepping out into the unknown, I decided to create my own world and let go of what I thought I should be doing and looked for different paths that would take me to what I could be doing if only I could take that leap of faith. I did just that and allowed myself the freedom and the pleasure of creating my own secret world that would become more fulfilling, a bit scary and ultimately self-developing.

Ultimately, I have learnt to like myself and even to love myself. The inner dialogue is continuous. What would make me happy today? Okay, I am luckier than most I have had a dream and I have followed it. The detractors may say, 'Well it is alright for her, but what about me... this, this and this is stopping me.' I agree that we all have different views, paths and seemingly different directions in life. But I think that everyone of us could ask the question: What would I really like to do with my life? What would make me happy? What could make my stomach flip with excitement and challenge me?

If you can't write a book, then write a poem, tell your story. If you can't paint a picture, then take a memorable photo. If you can't climb a mountain, then go on a favourite walk or try out a new activity. Live the life that is being offered to you.

Have patience with yourself. Nothing happens overnight and small changes leads to bigger changes. Try and stay in the moment as much as possible. I have heard this said many times, if you are doing the washing up, just do that. Don't think about anything else. Apparently, the happiest people are those who can just lose themselves in the flow of whatever they are doing.

I remember when my dad was elderly, and his health was deteriorating, I had picked him up for a day out. I was driving and probably not really connecting to him or myself. 'It would be nice to see the scenery,' he said. I realised that I had been just getting from A to B. This can be a metaphor for life, it you rush through it and really see it you will miss life's nuances and beauty. Take the B roads and look around you. Notice something different and new every day. As I do now.

Here is a small list of things that have helped me to combat loneliness and feel comfortable and more in the moment with myself:

- Do things that are character building. Go out on your own. Have a prosecco or a coffee. Sit and watch the world go by as an observer, without feeling the need to belong to the throng. Have a date with yourself.

- Be in the moment. Connect with nature, go for long languorous walks. Notice the sights, the sounds and the smells. Stay in the moment and notice the dipping sun and the smears of oranges, pinks and purples. The scurrying of a gecko into a crack in the wall and a cat that sits patiently waiting for it to come out again for a chance of an early supper. Smell the air and take long lungfuls of it, in slow, deep inhaling breaths.

- Enjoy the freedom of when to eat, what you want to eat and where you want to eat.

- Talk to yourself, out loud if necessary. Process your thoughts rather than your thoughts owning you. Talk to the dog or the cat– although if you answer yourself as the dog or cat you may be getting into problems.

- Take your own bins out – why is this always such an issue with couples? – if you live on your own, you have no choice. But I mean this as a metaphor.

- Enjoy the silence and the solitude and the unravelling of thoughts and ideas.

- Take time to daydream without the minutiae of life getting in the way if only for a few minutes.

- Meditate. Concentrate on your breathing and cut out the left brain chatter and let the right brain just be. Put on meditation music, even if you are not meditating, it's wonderfully soothing. Ask the question, 'Who am I and where am I going?'

- Self-fulfilment is like a man's erection – if you give too much thought to it, then it flops. Take your time and take pleasure in the small things in life. Move in small steps towards what you want to achieve and the bigger things will come – if you pardon the pun!

- Grow your lady garden, because there is no one or reason to get out your mower.

Society seems to be telling us that being alone is a negative thing, accompanied by fear and that it can be a cold, despairing place. If you can immerse yourself in potential joys and slowly peel off the layers that seem to be fearful, it can be a very free and comforting place to be. To be alone, but not lonely. *Mi sono trovata* – I have found myself. And if you haven't yet, just keep looking.

I have developed an interest in photography, and now I see things more clearly, colourfully and texturally. The curve of a boat; the cast of a shadow; a profile of a face; a walk in the woods and the light shining through the trees; the honeyed light that always seems to kiss the buildings here in Italy as the light fades. I can not only appreciate the beautiful creamy baroque buildings in Lecce but take better photographs of them from different angles and using different lenses; as I now look at life through a much wider lens.

I have transformed from the woman who felt desperately alone and cried and howled deep into the night and who felt lost and broken. It took me over eight years to get over the hurt and to step into a new life here in Italy. I have learnt to laugh at myself and at the situations that I have found myself in. And although I haven't found love with another person, I have learnt to love myself and my dark corners and all my imperfections. I have learnt to embrace every new day with the freshness and newness that it deserves. I have truly found myself and decided that I am an okay person and know that ultimately, I can live life alone, without feeling lonely.

Dream, dream and dream some more. If you dream enough and manifest some action towards that dream, you will open a door. Step through the opening and experience something new. It may be scary, but you can hold your own hand and be your own best companion.

If I were to sit on top of Maslow's Hierarchy of Needs, I would aspire to be on top of my game in the self-actualisation stakes and hope that the point of the triangle wouldn't be too painful on the nether regions. Finally, I hope to grow old gracefully and into my big pants.

Remember life is only boring when we want to be somewhere else, start by being the person that you want to become.

Chapter 23

৵৵

The Last Summer, Wine and Endings

'Wine is the most civilised thing in the world.'
Ernest Hemingway

I have six bottles of wine in a box on the floor in
the spare room; all organic which will be drunk over
the coming Christmas period (the last Christmas
here). My daughter, Elisa and her partner Dean,
myself and Anna (Anna planted and cultivated
her own vineyard in England and did a sterling
job considering the weather isn't always conducent
with growing grapes), went to a wine tasting at a
vineyard in Cisternino recently, called Vini Semeraro
who produce 24,000 bottles of wine a year. Franco,
one of the vineyard owners – who spoke excellent
English and had his iPad in his hand – took us down
to the cellars where dark bottles were resting on
their sides, their corks pointing outwards in order to
allow the wine to 'breathe'. Franco went on to tell us
that, when the wine is fermented in the huge steel
containers that they play Mozart in order to aid with
the fermentation; three hours of acoustic energy
at 70 decibels, (this has been scientifically proven

apparently, and the music affects the yeast in the wine and increases the oxygen levels in the wine). Franco showed us a video of particles dancing and moving in waves and patterns when music is played. Mozart is used because of the harmony and the melody in the music of the composer. All this Mozart assisted fermentation technique, develops the soft taste of the wine from this vineyard, Franco tells us. Franco is also a musician, and so all this Mozart and wine synergy is of particular interest to him. He also plays Mozart to his seven-year-old son to calm him down (possibly after Italian pop music has wound him up).

It is a family run vineyard dating back through five generations. 'The sun is our friend,' Franco alludes. And goes on to say, how the grapes are all cut by hand at the end of September and taken for processing as soon as possible. The pre-fermentation stage lasts one week in order to control the sugar content. No antioxidants are used in the winemaking or sulphites, so presumably there is not nasty headache hangover after too much consumption, which is usually due to sulphites. My sister is allergic to sulphites and gets breathing problems when she drinks wine, although she likes wine and still drinks it (despite the danger of possible respiratory complications), maybe she should switch to organic wine?

We sat in the light and airy restaurant. The white tables laid out with large Bordeaux glasses, big enough to get our noses in for a good sniff and perhaps our whole heads! Apparently, the aroma of the fruit hits the nose first and then the tannins (ooh the tannins that lay so heavily in homemade Italian wine). And

waited patiently and eagerly for Franco to open the
bottles of wine one by one that we were going to
taste. My daughter had always wanted to go to a wine
tasting at a vineyard in Italy, and I wondered why we
hadn't experienced this sooner? Vineyards surround
me and yet I have never visited one. It is strange how
things that are right under your nose can be ignored,
just because they are there and taken for granted.
So, we came to Cisternino in a village called Casalini,
to experience some of the wonderful wines that are
produced in this region.

The first bottle was a sparkling wine called Brioso
(apparently this wine likes to listen to Joseph
Mahler), which tasted of peaches, melon and lemons.
Gorgeous! We were served bruschetta with toasted
fava beans. Each little dish of food was matched to
compliment and enhance the flavours in the wine.
More wine followed, Canzone, a dry white which had
a hint of almond in tasting it; more bruschetta was
served this time with preserved peppers, in oil garlic
and chilli.

Next was a red called Opera made from 100%
Primitivo grapes. This grape variety is not only one
of my favourites, but has also been recognised as one
of the best wines in the world, and because it is not
preserved in barrels at this vineyard, the fruit slices
through the wine, softly and melodiously. Deliciously
velvety, yummy and jammy! After two minutes of
this wine being poured, it became even smoother and
highly drinkable. Pasta, *orechiette*, little ears; was served
with tomato and basil (I just played with dish as wheat

is still not my friend).

The next bottle was called Cantus and was 50% Primitivo, 40% Mantuzia and 10% Cabernet. This wine was 13% and had quiet a smoky taste; this was served with *capo collo*, the neck of the pork from Martina Franca and *pancetta* to enhance the flavour of the wine.

We then tried a *rosé* called Cantabile which has a shorter fermentation time in order to produce the light colour and the food served consisted of emmental cheese and *vincotto*, pickled artichokes and *cacio cavallo* cheese which was quite a salty cheese. *Vincotto* is the syrup from large amounts of wine that have been boiled and reduced into a delicious sticky sauce that goes really well with cheese. I would recommend *vincotto originale*, but you can buy it in different varieties such as fig.

The last bottle of wine was called Notturno and was a sweet dessert wine which tasted of honey, figs, and almonds and the grape variety was Fiano Minute, and less water is used in the pressing which accounts for the honey taste. The food consisted of a birthday cake for Elisa (it was her birthday the day before), freshly baked that morning. A light sponge with cream. And lots of oohs and aahs from us as we tasted the sweet elixir. Although in truth I only had one swallow from each glass as I was driving, this didn't really diminish the whole experience.

The tasting cost £25 a head, and the wine cost 7.90 euros per bottle with the sparkling wine being slightly more expensive at 15 euros. This is how wine should be made and drunk. A wonderful and unique experience, perfect for the last summer.

Italy has over 2,000 varieties of grapes, compared to France's 200. Wine used to be transported up to the north to be mixed with Brunello and Chianti, because of the superior quality of the grapes down here. Would anyone admit to this, probably not? But I have heard this from winegrowers down here that this used to be the practice. Why aren't Puglian wines really on the map? Even though wine connoisseurs and winegrowers know about Puglian wines and recognise their quality, the general consumer will still plump for a French, South American or New World wine. I urge everyone to start accessing and drinking Puglian wines and to help this region of Italy put these wonderful wines on the international map. Cin, cin!

According to my calendar tomorrow, is the 22nd of September 2016 which will be the start of autumn. Yesterday was the autumn equinox when the night and the day have equal hours and now the nights will become longer. My fourth and last summer here has finally come to a close, and I am thinking about putting my thick duck down quilt back on the bed and socks on my feet – my feet are always cold in bed. The beach umbrellas that gave a splash of citrus colours are now disappearing, and only the foolhardy and the stoic are now attempting to swim in the much cooler and more choppy Adriatic waters.

A spate of thunderstorms last week cut through the heat and humidity and allowed the air to cool. The storms were daily and persistent. Thunder cannoned through the sky, and the window panes rattled. Rivers of water sped down the terracotta tiles on the patio, and the lawn drank in the water thirstily. The best thing of all that in between the storms, all was quiet. And eventually everyone headed back to town, and I was left in peace. The selfish peace that I desire at the end of every summer here.

In my head, I have promised myself an early morning swim when the sea is calm, and no one can witness me drowning, or save me from drowning for that matter. I will drive to the Mezzaluna beach with just a towel and wearing my bathing suit and walk lithely and swan-like into the sea and swim effortlessly through the aquamarine waters, breathing steadily and comfortably. So far, I swam twenty feet (a ladylike breast stroke with my head out of the water), when my daughter was here and have ventured in up to my thighs with Basil on the lead. Basil, quickly being out of his depth had to swim with a look of panic on his face as he scrambled to the shore. And then I realised that is me (at least in swimming terms) when I am out of my depth I too, quickly scramble to a depth where I can put my feet on the ground and feel safe. If I don't do this solo swim soon, the water will be too cold, and I will have lost my chance to really push myself into doing something that I am not only uncomfortable with but also a bit fearful of doing. They say, 'Feel the fear and do it anyway.' But also the most famous last words of many a daredevil is probably, 'Hold my drink and watch this.' Before some idiotic, drunken and not death-defying feat, that then inevitably results in an untimely death. If I do die during my pursuit of a solo swim, I want my obituary to be, 'She had a good innings. Always up to bat and was hardly ever stumped.'

Hopefully, if I do pluck up the courage and don't get carried away by a riptide, it will be another challenge that I have faced and a fear overcome. This really is a big fear of mine as I nearly drowned when I was seven years old in Spain, and a man waved maniacally at me to warn me of a ten-foot wave that was quickly advancing just behind me. It hit me hard, and I found myself face down in the sand and ever since then I have had a fear of water.

Only this morning I watched a woman in her late seventies shuffle down to the water's edge on crutches. She was wearing a brightly coloured dress and a straw sun hat and bright pink plastic Crocs. One leg was swollen and despite her limitations, she paddled in the sea and leant against the rock to steady herself, which made me realise that I don't have to swim in the sea I just have to greet it and to know that it is there. Everything that I do in life is always my choice, whether it is how I react to a situation or how I adapt to a new one. For me, it is about looking at my fears and challenges straight in the eye, and even if I don't always swim into the depths of life's waters, I will always base my decisions on what I really want to do and not because I feel as though 'I have' to do something.

I think that my PE teacher gave me my swimming Confidence Certificate out of pity, rather than out of ability, and I never understood why we had to swim for bricks in our pyjamas, as to me, the likelihood of drowning whilst wearing pyjamas was a very remote possibility. I concluded at an early age that I was more likely to drown in a bathing suit. Unless I went sleep walking beside a canal.

Another weird fear I have is the blinking icon of the cursor at the end of every sentence, a full stop or a pause and there it is blinking and daring me to write a few more words, a sentence and eventually a paragraph. 'Hold my drink, whilst I finish this sentence…'

In order to stop the cursor blinking at me for too long, I have composed a couple of lists. Things that I will miss/I will not miss about Italian summers:

Things That I Will Miss
ঙ৽ৎ

- Paddling in the sea, but only up to my thighs and bringing the reluctant Basil in with me.

- Not paddling in the sea, but admiring it and watching with envy the competent swimmers glide through the water with ease.

- Having lots of visitors and being a tourist in my own temporary country of residence even though I have visited these lovely towns dozens of times, I never tire of it.

- *Pistacchio* ice cream (which is pronounced *pist-akio*) or my son's favourite which is *cioccolato fondente* which is a thick and creamy dark chocolate which seems to be an Italian favourite too. I once had a white chocolate ice cream from Polignano a Mare which tasted like whipped cream white chocolate Milky Bars, ice cream heaven in a tub.

- *Caffè ghiacccio con latte di mandorle*, which is an espresso with chunks of ice and almond milk with is the perfect cool-down and pick-me-up drink on a hot summer's day.

- *La passeggiata* in Ostuni and browsing through all the shops and boutiques followed by an *Aperol spritz* whilst sitting on giant lime green bean bags on the steps of the old town and perhaps supper in the restaurant below, *La Bella Vista*.

- Early morning walks and taking photos of the sunrise and the people who are up early enough to be my companions. A fisherman with a Roman nose (who had an amazing profile in the shot), who was waiting for the boats to come in. Two old men sitting on the bench at the sea front, chatting and their arms gesticulating madly as though they were conducting an orchestra.

- Dawn bathers cooling down in a calm sea up to their necks and also deep in conversation; probably about nothing in particular.

- A 6 am cappuccino at the Summer Café (the owner opens up at 5:30am in the summer), my camera in hand reviewing my photos and knowing that nearly everyone else is still deep in slumber.

- A man who I see every morning walking his dog -

and we always have a short conversation – he tells me he has ten cats, and one of them is pregnant. *'Questa è la vita.'* 'This is the life,' I say in Italian and hold my arms up in the air to emphasise the fact and realise that perhaps a very small part of me is Italian.

- Mojitos. Especially the ones that are made at the whitewashed wooden bar on the Mezzaluna beach, which is always packed in the summer. But somehow one of these mojitos seems to wash away all the effects of the chaos and leaves me feeling tranquil and a little bit inebriated.

- Clean beaches. The beaches are cleaned at 6 am between May and September. The rest of the year the debris collects. There is always one shoe lying washed up on the beach next to a bit of polystyrene and the ubiquitous plastic bottles.

- Little supermarkets and bakers are open. And my favourite a vegetable van which parks up a couple of minutes' walk away from my house. Organic, misshapen and fresh, but most of all cheap fruit and vegetables.

- Popping into Lili's for a little tot of homemade limoncello, mandarincello or homemade wine on my way back from an evening walk. Occasionally, I have had a mojito pressed into my hand as made by Mimo, who is becoming a bit of an expert in cocktail making.

- Dry walls and no damp in the house. Dry, aired and brown feet from wearing flip-flops for six months. The good weather really does last from April til October.

- Summer concerts (Ostuni puts on free concerts in the summer). One particular concert Anna and I attended was a tribute to Tito Schippa who was local Puglian opera singer. Opera and the tango, a winning and wonderful combination for an evening's entertainment.

- Food festivals and *Sagras*. Carovigno always puts on food festivals in August. Music, fire-eaters, street food and a quartet playing, *O sole mio*.

- The parade of La Madonna through the streets of Santa Sabina. The local priest leads the procession, and the Madonna is taken to the water's edge to bless the sea and its bounty for the people in the coming year. An Italian marching band plays *Godfatheresque* music, and it all reminds me that I really am in Italy. And all is well.

- Lunch at Anna's in the Puglian countryside of Pascarosa. *Patate, cozze e riso*, which is a dish cooked in the oven with potatoes, mussels and rice and is a traditional Puglian dish. Accompanied by fresh peas from the countryside with fresh mint. Spirals of courgettes served with oil, salt, pepper and a little garlic. The whole meal finished off with homemade coffee ice cream. A guest might arrive in the form of a black snake winding its way across the patio and then hiding in the flower beds. An Italian wall lizard basking in the sun on a rock and then darting away into a crack in the wall. The table where we sit and have lunch has a pergola that is covered in grape vines and an orange tree hanging low and heavy with fruit. The sun glancing off the top of the white *trullo* cone and the crickets singing their songs as background music. Even a nearby hornets nest in an olive tree doesn't put us off our lunch. I will definitely miss this, all of this...

Things That I Won't Miss
⋙⋘

- Mosquitoes. Although they are not so partial to my flesh as they used to be.

- A gecko in my bedroom. Geckos getting squashed in door frames.

- Hot, humid, sticky and sleepless nights when I find myself waking up upside down in the bed. My unconscious body trying to find a cool spot on the sheets.

- Feeling too exhausted by the heat to do anything and then getting my air conditioner fixed so that I can wear a jumper indoors.

- Two days every year of a climbing temperature that peaks at 46c, which burns my nose hairs when I breathe in.

- Screaming kids. You know who you are, stop it!!

- Arguing and screaming teenagers who can also be heard trying to hock up a good gobby, presumably to add a little liquid to the fights. You know who you are, stop it!!

- A cacophony of Italian conversation late into the night (usually taking place on white plastic chairs facing the street). You know who you are, stop it!!

- Fireworks at midnight. Celebrating what? If it's nothing, in particular, stop it!!

- Being punched in the chest by a gesticulating Italian as I walk by (this isn't just a summer event).

- Another, not just a summer event. 80 and 90's power ballads and pop rock being blasted out at my local supermarket. Since Puccini and Verde the musical virtues of the Italians has plummeted in my estimation.

- Speedos. I have written about this before. You look naked in them Italian men. You know who you are, stop it!!

My sister recently sent me a book called *The Wordsworth book of intriguing words*, by Paul Hellweg (whose surname is also intriguing). Just the sort of book that I need to while away a few hours and be intrigued and also amazed by some of the words that may or may not have dropped out of English usage. For example, *Tipsycake – cake saturated with wine or liquor*; my mum has already baked her Christmas cakes and is giving them a daily dose of brandy whilst they lie quietly in the garage, 'They will be intoxicated by Christmas,' she tells me. And there you are, it is still a relevant word tipsycake or thoroughly pissedcake.

One of my favourites is the *Grangousier – one who will swallow anything*. No comment. Or the *Tenterbelly – a glutton*. Ten people around a Christmas dinner table eating 1,500 calories in one sitting, ten tenterbellies.

Dipfiddle – someone who just fiddles with their food. Okay, I just made that one up, but this is what I tend to do if I am surrounded by tenterbellies.

Pogonaphile – someone who loves beards. And apart from the latest hairy hipster craze, everyone loves Santa, so we are all pogonaphiles. And lastly; *Pygalgia* – a pain in the arse, which is what I have become, so I'll stop now.

As I am writing this, I have a kitten on my lap, purring contentedly. Is she just visiting or will she stay? A few days ago I rescued her from the top of one of the Yukka trees. She mewed and scrambled further up the tree as Basil was waiting at the bottom of the tree, hoping that she would fall and then he could chase her out of the garden victoriously. I managed to grab her before she ventured even further up the tree and cooed to her, 'What are you doing up there, little Munchkin?' I stroked her back and intended to put her outside of the gate to join the local cat community, but she snuggled into the crook of my arm and started purring. I then realised that she had been handled and was tame.

Everyone was leaving Santa Sabina as the summer was over and she must have been a house guest, before being left to fend for herself; abandoned. She is some sort of tabby mix with long hair and wispy white fur sprouting out of her ears, a lioness face and black silky paws. I am ashamed to say this, but I have called her Munchie, short for Munchkin and unlike Polly and Lizzy who weren't particularly cuddly cats and did their own thing. Munchie is curious and wants to see what I am doing all the time and follows me around, being very vocal and mewing constantly, begging to be picked up, so that she can snuggle in the crook of my arm or nestle under my chin. Although I am convinced that she doesn't say, 'Meow.' But, 'Ow, ow, ow.' She does repeatedly, maybe she is just meowing with an Italian accent.

She started sleeping outside on the swing seat and was then promoted to the beige faux-leather writing chair, and now she sleeps at the end of the bed. Occasionally being booted off by my nocturnal restless legs.

Will she stay, who knows? I am trying not to get too attached in case she sods off one day, but at the moment I am smitten with a kitten. And if she does hang around, perhaps she will end up in a cat basket flying back to Blighty with a pet passport in her paws and an English phrasebook.

A month on and she is still here. She has just sat on some papers and farted. Maybe I should change her food? She also likes to walk over the keyboard and delete a few paragraphs. Occasionally, she goes for a wander and comes back smelling of expensive perfume, and I know that she has been schmoozing and nestling under someone else's chin. What a tart!

Lili rang me yesterday to say that the Munch-tart was schmoozing with her and to evidence this; Lili took about a dozen photos. Lili is also feeding her dog biscuits which may account for the farting. Well, she can't have her. I scooped her up and took her back to my place. What a tart!

I must admit it is nice to have a companion whilst I write; even if I can't read my notes and she is constantly pulling my fingers towards her so that she can bite them or she climbs onto my shoulder so that she can get a better view of the funny little wiggly things that are moving across the screen. I may never get this finished. Maybe I could distract her by putting on cute kitten video... *'Oh look there's cat in a jar, again.'*

You know when a cat is going to be a permanent fixture in your life when they gain a plethora of name changes, Munch-tart, Munchie-crunch, Mrs Munch or just Munchie. She is still here and has a big fat belly as she seems to be permanently hungry. I am hoping that Dave will save her a seat on the van if I can train her on a leash (I looked into flying her back and realised that the Captain might forget the turn up the heat in the hold and she could freeze to death). Her fur is growing thick and fast (even Chewbacca would be envious) and she is now resembling a Norwegian Forest Cat rather than a Puglian Mog-cat.

She is now almost fully vaccinated and had treatment for ear mites. Although I thought the vet was going to give her a brain injury when he cleaned her ears with a cotton bud, dug deeply into her little ears and came up with some unedifying brown goo.

'Is she of good character?' he asked as she was trying to escape the deep probing cotton bud. I said she was and thinking maybe he shouldn't dig that deeply and then she wouldn't be trying to escape like the cartoon cat from the unwanted embrace of *Pepe Le Pew*.

I often find her lying in a pocket in the duvet in the mornings and she initially gently taps me on the face to remind me that she hasn't been fed yet and that she could possibly die of starvation fairly soon. If I don't rise immediately, the taps increase and become a bit more incessant and finally if she thinks I am dead and she will have to find another owner, she punches me in the eye. Despite all of this, she is staying.

It'll be four years that I have been in Italy this coming January and it feels likes four minutes. Time passes so quickly when you are not looking. And in the spring I will leave a country that has been my home, my life, my comfort, and provided my path for journeying and discovery both internally and externally.

Last week I took Anna to the airport. Only twelve litres of olive oil in her suitcase this time. No clothes, just olive oil. I asked her what she would miss about not living in Italy, and she said, 'Waking up amongst the trees and in the countryside. The stillness and the blissful peace.' I have been thinking about what I will miss. I sat on the rocks at dawn the other day (which makes a change from falling on the rocks), and took photos of the sun rising above the waves; a myriad of oranges, yellows and reds and I know that wherever I end up next, I have to live near the sea. I will miss the sea here in Puglia, whether it is raging or calm. I will miss the amazing cloud formations; that can look like mountains in the sky with huge plumes and flares of vapour and the fishing boats go out early in the morning skitting across the water and witnessing the awakening of the day. Can't I get up early and take photos anywhere? I looked up at the sky, and a plane was leaving a contrail, a white streak of vapour in contrast to the blueness of the sky, and I went home and emailed Dave to see if he was available for the trip back next March; a man, a van, a basset and a fluffy Munchie. Time to move on, back to baths and the cinema (the only two things that I miss about England as I have said before). But maybe I do miss more things about England; English pubs and a crackling fire on a winter's evening; bluebell woods and daffodils in the spring and the fact that the Brits love queueing and complaining about the weather. And perhaps the fact that an English summer only lasts for two weeks and because of this, there will be no more sweaty, confusing summers that seem to go on forever. How am I even complaining about this? Quite simply, because I am a Brit and it is instilled deep in my psyche to complain.

And there are things that have happened since I have been gone; Brexit (bog off Boris); the definition of surprise, Jeremy Corbyn; a female Prime Minister (go girl!) and worst of all *The Great British Bake Off* going to Channel 4, English baking fascination culture in a tent with flour, ovens and a Pillsbury Doughboy.

One more word from *Intriguing Words: Omphaloskepsis – the act of contemplating one's own navel.* I think I am guilty of nearly four years of doing just that. No regrets. I jumped right in and savoured every moment. I never did go for that solo swim, but I wonder if it really matters now. We all have our challenges, but on this occasion I think that it was better for me, at least, to conquer my fears on dry land.

I spoke to Anna on the phone yesterday and we talked about what a nice summer we had had together.

'Oh yes, it was lovely,' she said and went on to say, 'I can't bear the thought of you not being here.'

And just to add a little more sadness into the mix. Lili sat in the garden the other day and said how much she felt that I was part of her life. Tears pricked her eyes and she said that she wouldn't be able to come to the airport to say goodbye as she would find it too emotional. A few years before, it had been my emotions that had been rising, as I asked her if I could stay here in this little piece of Italian heaven. She and Italy have also become part of my life, a different life that was once a dream and became a reality.

Endings are nearly always sad, but everything has to come to an end, and I am ready for a new beginning. All these experiences that I have had, the people that I have met and the struggles that I have had and sweet precious moments that I have savoured have all led up to finally, finding myself in Puglia.

And I am never going to lose myself again.

And as JRR Tolkien once said, *'Not all those who wander are lost.'*

Postscript

❦

It's All in a Name

I was baptised Elaine in a church in Beaconsfield
Buckinghamshire on a cold December day in 1960;
my father wore a heavy black overcoat and my mother
a fur coat to keep out the winter's chill. To my close
friends and family, I am known as Laine or Lainey.
Living in Italy, I became Elena, Eleanor or Helen –
no Italian seemed to be able to pronounce Elaine.
Although to complete strangers who just knew 'of
me' I became *l'inglese*, the English. I would often hear
snatched bits of conversation *l'inglese* this, or that and
often wondered what the full gist of the conversation
was, but in the end, I didn't care.

I found myself in Italy and carved a new and
uncharted path for myself. I traversed its twists and
turns and left an old self behind. I became a new me
and thus became lainebbrown writer and memoirist,
and if you are reading this I thank you for coming
on my bittersweet journey and for that, I am truly
grateful.

Italian Observations

❧

- There are no carpets in Italian homes. Floors are nearly always tiled, or wooden floors have been laid, and they are always spotlessly clean. Cleanliness is next to godliness. I couldn't find a quote that was near to that, so here is something else:

  Spazzotoio nuovo spazza bene la casa – A new broom sweeps the house well. Which could be applied to any situation really; especially in reference to politics in Italy and I would say, *'What new broom? Same shaft, same head and no sweeping.'*

- The Italians have a love affair with plastic plates and cups. Although plastic knives and forks are less common. Post-picnics the woods can be littered with plastic discarded discs as though dropped from the sky. I can't really understand the fascination with the plastic plate thing.

- The Italians who are just 'curious' will invite The *Inglese* for dinner or coffee just once in order to fuel the *Quattro chiacchiere,* four talks or gossip in English. They may say, 'She eats like a bird and doesn't have a *buona forchetta,*' a good fork, meaning that she doesn't eat well. 'She didn't say how old she is.' It seems to be an Italian local occupation to wonder how old I am. And they say, 'She is always alone.' As though being alone is some sort of affliction, something to bear rather than something to be enjoyed. Other people will invite you more than once and treat you like a member of the family.

- Your Italian will be corrected relentlessly, even though their English will be non-existent or consists of 'Lovely jubbly.' 'You cheeky monkey.' I blame David Jason for this.

- Everyone outside the local town is considered to be a *straniero/a/e* – a stranger/foreigner. I must, therefore, be considered an alien, an out-of-this-world creature.

- Everyone has a cell phone, but internet use is low. The outside world is a lot less important to a Southern Italian and if it doesn't affect the food on the dinner table and then it is probably of no significance.

- Italian people are friendly and helpful. But an Italian shopkeeper – if he sees you coming – may charge you more. I bought a watch strap which was made of leather, and it was faulty and broke after two months use. It cost me 23 euros. I took it back to the shop, and although the shopkeeper spoke some English, I decided to be polite and converse in Italian, and this is how it went:

'Do you remember me?' A receptive nod...
'I bought this watch strap two months ago, and it
has broken.' Another nod...
'Did you wash in it?'
'No.'
'Did you put it on too tight?'
'No.' And how do you put a watch strap on too
tight anyway? I am thinking you can only tighten it
as far as the holes. How do I say this in Italian...?
No answer from brain, therefore, I say, 'Can I
have another strap.' Meaning a replacement.
'Yes,' said the amicably nodding shopkeeper.
'That will be 23 euros.'
He definitely saw me coming, and I didn't buy
another strap.

- The local English woman will be the only one
  wearing shorts and a T-shirt on a pleasant April
  day. Temp 22c and a light breeze whilst her fellow
  Italians will be wearing coats and a scarf to protect
  them from:

  'colpo di stregha o colpo d'aria', the hit of the witch
  or the hit of the wind which can both lead to
  – apparently – *cervicale*, a bad neck which tends
  to happen when winds and witches are around.
  A bit like your mum saying that you will get
  haemorrhoids if you sit on a cold floor.

- Italians – on the whole – never admit that they are
  wrong as this would result in a loss of pride, face,
  and dignity, *brutta figura* – at all times the face that
  you put out to the world the *bella figura*, must be

maintained. Which is why I didn't get a replacement watch strap!

- Driving requires nerves of steel and white knuckles. And if you do have accident then things may be settled without the intervention of the insurance company, as premiums may rise astronomically. The accident will be your fault. And although all children and babies are beloved by the Italians; you will often seem them in the front seat of cars on someone's lap, their heads dangerously close to the dashboard (I broke my nose on a dashboard of a green Mini Traveller when I was three as I was untethered and on someone's lap; the treatment, if I remember correctly, was a thick application of butter to reduce the swelling).

- Tax is paid by the honest Italians...

- All food is cooked from scratch with seasonal ingredients. Apart from the butter.

- In the land of pasta. Coeliac disease is only just being recognised and accepted. Gluten free pasta is now more widely available. Lovely.

- Apparently, in Italian, there are over 3,500 sexual swear words, which is quite a lot emanating from a Catholic country. For the innocent *Inglese* it is easy for a minor vowel slip to change the whole word:

  Tetta – Tit. *Tetto* – roof. One small vowel mistake can change the whole sentence:

'Le tette sono coperte di neve.' The tits are covered in snow, instead the roofs (or is it rooves?).

I do know of an English expat, who told a tale about when he had required the emergency services in Italy and instead of saying he needed a *Pompiere*, a fireman, he said that he needed a *pompino*, a blowjob. Be careful with your *ere's* and *ino's*, is all I can say.

To avoid any sexual swear words. Mimo will replace the offending word with, *Francesca*. Especially when he is having an argument with Lili. Thus avoiding offending God and the Holy Mother Mary.

- In summer most of the beach loving Italians will become the colour of a deep mahogany sideboard. Giving the impression that skin cancer is a myth perpetuated by the sun cream industry.

- Public drunkenness is frowned upon. I have never seen an inebriated Italian. Inebriation would lead to displaying a *brutta figura*.

- A majority of Southern Italians have a *campagna*, land that they own in the countryside where seasonal fruit and vegetables are picked along with the olives and a lot of families make their own olive oil. They also make enough tomato sauce for pasta dishes for a whole year!

- *La passeggiata*, the daily early evening walk keeps

everyone connected and healthy. Although their daily walking ritual may be disrupted by an English woman who can't ride a bicycle in a straight line and threatens to disperse the walkers and at worst leave them running for their lives. Thankfully, peace has been restored, because I have had a flat tyre for six months.

- Cappuccinos are allegedly, not drunk after 11 am, but if you do want one at three in the afternoon – I can assure you that you will not be shot on the spot by the Italian Coffee Police.

- Italian homemade wine can give you an acute onset of Italian Inebriation Syndrome and is also guaranteed to remove all the enamel from your teeth.

- If something cannot be fixed immediately, then it becomes *un mistero*, a mystery and you may never see the mechanic, electrician or plumber again.

- Get used to being stared at – it happens all the time. And as time passes you may find yourself doing the same thing. I know I do.

- The Italians don't do project planning. A few days can become a few weeks or a few months. Don't expect anything to be finished on time. A friend once called it the 90% syndrome. The last 10% just becomes a horizontal 8 – an infinity symbol.

- During the *pisolino*, siesta or afternoon nap or as I

like to call it a nanna nap – nothing is open, and nothing gets done. In the summer, nothing gets done. Everything shuts down especially in August.

- Italian bureaucracy is eye-bleeding and painstakingly slow. Every local commune has offices full of box files and grey steel cabinets carrying yards of paperwork – the more paperwork there is, the less accountability there is - try following an Italian paper trail, a) You won't live long enough to see the end of it and b) You would be more likely to find Big Foot. Although you can pay a parking fine at the local *Tabacchi* on a computerised till within about thirty seconds. Funny that...

The family is everything in Italy. This is where the love is seated and usually around a very long and happy table. If you get invited into a family home more than once – then you have made it!

Acknowledgements:

໑໑

I would like to, first of all, thank my friend Deborah Gould who told me that my things were only things and that I could let go of all of that. Linda Brash, who encouraged me to follow my dreams and said that she didn't want to see me in the hospital car park in a few years' time and not having achieved anything, apart from still being in the car park.

Much love and gratitude to my daughter Elisa and her partner Dean and my son Christian who never questioned my decision to uproot and change my life. Their frequent visits to Italy I treasured, we shared experiences, and I wrote about them.

Thank you, thank you to Debz-Hobbs Wyatt who supported me and professionally edited my book and encouraged me along the way.

A big thank you to Ally Partington who first accompanied me in 2010 to Italy and shouted, 'Fuck!' frequently and very loudly in my ears as I drove around Puglia tearing off the wing mirrors of unsuspecting Italian vehicles. My sister, Stella who followed me the following year to Puglia, swore less and supported my journey into an unknown world and encouraged me to have a five-minute conversation with Lili that changed my life. Grazie mille to Lili, Mimo and their daughter Simona and their extended family, who made me feel at home in Italy; fed me, helped me with my everyday needs and became my Italian family.

Grazie to Tim Pratley, who shared my love of English humour and kept me sane by sharing Graham Norton stories and love to his sweet daughters, Elisabeth and Caroline who gave me hugs.

Much love to Anna Rossi, who taught me Italian, looked after Basil and also fed me delicious Puglian cuisine and became my Italian mother. If you are in Italy, everyone feeds you, emotionally, spiritually and physically.

Thanks and gratitude to Julie Shearer whose shoulder I cried on in the first few difficult years post-divorce. Debbie (Dee) Oakes who introduced me to Tuscany and Umbria and welcomed me into her gorgeous home. Also, my friends Georgie and Steve Priestly, who visited me in Puglia and laughed out loud at my writing and made me feel as though at least, I had an audience with them.

Grazie mille to all my expat friends, especially Christine (who contributed towards the book) and Angela who were always there with a glass of wine or a cup of coffee and a walk by the sea. And to Maureen Rose who contributed her story to the book.

Finally, grazie to my Italian neighbours Lina, Mariella, Frankie, Maria, Rosetta, Ferdinando and Narucia who made me feel welcome and were eternally patient with my nascent Italian. And to the people of Torre Santa Sabina who waved, smiled and probably wondered why the *Inglese* was always on her own, not realising that the *Inglese* was happy just simply, being alone. It was a choice.

Oh (nearly forgot and how could I?) and thanks, big time to my dog Basil who kept me company and walked with me for miles over sandy beaches and craggy rocks. Also cat kisses to the fluffy one - the new arrival six months before I left - the kitten I found up a tree, Munchkin.

Text Acknowledgements:

'Resolve' Ian Hamilton Collected Poems, edited by Alan Jenkins. Faber & Faber (2009).

'What Solitude is' taken from Intimacy and Solitude by Stephanie Dowrick, Women's Press Ltd (1992).

'Christ Stopped at Eboli' by Carlo Levi, Penguin Classics, New Edition (2000).

'The Italians' by John Hooper, Penguin Random House (2015).

When I first saw Munchkin up the tree in 2016.

The last day in Italy March 2017, before Dave's road trip across Europe and back to England with Basil and Munchkin